A GUIDE TO FOREIGN LANGUAGE GRAMMARS AND DICTIONARIES

Second edition, revised and enlarged

Edited by A. J. Walford,
M.A., Ph.D., F.L.A.

LONDON
THE LIBRARY ASSOCIATION
1967

Published by
The Library Association
7 Ridgmount Street, London, W.C.1
© A. J. Walford, 1967
SBN: 85365 040 3

First edition, 1964
Second edition, revised and enlarged, 1967

Made and printed in England by
STAPLES PRINTERS LIMITED
at their Rochester, Kent, establishment

CONTENTS

INTRODUCTION

The present British interest in foreign languages owes much to the travel habits of our post-World War II affluent society and something to the universality of television. In the teaching of modern languages the classical tradition has been the dominant influence. French is accepted as the second language to be taught in secondary schools.[1] German and possibly Spanish may appear in the upper-form curriculum, but the pattern is changing somewhat now that Russian is being taught at secondary-school level.

This *Guide* provides an annotated list of grammars, dictionaries and audio-visual aids for the major foreign languages of Western Europe, plus Russian and Chinese. It is intended for teachers, students, graduates who may be taking up a particular language for the first time, scientists (for acquiring a reading knowledge of a language on a minimum of grammar), tourists, and librarians (for book-selection and stock revision).

The aim is to cover as many as possible – good, indifferent and some bad – of the relevant grammars, dictionaries, disc and tape courses in print. Because of the volume of output (on French, in particular), coverage has been more selective for some languages than for others.

In this second edition three languages have been added: Chinese, Dutch and Finnish. More emphasis is placed on gramophone records and audio-visual aids. The chapter on French has been considerably expanded, an introductory chapter prefixed, and the whole brought up to date.

[1] This pattern seems also to apply to scientists. "The present position in the United Kingdom is that most graduate scientists and engineers have learned French at school, and probably more than half of them can, later in life, make sense of French technical papers. Reading ability in German, which is less often taught in school, is less common. In other languages it is still less common, probably under 5 per cent for any one language. In 1956 [quoting Dr. J. Urquhart] only 2 per cent claimed to be able to read Russian, although this figure may well have been doubled since then." (ASLIB. *The foreign language barrier in science and technology* (1962), p. 3).

I

GENERAL

Grammars – Dictionaries – Bibliographical note

Grammars. For A. H. Sweet[1], grammar was not a piece of dead mechanism or a Chinese puzzle of which the parts must be fitted together in accordance with certain artificial rules, but "a living organism which has a history and reason of its own". In the more familiar foreign languages writers of grammars have, after years of trial and error, presented linguistic material in a digested and attractive form. Certainly this applies to French, but not to Russian as yet, and even less to Portuguese.

Grammars cover a multitude of forms, from the two-page card guides published in 1963 by Edward Arnold to the multi-volume course books (usually one book per course-year) and reference grammars. Some grammars concentrate on a command of the written language; others stress conversation and oral fluency. Some so-called grammars of the "German in three months" type give no more than a smattering of the language[2]; others, of *la plume de ma tante* type, have stilted and unrealistic examples and exercises; others, again, need to be reinforced, for full value, by gramophone records or tapes. We have got beyond the stage when a Spanish grammar for Frenchmen needs only to be translated into English to make it acceptable to Englishmen. Each language must be approached on its own terms.

Points to be considered in selecting a foreign-language grammar:

1. Declared purpose. A clear statement of the level or standard and class of user aimed at; the accuracy of the claims made by the author.
2. Accuracy and general reliability; up-to-dateness (*e.g.*, current official orthography).

---

[1] On "Grammar", in *Encyclopædia Britannica* (11th ed.), v. 12, p. 332.

[2] How long does an adult require to master a foreign language? Much depends on background. The Aslib investigation found that the maximum amount of tuition necessary for adult scientists to reach a specified standard in Russian is about 200 hours and the minimum amount about 45 hours (*The foreign language barrier*, p. 15).

3. Presentation. Stress on points of grammar or the more modern 'direct method', encouraging oral fluency? A four-year course designed for 'O' level may run dry of ideas and interesting material in later stages.

4. Systematic and graduated treatment of material; comprehensiveness within stated limits. First things first, – not blinding the student with out-of-the-way vocabulary, exceptions to rules or difficult exercises before he has been adequately prepared for them.

5. Interesting material, *e.g.*, lively and up-to-date passages for reading and translation; practical examples; numerous and relevant illustrations; adequate range of exercises.

6. Aids to pronunciation. If the grammar is a self-tutor, the author should state plainly what can and what cannot be learned from a book. (Gramophone records will be essential for cultivating a correct accent.) In Italian and Russian stress must be indicated. Pronunciation based on English-word analogy is a very rough-and-ready system.

7. Reference material on the grammar, *e.g.*, verb tables; summary of grammar.

8. Subject index to points of grammar.

9. End-vocabulary: each way; based on word frequency.

10. Typography: clarity; fairly generous type size (especially for Cyrillic characters) and attractive layout; judicious use of bold type.

11. Availability of a key (for self-tuition).

12. Price.

Dictionaries. If we accept the axiom that the unit of speech is the sentence, then the dictionary is clearly at a disadvantage. To quote the Chevalleys[1]: "Speaking in terms of life, there is no such thing as a 'separate' word. When you speak or write, none of your words stand alone; they derive their form, colour, functions, special meaning or strength from the context. . . . A dictionary is like a herbarium. It can only present words in a dried state, and must, for the sake of reference, give them in an alphabetical order." But the dictionary can give, with more or less exactness, the different senses of a word, discriminate between them, and enumerate them in order of frequency of use, with examples.

Points to be considered when selecting a foreign-language dictionary:

1. Authority of issuing body; reputation of publisher.

2. Aims, – as stated by publisher and compiler. How far are these met in practice? Are types of intended user stated?

[1] *The Concise Oxford French dictionary*, Introduction, p. v.

3. Scope. If a technical dictionary, how far are common words with non-technical meanings included? Are roots and derivatives, colloquialisms and country variations (*e.g.*, Swiss German, Brazilian Portuguese) included? Number of entries, assuming sub-entries to be counted separately. Extent of entries: frequency of idioms and sentences showing meaning in context; categorisation of nouns, etc. (pocket dictionaries, particularly, tend to give a take-or-leave-it equivalent or a string of undifferentiated equivalents).

4. Arrangement and balance. Alphabetical order of entry words is not necessarily the best arrangement for a technical dictionary. A dictionary may be largely for use in the country of publication; the number of pages in the two parts will need to be compared.

5. Consistency (*e.g.*, a qualifying adjective with a noun should be entered under either (or both) the adjective or the noun, not sometimes one and sometimes the other).

6. Up-to-dateness (particularly applicable to technical dictionaries); current official orthography. Is a so-called later edition a substantial revision or merely a reprint?

7. Aids to pronunciation: use of international phonetic symbols; indication of stress in Russian and Italian; noting of quality of vowels and sibilants in Italian; syllabification.

8. Indication of genders (omitted in some technical dictionaries).

9. Appendices: verb and other tables; abbreviations and proper names (if not in main sequence); conversion tables of weights and measures.

10. Illustrations, particularly if keyed parts are shown.

11. Legibility and ease of reference, usually involving adequate use of bold type, the numbering of different meanings of entry words, use of italic for examples of usage, and avoidance of too many symbols and other abbreviations. Portability is, unfortunately for the user, in inverse ratio to comprehensiveness. Whiteness and opaqueness of paper make for legibility, and a stout binding ensures a longer life for the dictionary.

12. Price.

Polyglot dictionaries

The Schlomann-Oldenbourg series of technical dictionaries in six languages[1] set a standard of excellence in multilingual dictionaries that has rarely been attained since. The series also provided a pattern for later dictionaries of this type to follow: (a) concentration on the major European languages (German – English – Russian – French – Italian – Spanish); (b) specific subject coverage for each volume; (c)

[1] Schlomann, A., ed. *Illustrated technical dictionaries in six languages* (London, Constable, 1900-32. 17v.).

classified arrangement; (d) numbered entries and word indexes for each of the six languages; (e) numerous line-drawings, some with keyed parts. Thus v. 15, *Spinnerei und Gespinste* (1925. v, 951 p.) includes more than 1,200 small but clear illustrations. It contains *c.* 10,000 entry-words in 18 main classes, with *c.* 200 sub-divisions.

The nearest parallel to the Schlomann-Oldenbourg series is now the Elsevier series. Many of the volumes are edited by W. E. Clason. They are, on occasion, the only multilingual dictionaries in their specific fields, but they have their general faults: Russian is often not included (sometimes it appears as an afterthought, in a supplement); equivalents are given in one A-Z sequence in ruled columns (the eye should first run horizontally, not vertically, when we search for equivalents); illustrations are often lacking; and prices are invariably high. The Elsevier Glossarium interpretum series cover highly specific fields in some twenty languages. Thus, *Elsevier's lexikon of pressurized packaging (aerosols)*, compiled by A. Herzka (1964. 159 p. $7) contains 262 English terms with equivalents in 20 other languages. A point to note in the rendering of an equivalent to, say an English/American technical term is that it may not exist in, say, modern Greek. In that case the compiler should explain the meaning of the term in that language and not concoct a term that looks plausible.

A selection follows of well-known polyglot dictionaries. Some, like Medeiros, cover the whole of technology; others deal with self-contained fields such as aeronautics or medicine; others again, like Carrière, are limited to a few hundred terms in a highly specialised field. These include examples of trilingual (English, French and German) dictionaries.

ADLER, J. A.   Elsevier's dictionary of criminal science in eight languages.   Amsterdam, Elsevier, 1960.   xv, 1460 p.   £16 10s.

English/American, French, Italian, Spanish, Portuguese, Dutch, Swedish, German; 10,930 numbered terms. Mistranslations and omissions are noted in *Babel*, v. 9, no. 1-2, 1963, p. 110-1.

CARNELUTTI, D.   A technical dictionary of the automobile.   Lausanne, Spes; London, Macdonald, 1964.   180 p.   63s.

Italian, French, English, German, Spanish; *c.* 5,000 terms in 12 sections (97 sub-sections). On each verso, a clear line-drawing (*e.g.*, 'gear box': 2 illustrations; 33 relevant terms).

CARRIÈRE, G.   Detergents: a glossary of terms used in the detergents industry.   Amsterdam, Elsevier, 1960.   vi, [2], 141 p.   (Glossaria interpretum, 5).   21s.

19 languages; 257 numbered terms in 10 classes with sub-divisions. The 1966 edition adds an 8-language glossary of terms used in cosmetics and toiletries.

CLAIRVILLE, A. L.   Dictionnaire polyglotte des termes médicaux. Paris, SUPCO.   v. 1. 2nd ed., 1955.   6,500 fr.

French-English-German-Latin (v. 2–4 are Portuguese, Spanish and Italian supplements, respectively); 14,534 terms. Considered the best polyglot dictionary of medical terms.

CLASON, W. E.   Elsevier's dictionary of electronics and waveguides ... Amsterdam, Elsevier, 1957.   viii, 628 p.   90s.; Swedish supplement, 1960.   43 p.   20s.; Russian supplement. 1961.   iv, 57 p.   42s.

English/American, French, Spanish, Italian, Dutch, German; 2,056 terms. Updated by *Supplement to the Elsevier dictionaries of electronics, nucleonics and telecommunications in six languages*, compiled by W. E. Clason (1963, viii, 632 p. 100s.).

DE KERCHOVE, R.   International maritime dictionary.   2nd ed. Princeton, N.J., Van Nostrand, [1961].   1,018 p. $24.75; 155s.

First published 1948. About 12,000 terms in ship construction, maritime law, shipping and marine insurance, including many abbreviations. French and German equivalents are given of English entry-words, with indexes. Terms have not been completely updated and diagrams are distinctly old-fashioned. *Elsevier's Nautical dictionary* by P. E. Segditsas (1965–66. 3 v. £18 10s.) is fuller and up-to-date, and covers English, French, Italian, Spanish and German.

Dictionar technič polyglot romînă, rusă, englesă, germană, francezșă, maghiară.   Bucharest, Editura Tehnică, 1963.   xx, 1,235 p.   105s.

Rumanian, Russian, English, German, French and Hungarian; c. 30,000 terms. 45 subject categories indicated.

DORIAN, A. F.   Six-language dictionary of automation, electronics and scientific instruments ...   London, Iliffe, 1962.   12, 732 p. 105s.

English, French, German, Italian, Spanish, Russian; c. 5,500 terms. U.S. usage is not differentiated from British.

DURY, J.   Vocabulaire textile trilingue, français-allemand-anglais. Troyes, Centre de Recherches de la Bonneterie, 1962.   viii, 139, 166 p.

About 15,000 numbered French textile terms, with German and English equivalents. Systematically arranged in 9 chapters, each with language indexes.

HAENSCH, G., and HABERKAMP, G.   Wörterbuch der Landwirtschaft. 2nd ed.   Munich, BLV, 1963.   xxiv, 744 p.   DM.59; Ergänzungs-band italienisch. 1963.   x, 182 p.   DM.29.

First published 1959. German, English, French, Spanish; 10,057 entries in 14 main classes and sub-divisions. A 3rd revised edition of the main work appeared in 1966 (746 p. £7 15s.). The promised Russian supplement has not yet been published.

HERBST, R.   Wörterbuch der Handels, Finanz und Rechtssprache. 2. Aufl.   Lucerne, Thali, 1962–66.   3 v.   (v. 1: English-German-French, v. 2: Deutsch-Englisch-Französisch. v. 3: Français-anglais-allemand).   ea. Sw.fr. 98.50.

Each volume has c. 50,000 entry-words on banking, stock-exchange, finance, foreign exchange, taxation and customs, law, sea and air transport, postal services and insurance. British and U.S. English, and Swiss usage are differentiated.

HOYER, E. von, and KREUTER, F.   Technologisches Wörterbuch. 6th ed.   New York, Ungar, 1944.   3 v.   ea. 152s.

Reprint of the 1932 ed., edited by A. Schlomann. V. 1, German-English-French; v. 2, English-German-French; v. 3, French-German-English. Each volume has c. 20,000 entry-words, with many sub-entries. A well-compiled, reliable dictionary, now much overdue for revision.

INTERNATIONAL ELECTROTECHNICAL COMMISSION.   International elec-trotechnical vocabulary.   2nd ed.   Geneva, the Commission, 1954–.

Planned in 22 parts; 19 published by 1965, each covering a specific topic (e.g., *Lighting*) in 8 or 9 languages, including Swedish, Russian and Polish. Group 07, *Electronics* (2nd ed. Moscow, 1959. 335 p. 12s.) consists of a classified list of terms in French, German, Spanish, Italian, Polish and Swedish, with definitions in Russian and English, and reverse indexes.

JACKS, G. V., and others.   Multilingual vocabulary of soil science. 2nd ed., rev.   Rome, F.A.O., 1960.   xxiii, 428 p.   22s. 6d.

First published 1954. English, French, German, Spanish, Portuguese, Italian, Dutch, Swedish and Russian; c. 350 terms in 22 sections. Includes marginal subjects such as irrigation.

JAMES, G., and JAMES, R. C.   Mathematics dictionary.   Multilingual ed.   Princeton, N.J., London, etc., Van Nostrand, 1959.   [iv], 546 p. $15; 112s. 6d.

First published 1942. The first part (p. 1–423) is an English dictionary, defining *c.* 7,000 mathematical terms. It is followed by logarithmic tables and formulae. The second part consists of French-English, German-English, Russian-English and Spanish-English indexes.

MEDEIROS, M. F. da S. de. Dicionario téchnico poliglota. Lisbon, Gomes & Rodrigues, 1949–54. 8 v. £29 14s.

68,193 terms (Portuguese-Spanish-French-Italian-English-German) in v. 1–3; v. 4–8 are separate language indexes and include Latin. Particularly valuable for its coverage of the Romance languages.

NATO/AGARD. AGARD aeronautical multilingual dictionary. Edited by G. H. Frenot and A. H. Holloway. London, Pergamon Press, 1960. 1,072 p. 140s.; Supplement 1, 1963. 70s.

English, French, German, Spanish, Italian, Dutch, Turkish and Russian; 1,574 numbered entry-words and expressions in 15 sections. Supplement 1 adds 1,287 entries and a further language, Greek.

NIJDAM, J. Horticultural dictionary in eight languages. [3rd] rev. and expanded ed. New York & London, Wiley, 1962. 504 p. 57s.

First published 1955. Dutch, English, French, German, Danish, Swedish, Spanish and Latin. In one alphabetical sequence, for which it is criticised in *The incorporated linguist* (v. 3, no. 4, October 1964, p. 120).

PERMANENT INTERNATIONAL ASSOCIATION OF NAVIGATION CONGRESSES. Illustrated technical dictionary in six languages . . . Brussels, the Association, [1934]–.

Compiled on the Schlomann pattern; separate volumes for different subjects (e.g., v. 5 *Materials*, 1951. 2,022 terms); diagrams with keyed parts. The languages are: English, German, French, Spanish, Italian and Dutch.

SERVOTTE, J. V. Woorderboek voor handel en financien . . . [3rd ed. rev. and enl.]. Brussels, Brepols, 1964. ix, 960 p. 395 Belg.fr.

French-Dutch-English-German; over 22,000 entries. A trade and financial dictionary with a good reputation. The arbitrarily chosen appended list of abbreviations is criticised in *Babel* (v. 12, no. 1, 1966, p. 52).

SOBECKA, Z., and others. Dictionary of chemistry and chemical technology . . . Oxford, Pergamon Press; Warsaw, Wydawnictwa Naukowo Techniczne, 1962. vii, 724 p. £10.

English, German, Polish, Russian; 11,987 numbered entries.

Tekniikan sanasto . . . [2nd ed.], edited by V. Airas [and others].
Helsinki, Kustannusosakeyhtiö Otava, 1950-2. 2 v. 108s.

German-English-Finnish-Swedish Russian technical dictionary. V. 2
provides indexes.

THALI, H. Technical dictionary of the terms used in electrical
engineering, radio, television, telecommunication. Lucerne, Thali,
1960–.

V. 1, English–German–French (6th ed. 1960): c. 17,000 entries, categorised;
appendix of abbreviations. V. 2, German–English–French (4th ed. 1961);
c. 24,000 entries, categorised. V. 3, French–German–English (in preparation).

THEWLIS, J., ed. Encyclopaedic dictionary of physics. v. 9. Multilingual dictionary. Oxford, Pergamon Press, 1964. xvi, 988 p.
£10.

English, French, German, Spanish, Russian, Japanese (romanised); 13,675
numbered terms, mostly drawn from headings in the *Encyclopaedic dictionary
of physics*. The English terms are accompanied by numbered references to
French, German, Spanish, Russian and Japanese equivalents, each in a
separate list. Each word in these lists carries a reference to the numbered
English terms, – a cumbersome device to save space.

UNION INTERNATIONALE DES CHEMINS DE FER. Lexique général des
termes ferroviaires. Paris, Bureau International de Documentation
des Chemins de Fer, 1957. 829 p. 2,200 fr.

French, German, English, Italian, Spanish; c. 10,000 railway and engineer-
ing terms. Distinguishes between British and U.S. English, Castillian and
Latin American Spanish, French and Belgian usage, and the variations of
German, French and Italian used in Switzerland.

Other polyglot aids

*Manual of foreign languages for the use of librarians, bibliographers,
research workers, editors, translators and printers*, compiled by G. F. Von
Ostermann, (4th ed., rev. and enl. New York, Central Book Co., Inc.,
1952. [xii], 414 p. $12.50) deals with about 130 languages, some of
them sketchily. Points covered in each case may include alphabet,
capitalisation, syllabification, word formation, gender, articles, cardinal
and ordinal numbers, months, days, seasons, time. Japanese, Chinese
and other non-romanised characters are reproduced.

For those who wish to translate into and type in foreign languages,
and who are at a loss on the rules for capitalisation, syllabification and
other such matters in the languages concerned, there is the admirable

A guide to foreign languages for science librarians and bibliographers (compiled by J. R. F. Piette. Rev. ed., revised and enlarged by E. Horzelska. London, Aslib, on behalf of the Welsh Plant Breeding Station, Aberystwyth, 1965. iii, [1], 53 p. 21*s*.). First published in 1959, this aide-mémoire now covers 25 languages, in five groups, plus Turkish and Esperanto, with notes also on Chinese and Japanese.

Sir A. Lyall's *A guide to the languages of Europe: a phrase phrase-book* (2nd rev. ed. London, Sidgwick & Jackson, 1935 and reprints (e.g., 1960). viii, 315 p. 12*s*. 6*d*.) is a pocket vade-mecum for students, tourists, salesmen and especially motorists who travel through half-a-score of countries in a single trip. It covers 25 foreign languages (including Turkish, Arabic and Esperanto) in 5 sections, each section dealing with 5 languages plus English, in 6 columns across the double page. For each language useful phrases, a basic vocabulary of *c*. 800 words and 30 sentences are provided, plus imitated pronunciation. All scripts are romanised. The 30 sentences, which cover a number of contingencies, are intended as transposable models. A third revised edition is being issued in 2 parts; part 1 covers the Romance and Teutonic groups of languages (1966. 165 p. 7*s*. 6*d*.).

Bibliographical note

(a) *General.* The following have proved their value as checklists:

ULLMAN, M. J., ed.   MLA selective list of material for use by teachers of modern foreign languages in elementary and secondary schools. New York, Modern Language Association of America, 1962. vi, 162 p. $1.

A systematic and detailed survey of language materials for French, German, Italian, Modern Hebrew, Norwegian, Polish, Portuguese, Russian, Spanish and Swedish. Specialist teachers describe and evaluate nearly 2,400 items grouped usually under these heads: Basic texts – Bibliographies and resource lists – Books of culture and civilization – Books of songs – Books on methodology – Conversation books – Dictionaries – Discs and tapes (cultural; language; literary; songs) – Elementary readers – Films (documentary; language) – Film strips – Linguistics – Literary texts – Maps – Periodicals – Picture and wall charts – Reference grammars – Review grammars – Supplementary materials – Teachers course guides. Level and class grades are allotted for each item. Appended are annotated lists of books on cultural backgrounds, criteria for evaluation and a list of publishers. Heavily slanted to U.S. needs; U.S. imprints and prices only. No index. Apparently the only detailed survey of its kind.

FERGUSON, C. A., and STEWART, W. A., ed.   Linguistic reading lists
for teachers of modern languages: French, German, Italian, Russian,
Spanish.   Washington, D.C., Centre for Applied Linguistics, 1963.
ix, 114 p.

Items include dictionaries, bibliographies and journals, as well as periodical
articles, and are usually annotated. The fullest chapter is that on French
(p. 7–30), specially recommended works being asterisked.

KENT EDUCATION COMMITTEE.   Catalogue of recommended books
and publications for secondary schools (grammar, technical and
modern): modern languages.   Maidstone, Kent County Education
Offices, 1962.   40 p.   4s.

Serves roughly the same purpose as the *MLA selective list*, on a modest
scale. The languages are French, German and Spanish. Categories are:
Dictionaries and Vocabularies – Grammars – Courses – Translation – Free
Composition, Comprehension Tests and Oral Practice – Readers (junior,
intermediate, senior) – Plays – Verse and Song Books – Classroom Aids. The
final section lists items on teaching of modern languages. Index of authors.
Does not include films and gramophone records; for lists of these the user is
referred to the Catalogues of the Kent Education Committee's film and
gramophone record libraries.

Booksellers' lists are issued by Stechert-Hafner (*The world's languages:
grammars, dictionaries*. 14th ed. 1966. 173 p., covering some 160 languages, arranged alphabetically; U.S. slanted and U.S. prices only),
Bailey Bros. & Swinfen (*Bailey's Catalogue of dictionaries & grammars in
the European languages*... 1961. 44 p.; and *Bailey's Oriental-African
catalogue of dictionaries, grammars and phrasebooks*. 1965. 56 p.), and
Blackwell (*European philology*. 1961. 53 p.).

(b) *Dictionaries*. The fullest list of current language dictionaries is
K. O. Saur's *Technik und Wirtschaft in fremden Sprachen. Internationale
Bibliographie der Fachwörterbuch* (3rd ed. Munich, Verlag Dokument-
ation, 1966. cxlvi, 304 p. DM.88) which lists 3,632 items in 12 sections;
Supplement, 1967 (967 entries). No annotations, but languages
covered are stated; sometimes the number of entries is given. Author,
publisher (by country), subject and language indexes precede. The
Unesco *Bibliography of interlingual scientific and technical dictionaries*
(4th ed. 1961. xxxvi, 236 p. 17s. 6d.; Supplement, 1964. 83 p. 10s.)
lists about 3,000 items in U.D.C. order; language, author and subject
indexes. Complementary to it is the Unesco *Bibliography of monolingual
scientific and technical glossaries*, by E. Wüster (v. 1, *National standards.*

1955. 219 p. 14s. 6d.; *Miscellaneous sources*, 1959. 146 p. 12s. 6d.). V. 2 lists 1,043 privately published monolingual glossaries in 26 languages. Both volumes are definitely dated, but addenda appear in the quarterly *Babel. Bibliography, documentation, terminology* (Paris, Unesco, 1961–. 6 p.a.) provides supplementary lists of both interlingual and monolingual scientific and technical dictionaries.

W. Marton's *Foreign language and English dictionaries in the physical sciences and engineering* (U.S. National Bureau of Standards. Washington, U.S. Government Printing Office, 1964. ii, 189 p. $1.25) covers more than 2,800 items published 1951–1962. Most items are English-based. The alphabetical arrangement of the 49 subject classes leads to some unnatural separations. Approximate number of entries is often stated; author, language and subject indexes are appended. A handy, inexpensive list.

Notable short lists are included in the Institute of Linguist's *Year book* (1967, p. 148–178), with supplements in later issues of *The incorporated linguist;* and in *The Manchester review* (v. 9, Summer 1962, p. 267–300: "Technical translating dictionaries", by F. R. Taylor).

(c) *Reviewing journals.* Some current journals that can be recommended are: *Modern languages* (London, Modern Language Association, 1905–. Quarterly); *The incorporated linguist* (London, Institute of Linguists, 1962–. Quarterly); *Babel* (Bonn, International Federation of Translators, 1955–. Quarterly); *Lebende Sprachen* (Berlin-Schöneberg, Langenscheidt, 1956–. 9 p.a.); and *Technical translation bulletin* (London, Aslib, Technical Translation Group, 1961–. 3 p.a.).

(d) *Audio-visual aids*

DUTTON, B., ed. A guide to modern language teaching methods. London, Cassell, 1965. (Audio-Visual Language Association. Publication no. 1).

LOWE, M., and LOWE, J., ed. On teaching foreign languages to adults: a symposium. Oxford, Pergamon Press, 1965.

NATIONAL COMMITTEE FOR AUDIO-VISUAL AIDS IN EDUCATION. Audio-visual aids and modern language teaching: a symposium. London, N.C.A.V.A.E., 1962.

TURNER, J. D. Language laboratories in Great Britain, 1965. 3rd ed. London, University of London Press, 1965.

2

FRENCH

by PETER PLATT, M.A., PH.D., F.L.A. and A. J. WALFORD, M.A., PH.D., F.L.A.

I think then that it is merely waste of time to learn more than a smattering of foreign tongues. The only exception I would make to this is French.
(W. Somerset Maugham. *The summing-up.*)

Whether or not one agrees with either part of Maugham's statement, French will go on being taught and learned in this country and is likely to remain our most common second language. It follows from this that there is a wide range of grammars, courses and dictionaries devoted to the teaching and learning of French. It would take longer, but in some ways it would be more satisfactory, to produce an exhaustive list, because selection is always a highly personal matter and others would doubtless have chosen differently. However, it is felt that those for whom this work is intended will find here a *representative* selection from which to choose.

For some, the formal approach to a language through the conscientious assimilation of the basic rules of grammar will still be the most satisfactory method. Others may prefer the more modern Direct Method approach, whereby the pupil pronounces and writes the word simultaneously, but the teacher uses the foreign language as the medium in which the lesson is taught, *instead of English*.

As a development of this method many people, both children and adults, are now learning French and other languages in a language laboratory where students can learn to speak a language quickly and without the agonies which some of us will have suffered through repeated attempts at a difficult pronunciation in a strange language in front of an unsympathetic class. Even so, the language laboratory is more suitable for adults than for children, who need the personality of the teacher to keep the subject interesting.

Where a language laboratory is not available it may still be possible to supplement formal study by use of other audio-visual aids such as gramophone records, tapes and film strips. As will be seen from some of the annotations which follow, records and tapes are now available to accompany a number of text-books, a particularly useful aid to the student trying to learn by himself. But such aids are only 'audio' and not 'visual'. Pupils are dependent on the film-strip for understanding the meaning of the tape. The audio-visual method is particularly useful in secondary modern schools where pupils may be unable to tackle the grammatical side of the language.

The best known audio-visual method of teaching and learning French is the Tavor system. Writing about this in 1962, S. R. Ingram said:

. . . the aim of the course is to bombard the eye and ear of the pupil with situations which are immediately comprehensible . . . [and] to give the pupils mastery over enough elements of the spoken language to enable them to approach its grammatical study through material which is completely familiar.[1]

This is a modern recognition of the natural way of learning a language, although as a method it is very much in the experimental stage: nothing is proved. In general, audio-visual aids, whether records, tapes, radio, television or language laboratory, will supplement or will be supplemented by the printed word. And here it is encouraging to note that a growing number of authors of grammars and courses are recognising that the text-book is no longer unchallenged.

In the entries which follow, the availability of audio-visual aids is indicated in the appropriate annotations and a separate section at the end covers gramophone records. Other criteria which have been considered include standard or level, coverage, exercises, help with pronunciation, indexes and vocabularies, typography and price.

The authors of this chapter are much indebted to Mrs. S. Julyan for her critical comments on some of the more recent grammars.

GRAMMARS

ALDEN, D. W.   Collins' Cortina French in twenty lessons.   London, Collins, 1962.   382 p.   12s. 6d.

Based on the 80th Cortina (New York) edition. Method is that invented by

---

[1] S. R. Ingram. "Audio-visual French: the Tavor system." In National Committee for Audio-Visual Aids in Education. *Audio-visual aids and modern language teaching; a symposium* (London, N.C.A.V.A.E., 1962), p. 23-24.

R. Diez de la Cortina, who founded the Cortina Academy of Languages in
U.S.A. in 1882. A self-tutor for beginners.

20 lessons, followed by reference grammar and vocabulary, each way
(English–French, 30 p; French–English, 24 p.). Separate vocabulary with
each lesson, together with conversational exercises. Vocabularies and
exercises of lessons 1–16 are transcribed by simple phonetic symbols based
on English spelling. Two chapters in addition on pronunciation. Most pages
in lessons section have at least one line-drawing. Some pages are cramped
to keep volume to a reasonable size. Similarly, parts of the reference grammar
are set in very small type which is difficult to read. Otherwise, excellent value.
Deals with familiar social topics. One of the best of the self-tutoring courses.

BEARDSWORTH, P.   French; first year G.C.E. course.   London, Dent,
1964.   v.p.   (New Master series).   7s. 6d.

A self-tutor which describes itself as "an entirely automatic textbook
system for schools and private students". Is modern in its use of programmed-
learning techniques. Each page, headed by a four-figure number, contains
a certain amount of teaching and four questions with numbered alternative
answers. By writing down the numbers of the correct answers in the same
order as the questions, the learner will move on to a further page headed by
the four-figure number arrived at. May appeal to the G.C.E. pupils for
whom it is intended, but adult learners could be irritated by the possibility
implied by the warning at the front: "Always write down your four-figure
numbers at every attempt – otherwise you may lose your page and your
position in this book". Teachers and *bona fide* private students may obtain an
index to the 'scrambled' text.

This volume includes nouns, adjectives, present tense and regular impera-
tives, pronouns and numbers, etc. Layout is very clear and the typography
is good, with bold well used. Slated in *Modern languages* (v. 46, no. 1, 1965,
p. 43) as exemplifying "all the worst features of the teaching we are striving
today to abolish".

BEARDSWORTH, P.   French; second year G.C.E. course.   London,
Dent, 1965.   v.p.   (New Master series).   7s. 6d.

Same presentation as first-year volume. Introduces reflexive verbs and
certain irregular verbs. Contains a short revision of first-year work, additional exercises, verb tables and a short, each-way vocabulary.

BROOKS, K. G., and COOK, H. F.   Modern French for adults.   London,
Dent, 1941–42 (reprinted 1963–65).   x, 150 p.   2 v., each 19s. 6d.

20 lessons in v. 1, 14 in v. 2. Each lesson consists of grammar, vocabulary,
conversation and exercises. Emphasis on the verb. Avoids exceptions to
rules if they would tend to hinder progress. Each-way vocabulary at end
of each volume. Index also at end of v. 1. Occasional use of phonetics and
four pages of "Hints on speaking French". A few illustrations. Layout is
clear. Bold type not used. Could be used as a self-tutor by older students

brushing up a knowledge of the language, but perhaps a little too 'solid' for some adult learners.

BYRNE, L. S. R., and CHURCHILL, E. L.   A comprehensive French grammar.   Oxford, Blackwell, 1956.   xxi, [1], 515 p.   £1 15s.

Revised edition of a work first published in 1950. A detailed reference grammar, with index. No exercises. Good use of bold type.

Also available: *Exercises and vocabulary* (1951. vii, 320 p. 16s.).

CHÉREL, A.   French without toil. Paris, Assimil, 1940 (reprinted 1962). vii, 504 p.   18s.

For those with no previous knowledge. 140 lessons. "About 6 months at 1 lesson a day." Has accompanying gramophone records which are desirable but not essential. (Details of these may be obtained from Assimil, Pitman's Correspondence College, Farncombe, Godalming, Surrey.)

Grammar introduced gradually through conversation exercises with short appendix of grammar at end. Vocabulary is acquired by comparing French on left-hand page with English equivalent on opposite page. Exercises with each lesson.

French pronunciation indicated by means of English sounds for those who do not have the records. Text has typically French line-drawings throughout. Pages are slightly cramped but fairly easy to read. Type is a somewhat untidy mixture of ordinary, bold and italic. Claims to be based on the process of intuitive assimilation. Has the advantage of using the everyday language of French life rather than 'school' French.

CHEVALIER, J. C., and others.   Grammaire Larousse du français contemporain.   Paris, Larousse, 1964.   494 p.   £1 15s. 6d.

Successor to *Grammaire Larousse du XXe siècle* (1936). Very full treatment of the whole of French grammar. Would not suit a beginner, but excellent at university level or for revising a 'rusty' but otherwise good standard of French. Has an exemplary index. No illustrations, but very clearly presented. Some of the small type used in places would not be easily read by everyone.

Even fuller is *Le bon usage: grammaire française*, by M. Grévisse (*q.v.*).

COLLINS, H. F.   A French manual for the examination form.   London, Macmillan, 1961.   ix, 224 p.   8s. 6d.

For the G.C.E. 'O' level final-year class. 23 sections cover passages for translation, composition, poems, grammar and exercises. Outline of grammar and verb tables are appended. Vocabulary, each way. No index to grammar.

CRAMPTON, E. B., and others.   Nelson's modern method French grammar.   London, Nelson, 1955–59.   5 v.   £1 16s.

A graduated 5-year course working up to G.C.E. 'O' level. Book 3 (1956) consists, e.g., of 18 chapters, each with passages for translation and grammar notes. Survey of grammar, p. 170–95. Crossword puzzles, with solutions. Vocabulary, each way.

DONALD, W., and HUTCHINSON, J. C. French: a new approach. London, Longmans, [n.d.].   3 v. illus.   £1 4s. 6d.

Authors maintain that most grammars try to instil ability to *write* French far too early. A 3-year course, with emphasis on the oral approach which is now finding more favour than hitherto. Three types of French text: texts based on French stories, passages on French life and adapted tales for listening to. Book 1 has 15 lessons. Amusing illustrations. Book 3 has refresher exercises and music.

DUFF, C. French for adults. London, English Universities Press, 1952 (reprinted 1966).   xix, 387 p.   7s. 6d.

Specifically written for adult learners. 26 lessons, 5 sections each.

Each lesson contains points of grammar, examples and vocabulary. Exercises consist of translating extracts from literature.

No index and no use of phonetics. Brief references to pronunciation (in lesson 20), with suggestion that those lacking a teacher should use the course in conjunction with records and radio listening. A few illustrations. Layout is fairly clear but rather solid in parts. Type is a tiring mixture of sizes and kinds. In general a very practical working course devoted to practical needs (e.g., hotels, eating, post office, camping, etc.).

EMERSON, H. O. A practical French course. London, Hachette, 1962.   3 v.   £1 8s. 6d.

A 3-year course designed for evening, technical and commercial schools. Intended for class use with teacher, but could be used as self-tutor.

Treatment of grammar is comprehensive. Each lesson consists of appropriate text matter with the necessary grammatical explanations. Summaries of grammar learned occur at intervals. Index of vocabulary, each way. Exercises with each lesson.

V. 1 opens with a chapter on phonetics and pronunciation. All three volumes are illustrated. Clearly laid out, although use of bold type would have been an advantage. A useful approach for those who find the "formal grammar" method difficult. An extremely varied selection of texts is used.

FERRAR, H. A French reference grammar. London, Oxford University Press, 1955 (reprinted 1960).   352 p.   12s. 6d.

Written with G.C.E. 'O' level candidates in mind. Covers approximately 3rd–5th forms of secondary school course. Could be used as a self-tutoring course.

Grammar treated very fully, as title of volume would suggest. No separate vocabulary, but many different words used in examples. Exercises are given. An edition without exercises is available at 11s. 6d. (296 p.), with separate exercise section at 2s. 6d. (56 p.).

Excellent index at beginning of volume. Introduction contains phonetic alphabet and guidance on pronunciation, spelling, etc. No illustrations. Extremely clear and attractive layout. Good typography, with excellent use of bold and italic. A very full and sensible grammar. Many of the interesting examples are taken from modern French authors.

Fox, J. R.   A School Certificate French grammar.   London, Grant Educational Co., Ltd., 1946.   viii, 244 p.   5s. 6d.

Written for School Certificate candidates, presumably in pre-G.C.E. days. Preferably to be used with a teacher.

Thorough treatment of grammar. English-French vocabulary at end. Set of exercises to illustrate each point of grammar.

Excellent index at end referring to number of appropriate section. No phonetics or guide to pronunciation. No illustrations. Clear layout and typography with good use of bold and italic. A very full grammar and one of the very few to have a really good index.

Grayson, D.   À la page.   Book 3.   London, Ginn, [1965].   304 p.   10s. 6d.

An 'O' level course with a difference. It aims "all the while to encourage an active and creative use of the language rather than simply equip the pupil for the 'O' level examination", and this it does with success. Excellent exercises and drawings. Reading matter concentrates on significant events in French history, from Charlemagne to the present day. Highly recommended in *Modern languages* (v. 46, no. 4, 1965, p. 167), and found from experience to be the best book at the moment for first to fifth year courses in grammar schools.

Grayson, D.   À propos.   London, Ginn, 1956–58 (and reprints).   2 v. illus.   £1 2s. od.

Attractively produced 2-year course "for adults, specially intended for those enthusiastic but heterogeneous groups in evening classes for whom the teacher needs interesting material which the students can occasionally work on their own" (Preface). Book 1 has 13 chapters, the last being "vocabulary revision". Appendices include "some suggestions for a gramophone library" (spoken passages only). Illustrations are both amusing and effective. Book 2 has skeleton grammar (p. 219–45). Both volumes have vocabulary, each way, and an index to grammar.

Grévisse, M.   Le bon usage: grammaire française, avec des remarques sur la langue française d'aujourd'hui.   8e éd. revue.   Gembloux (Belgium), Duculot; Paris, Hatier, 1964.   1,194 p.   55s. 6d.

A very detailed work of reference, with profuse examples drawn from French literature as well as from current usage. The section on the preposition alone occupies about 75 pages. 1,072 paragraphs, supported by a full subject index (p. 1,135–89). Primarily for those who have French as their mother tongue. *The* French reference grammar.

Gubb, F.   Points to watch in 'O' level French.   London Heinemann, 1959 (reprinted 1960).   38 p.   2s. 6d.

14 short chapters written for G.C.E. 'O' level candidates.

Treatment of grammar is clear and simple within a brief compass. Deals with pitfalls only. Knowledge of vocabulary is assumed. Sentences quoted to illustrate points mentioned.

No index, phonetics, guide to pronunciation or illustrations. Clear layout with bold type for key words. Good, concise revision of difficulties of grammar. Makes no mention, e.g., of formation or uses of the basic tenses of the verb, but sets out, e.g., on one page the essentials of *Commands and the subjunctive*. Useful for those with a French vocabulary and 'rusty' knowledge of grammar. Excellent value.

Hermus, C.   French.   London, E. Arnold, 1956–61.   5 v.   8s. 6d., 8s. 6d., 9s., 9s. 6d., 10s. 6d.

Illustrated course aimed at G.C.E. 'O' level candidates and those taking similar examinations. Claims to be practical and adaptable. Each volume has about 140 one-page lessons. V. 1 includes oral practice and French–English vocabulary. V. 2 has similar pattern but omits oral questions and adds index to grammar. V. 5, by Hermus and D. N. R. Lester, is also a revision volume for the four earlier parts of the course. An alternative to this, by the same two authors, is *French for first examinations* (9s. 6d.), which includes examples of examination questions.

Hugo's Language Institute.   French grammar simplified.   London, the Institute, [1954].   124, 32, 24 p.   6s.

1954 revision of a popular and established volume. One of a famous series of language grammars and courses. 26 lessons intended to teach French to beginners in 3 months.

Selective treatment, as title implies. Enough for a working knowledge. Vocabulary (4 p.) of words which occur more than once in text plus other words used in examples. Exercises with each lesson. Third section of book is key to these exercises.

No index and no use of phonetics. Introduction and p. 3–31 of second section are examples of imitated pronunciation. No illustrations. Layout is very cramped. Bold type is used but does not stand out. Chief defects are the unattractive appearance of the text (a very attractive text is required if the learner is to have any hope of teaching himself French in 3 months) and the imitated pronunciation which is designed to make the volume self-contained but which is not especially helpful.

Inman, T. B.   'O' level French.   London, Bell, 1965.   ix, 164 p.   8s. 6d.

The 35 lessons each consist of a passage of narrative prose (mainly by 19th and 20th-century authors), followed by exercises, vocabulary, questions on subject matter and suggestions for composition. A summary of grammar for 'O' level, with exercises, is included. The final vocabulary is French-English only. Solid and worthy, but a little dreary. "The book is worthy of consideration by teachers seeking a course for their 'O' level year" (*Modern languages*, v. 46, no. 3, 1965, p. 123–4). Prefer Hermus and Lester's *French for 'O' level examinations*.

JENKINS, E. S.   Teach yourself French grammar.   London, English Universities Press, 1961.   xxii, 167 p.   6s.

For those with some previous knowledge. Designed to follow on from N. S. Wilson's *Teach yourself French*.

Comprehensive treatment of grammar by the usual method of one part of speech per chapter. 50 pages devoted to verbs. Vocabulary introduced only to illustrate points of grammar. No exercises.

No index, phonetics, guide to pronunciation or illustrations. Layout is somewhat cramped and solid. Typography is reasonably good although the bold type does not stand out clearly. Type size of tables of irregular verbs is too small for the irregularities to stand out. This member of a famous family is good value if the learner can face the unattractive pages. Compares unfavourably with, say, Morle and Jammes.

KENYON, R. W.   La langue courante: a simple introduction to modern French for adults.   London, Harrap, 1963.   192 p.   10s. 6d.

19 lessons, each with text and a vocabulary of 50 words, and many exercises. Recommended in the Federation of British Industries' *Foreign language needs of industry* (1964), together with Alden's *Collins Cortina French* (q.v.), but it makes heavy demands on the beginner and, with its manipulative exercises, stresses reading skill rather than oral fluency.

KNIGHT, T. W.   Living French.   London, University of London Press, 1960 (reprinted 1962).   255 p.   9s. 6d.

2nd edition of a work intended primarily for day and evening students in commercial and technical colleges. 25 chapters plus 2 appendices. Can be used as self-tutor.

Full treatment of grammar with three main points explained in each chapter. Vocabulary attached to each lesson, together with list of idioms and phrases and list of useful words. Collected vocabulary, each way. Exercises with each lesson.

Phonetics not used; pronunciation covered briefly in introductory paragraphs. Maps on endpapers. Type and layout extremely clear and easy to follow. Covers fully but simply all the basic points of grammar. Useful reading material includes conversations, letters and stories. A rapid general course for those with no previous knowledge. Some outside help with pronunciation would be an advantage to the learner. Very pleasant volume to handle.

MANSION, J. E. A grammar of present-day French. London, Harrap, 1952 (and reprints). 400 p. *15s*. Key. *8s. 6d*.

First published 1919. "For sixth form pupils and university students study-ing 'the *mechanism* of present-day French' " (*Preface*). Praised for its arrange-ment, treatment and accuracy, in Harmer and Norton's *Manual of modern Spanish*. This fuller edition includes exercises, being bound with *Exercises in French syntax* (1925 and reprints. 152 p.).

MORLE, A. H. G., and JAMMES, J. R. J. A new French grammar for G.C.E. candidates. London, Hutchinson, 1960. 221 p. *7s. 9d*.

Written for G.C.E. 'O' and 'A' level candidates.

Very thorough and comprehensive. Makes a special attempt to simplify approach to irregular verbs. No separate vocabulary, but included in chapters in order to illustrate grammatical points. Special section on word traps. No exercises. 2nd ed., with exercises, 1964. *13s. 6d*.

Index of grammatical terms and English words. Separate index of French words and expressions. No phonetics, guides to pronunciation or illustrations. Layout is extremely clear and attractive. Times New Roman type, with good use of bold. Although intended for G.C.E. candidates, this would make an excellent course for someone with a working knowledge of French. One of the most useful and attractive examples of its kind.

MUIR, J. N. French examination practice. London, Blackie, [n.d.]. ix, 118 p. *5s. 3d*.

Produced for G.C.E. 'O' level candidates.

Selective treatment stresses basic rules of grammar only and gives practice in applying them. Vocabulary, each way, at end to cover needs of this volume. Also some classified vocabulary. Exercises to cover points mentioned.

No index, phonetics, guides to pronunciation or illustrations. Very clearly set out. Pleasing typography, but bold is used for headings only and not for emphasis of difficulties and differences. A very sound résumé of basic points of grammar which should appeal to those wishing to brush up an existing knowledge.

MUNRO, K. D. French revision. London, English Universities Press, 1965. xii, 84 p. (Teach Yourself revision text). *5s*.

Intended for quick reference and revision at about 'A' level standard. A good, solid book, but 'A' level students no longer revise in this manner. Exercises consist of 250 sentences from English to French, with answers. Useful 4-page guide to contents. No illustrations, cumulated vocabulary or help with pronunciation. Double-column layout on small page is not easy to read. Italic replaces bold where emphasis is needed and is not as easy to spot.

Pt. 1 is called "The simple sentence", pt. 2, "The complex sentence". Together they give good value for quick reference if, as the work assumes, the student already knows the elements of grammar, including the irregular verbs.

RAYMOND, M., and BOURCIER, C. L.   French in the primary school. Edited and adapted by R. P. A. Edwards.   London, Burke, 1964. 4 v. and Teacher's manual.   illus.   £3.

First published in U.S.A. by Allyn and Bacon, 1959–60. Although intended for primary level these volumes could be used by adults with no previous knowledge of the language (the teacher's manual enabling the course to be used as a self-tutor).

Volumes are based on modern Direct Method approach. First two volumes, *Bonjour* and *Venez voir*, consist of illustrations only. V. 3, *Je sais lire*, adds a few simple exercises to illustrations. V. 4, *Je sais lire avec joie*, is made up of reading matter with some illustrations.

Clear layout and attractively presented. Describes itself thus: "This course is designed to enable young children to express themselves freely in the French language and to understand it. If, at a later stage, an academic study of the language is made, the pupil will have the definite advantage of having first met it as a living medium of communication and will not regard it merely as an academic exercise." No better primer exists.

RESNICK, S.   Essential French grammar.   London, Hodder & Stoughton, 1966.   xiv, 15–157 p.   5s.

Paperback edition of a work first published in 1962 by Dover Publications.

Grammar is here treated as a means to express vocabulary. Difficulties are streamlined, if possible (e.g., the use of the subjunctive is covered in a few lines which merely indicate that one can manage without it, – which, of course, is true). No separate vocabulary, but there is a 50 p. list of words identical or nearly identical in both languages. No illustrations, but there is an index. No help with pronunciation, even though there is an emphasis on the spoken word. Layout is reasonably good within a small framework. Italic replaces bold where emphasis is needed.

Good value for those whose learning time is limited and who wish to communicate rather than be scholarly. Describes itself thus: "All the grammar you really need to speak and understand the language; designed for Teach Yourself enthusiasts or for class use, for beginners or for a refresher course; the ideal supplement to a phrase book".

SAXELBY, E.   Cours de français.   London, Ginn, 1937.   4 v. illus. £1 13s. 6d.

Volumes are: 1. *En route*. 2. *En marche*. 3. *En France*. 4. *Enfants de France*. Four-year course for G.C.E. candidates. Introduces students to French life and literature. Lengthy French passages, exercises, drill, grammar (p. 185– 215), verb tables, notes on translation, vocabulary each way, index to grammar. Also available are *Phonetic transcript of first five lessons of 'En route'* (2s.), and *Vocabulary booklet* (1s.).

SHOCKET, M. Cinq années de français. Cambridge, University
Press, 1958 (and reprints, e.g. 1964). 5 v. illus. £2 3s. 6d.

Course based on Direct Method approach. First four volumes cover
ground to 'O' level. V. 5 introduces subjunctive, consolidates and prepares
for first university examination.

French-English vocabulary. Index of grammar. Clear layout and typography.

SIMPSON, A. A simplified French course. London, Faber, 1953–59.
4 v. £1 7s.

Four-year course written especially to meet needs of secondary modern
schools. Better used with a teacher than as a self-tutor.

Treatment of grammar is fairly comprehensive. Points are introduced
gradually in context rather than in a vacuum. Very practical vocabulary in
text, but only collected vocabulary is 6 pages of French-English at end of
v. 4. Exercises at frequent intervals throughout.

No phonetics, no guide to pronunciation, but many useful illustrations.
Very well laid out, with helpful use of bold type. The whole is written from
the point of view of interest rather than academic performance. Contains
much interesting information about France and the French.

SKERRY'S COLLEGE. Modern Language Staff. A graded French
grammar. London, Pitman, 1954. viii, 264 p. 8s.

70 lessons. Part 1 (lessons 1–60), to smooth way for those unfamiliar with
English or French grammar. Part 2, for revision. Vocabulary with each lesson
and each way at end. Exercises with each lesson. Passages for translation.
Verb table. "Those who are taking up the study of French later in life will
find this an admirable book for their purpose. It anticipates and removes the
many 'snags' which so often hinder success in the early stages of study"
(*Foreword*).

SMITH, S. M. A modern French course. London, University
Tutorial Press, 1950–58. 5 v. £1 8s. 6d.

Volumes are *Ma première année de français*; *En deuxième année*; *En troisième
année;En quatrième année; En cinquième année*. 5-year course up to G.C.E. 'O'
level. Adequate drill and oral questions. V. 2 consists of 29 lessons. V. 4 includes classified vocabulary reprinted, for revision, from v. 2 and 3. V.5 is for
examination year.

SYMONDS, P. Let's speak French. London, Oxford University
Press, 1962–3. 2 v. 20s.

Aimed at teaching French to beginners, stressing the oral approach. Each
chapter consists of a page of illustrations related to a text, sets of questions,
and suggestions for classroom conversation. Good layout and typography.
Tapes and wall pictures are available for the two books. A very good book
for beginners, but expensive for school use.

TOMLINSON, L.   Nos voisins français.   London, Oxford University Press, 1951–63.   4 v.   £1 13s.

> 5-year course for secondary schools. Better used with a teacher than as a self-tutor.
>
> Treatment of grammar is very full. Points are introduced naturally and progressively. Collected vocabulary at end of each of first three vols. V. 3 only is both ways, v. 1 and 2, French-English only. Exercises throughout.
>
> Has general index also at end of each of first three vols. Phonetics not used and no guide to pronunciation. Illustrations, many of them decorative rather than useful. Layout is well up to usual O.U.P. standard. Clear typography with effective use of bold type. Essence of this course is that it attempts from beginning to make student speak and think entirely in French. It is thus in line with modern developments in language teaching. Grammar and vocabulary follow naturally from examples.
>
> V. 4, described as good material for the ambitious fifth-former, is highly praised in *Modern languages* (v. 44, no. 2, 1965, p. 84) as "a book which bridges the gap between the banalities of 'O' level and the heights of sixth form specialism".

TRAVIS, E. B., and TRAVIS, J. E.   Cours moyen de français.   London, Harrap, 1941–51 (and reprints). 2 v.   14s.

> Covers the third and fourth years of French. (Sub-title is *A French course for middle forms*). 22 and 21 lessons respectively. Vocabulary each way. Gramophone records available.

TRAVIS, J. E.   Cours élémentaire de français.   London, Harrap, 1960 (and reprints).   2 v. illus.   13s. 6d.

> Sub-title is *A beginner's French course for schools*. Covers the first two years of French. Part 2 consists of 24 lessons. Gramophone records, prepared by the Linguaphone Institute, may be used in conjunction with the course.

TRAVIS, J. E.   Cours pratique: an elementary French revision course.   London, Harrap, 1953.   248 p.   8s. 6d.

> Written for the third year of a grammar school course. Needs teacher, prior knowledge or some outside agent for guidance on pronunciation. 17 lessons.
>
> Grammar included is kept to a basic minimum. Vocabulary attached to each exercise, with chief words in bold type. Collected vocabulary at end. Exercises with each lesson.
>
> Phonetics not used and no guide to pronunciation. Illustrations of French countryside. Layout is clear and easy to follow. Easily read Baskerville type. A very useful refresher course for those with some previous knowledge. Contains much practical information.

TRAVIS, J. E.   A précis of French grammar.   London, Harrap, 1939 (reprinted 1962).   176 p.   5s. 6d.

Written for G.C.E. 'O' level candidates. To be used preferably with a teacher.

Contains all but the more advanced grammar. Points of grammar are introduced according to progressive difficulty. English-French vocabulary for use in exercises. These are grouped at end of volume to give practice on each point of grammar.

General index. No phonetics, guides to pronunciation, or illustrations. Layout and type are clear although bold type used in examples does not stand out particularly well. A straightforward statement of basic grammar which by itself would give a working knowledge. Could be used as a self-tutoring course with help on or knowledge of pronunciation.

TRAVIS, J. E., and AULD, D. M.   Études supérieures de français. London, Harrap, 1959–60.   2 v.   £1 2s.

Part 1 is a course for sixth forms and contains French passages and exercises. Part 2 is for 2nd year sixth forms and for those taking junior university examinations. Contains passages from and into French. Key available at 10s.

TRAVIS, J. E., and AULD, D. M.   Manuel de français moderne; French practice for the examination form.   London, Harrap, 1947 (and reprints, e.g., 1961).   405 p.   9s. 9d.

Consists of "texts and tests of every sort" designed to "round off the normal school course". 26 chapters, each following same pattern. Vocabulary each way, totalling 74 p. Includes examination questions from previous G.C.E. papers. Layout is clear and typography pleasing.

Begins with sound practical advice to examination candidates. An excellent revision course.

To accompany the volume, 5 double-sided 10″ records are available, prepared by and obtainable from Linguaphone Institute, 207–9, Regent Street, London, W.1.

WATSON, J. R.   French grammar in action; a collection of drills, games and ideas designed for the practice of grammar rules.   London, Harrap, 1958 (reprinted 1960).   80 p.   3s. 6d.

To give practice on difficult points of grammar. 16 lessons, 4 of them divided into several parts. Could be used in conjunction with a course as self-tutor.

Deals only with difficulties of grammar. Vocabulary incidentally in examples. Exercises to illustrate difficulties.

No index. Basic vowel sounds illustrated phonetically in French. Tape recording of introductory notes on French vowel sounds and intonation, together with many of the exercises, may be obtained from the author at Eagle House, Sandhurst, Camberley, Surrey. A few illustrations. Laid out mostly in double-column pages. Key words in bold type. Bright and interesting approach. Good value for those with knowledge of French grammar who need guidance on more difficult points.

WATSON, J. R.   La langue des français.   London, Harrap, 1963–66. 4 v.   256, 288, 320, 280 p.   illus.   12s., 13s., 13s. 6d., 16s.

V. 1–3 form a course to G.C.E. 'O' level standard. V. 1 has 18 lessons, v. 2 has 15, and v. 3, 16. Each lesson begins with a line or two of conversation, followed by vocabulary, reading matter, grammar, exercises and a brief game. Cumulated vocabulary, each way. Layout very clear. Bold and italic used for emphasis. Obligatory liaisons marked in the text, and tape recordings available of all texts and dialogues in the books. Tapes recorded in France by French adults and children. Three 5″ reels at 3¾ i.p.s. (cost: £5 5s.), from Harrap Audio-Visual Aids, 182, High Holborn, London, W.C.1.

Fourth book is independent of earlier three volumes. Intended for consolidation work or for the first year of 'A' level work. Contains summary of grammar, with an index. 6 sections: 1. Thirty extracts from modern French authors. 2. Thirty anecdotes. 3. Eighty passages for translation into French. 4. Sentences for translation into French. 5. Vocabulary difficulties. 6. Summary of grammar. A well recommended series.

WHITMARSH, W. F. H.   A first French book.   3rd ed.   London, Longmans, Green, 1965.   x, 182 p.   illus.   8s. 9d.

Third edition of v. 1 of a popular course by a well-known writer of French text-books. With companion volumes, constitutes a complete course from elementary to university level.

This volume has 34 lessons and includes only present tense of verbs as a starting point. Vocabulary of about 500 words. Exercises at end of each section.

Also available are *A phonetic introduction to 'A first French book'* and three L.P. records of excerpts from v. 1–3 of the course.

Third edition has been reset and newly illustrated, but text differs hardly at all from that of the 2nd edition (1953). A good solid book, with the virtue of clarity, but it lacks the 'spark' and imagination that distinguish Grayson's *A la page*.

WHITMARSH, W. F. H.   A second French book.   3rd ed.   London, Longmans Green, 1965.   ix, 211 p.   8s. 3d.

30 lessons intended for consolidation rather than advancement. 250 words of vocabulary added to the 500 of *A first French book*.

WHITMARSH, W. F. H.   A third French book.   2nd ed.   London, Longmans Green, 1965.   ix, 230 p.   8s. 9d.

28 lessons intended for middle forms of secondary schools. Introduces Imperfect, Past historic, Pluperfect and Conditional tenses, passive voice, present participle, infinitive with and without preposition, demonstrative

pronouns. Adds a further 250 words of vocabulary. Summary of grammar, with index.

WHITMARSH, W. F. H.   A fourth French book.   2nd ed.   London, Longmans Green, 1965.   viii, 247 p.   9s. 3d.

Fourth and final book of basic course. Adds reading matter from French authors to completion of a survey of the essentials of grammar. Emphasis in this volume is on oral and written expression of the language.

Like the three other volumes of the course, is clearly set out and reasonably attractive in appearance. Among the best of the orthodox grammar courses.

WILSON, N. S.   Teach yourself French.   London, English Universities Press, 1938 (and reprints, e.g., 1958).   239 p.   (Teach yourself language series).   6s.

Based on the work of Sir John Adams. 32 lessons. Does not claim to be a grammar. Exercises, translation, each way. Key, with notes, p. 149–208. French-English vocabulary. Also a list of more common irregular verbs.

Same author's *Everyday French* (London, English Universities Press. 4th ed. 1947, and reprints. 242 p. 7s. 6d.) consists of passages for translation each way and has short bibliography.

Grammars for Scientists

JACKSON, H. S., and STANDRING, J.   French course for technologists and scientists.   London, Harrap, 1960.   272 p.   16s.

Authors are lecturers in Department of Modern Languages, Manchester College of Science and Technology. For sixth formers studying science, undergraduates taking an examination in scientific French, and others. Grammar, p. 11–45; sentences for translation, from French, p. 49–54; 17 introductory passages; 150 passages for translation. These latter are extracts from French books and periodicals; they cover mechanical, electrical and civil engineering, chemistry and physics. Suggestions for further reading; French-English vocabulary of about 2,000 words; index to grammar. Clear, with good use of bold type.

MOFFATT, C. W. P.   Science French course.   London, University Tutorial Press, 1951 (and reprints, e.g. 1954).   viii, 332 p.   12s. 6d.

4th edition, revised by N. Corcoran, of work first published 1948. Wider in subject coverage and fuller, generally, than Jackson and Standring. Part 1: Elements of grammar (p. 1–44). 2: Notes on some important constructions (p. 45–53). 3: Irregular accidence and paradigms of verbs (p. 54–91). 4: Premières lectures. 5: Passages from periodicals and examination papers, covering physics, chemistry, mathematics, botany, zoology, geology, geography, physiology, psychology, anthropology, military studies. Vocabulary, French-English, p. 284–328; index to grammar.

GENERAL DICTIONARIES

CHEVALLEY, A., and CHEVALLEY, M.   The concise Oxford French dictionary.   Oxford, Clarendon Press, 1934 (reprinted with corrections, e.g., 1958).   xx, 895, [12] p.   illus.   17s. 6d.

Aims at being a worthy companion to the *Concise Oxford dictionary of current English*. Nearly 40,000 entry words, including proper names. List of irregular verbs; weights and measures. The introduction (p. iii–xii) includes notes on 'false friends' and pronunciation. Pronunciation of entry-words is given in International Phonetic Alphabet form. Appended list of proper and geographical names, plus 12 pages of line-drawings, showing named parts of aircraft, motor car and the like. The warning sign ⚠ is used to make the enquirer beware of an apparent analogy.

The companion volume is:

GOODRIDGE, G. W. F. R.   A practical French-English dictionary for English-speaking countries.   Oxford, Clarendon Press, 1940.   vi, 395 p.   9s. 6d.

The two volumes may be purchased bound together (1963 reprint. 20s.).

CURZON, A. de.   Cassell's French-English, English-French compact dictionary.   London, Cassell, 1962.   xi, 256 p.   10s. 6d.

43rd edition of a work first published in 1904.

In French-English section International Phonetic Association symbols given for each word. In English-French section simplified transcription adopted. Double column pages, somewhat cramped. Small type size makes reference slightly difficult. Up to date and reliable within the limits of a compact dictionary. Midway in size between Harrap's Concise and Pocket but not as easy to use as either of these two.

Dictionnaire usuel Quillet-Flammarion par le texte et par l'image, redigé par Pierre Goan.   Paris, Flammarion, 1960.   1,458 p.   c. 50s.

Combines dictionary and encyclopaedia in one sequence. Clear definitions. The illustrations are fewer than and inferior to those in *Petit Larousse* (q.v.). A 30-page grammar is included. There is a coloured version: *Dictionnaire usuel en couleurs* (1964). 1,708 p. 63s.).

DUBOIS, M. M., and CESTOE, C.   Larousse's modern French-English dictionary.   London, Macmillan, 1960.   [xiv] 768, [xiv] 752 p.   illus.   70s.

English-French, 768 p.; French-English, 752 p.; about 35,000 main entries, including geographical names, in each part. Phonetic pronunciation for both French and English entry-words. Gives U.S. as well as British usage. 27 word-lists and illustrations with keyed parts. Illustrations of more common objects such as flowers and trees would have been welcome.

Duden français. Dictionnaire en images.   2. éd. corrig.   Paris, Didier,
   1962.   672, 112, 128 p. illus.   20 F (London, Harrap. 30s.).

An all-French pictorial dictionary, adapted from the German edition
published by the Bibliographisches Institut, Mannheim. 25,000 illustrations,
including 8 colour plates.

The E.U.P. concise French and English dictionary.   London, English
   Universities Press, 1946 (reprinted 1960).   491 p.   8s. 6d.

Does not claim to be exhaustive, but French-English section has some
15,000 words; English-French section, over 20,000.

Lists of Christian and geographical names, weights and measures, irregular
verbs, idioms and phrases, all in French-English section.

No guide to pronunciation except that aspirated words in French-English
section are indicated. Double column pages and type both clear for easy
reference. Up to date. Within the limits of a concise dictionary contains
recent words which have become established. Covers most needs for conversation, reading, correspondence and translation.

FOURRÉ, P.   Premier dictionnaire en images; les 1300 mots fondamentaux du français.   London, Harrap, 1957.   255 p.   11s. 6d.

2nd edition of work published originally in France by Didier in series
De la langue à la civilisation française.

Basic French-French vocabulary. Contextual phrases for some words.
Not a work of reference.

Section on pronunciation, but entirely in French. One or more illustrations
per word, 2,000 in all. A very good way to learn or consolidate basic
vocabulary for those with some knowledge of pronunciation.

Gasc's concise dictionary of the French and English languages. New
   ed.   London, Bell, 1963.   xii, 775 p.   11s. 6d.

First published in 1901. Each part (French-English, English-French) has
c. 35,000 entry-words. Supplement of new words, these being footnoted in
the main sequence. No guide to pronunciation, apart from a one-page note
on "Peculiarities of French pronunciation". Equivalents are categorised.
Small type, but clear. Extremely cheap; much used in secondary schools.

GIRARD, D., and others.   Cassell's new French dictionary.   London,
   Cassell, 1962.   xvi, 762, 655 p.   £1 10s.

Based on Cassell's French-English English-French dictionary, first published 1920 and which had reached 35 editions by 1961.

Includes French-Canadian usage. New words put in and errors rectified.
Obsolete items omitted. Examples given wherever possible.

Phonetic pronunciation in brackets after each word. Key to pronunciation
at beginning. Double column pages. Word in bold, meaning in ordinary,
examples in italic. Well revised and up to date. Contains many recent
scientific and technical terms.

JAGO, R. P.   Harrap's concise French and English dictionary.   London, Harrap, 1949 (reprinted 1961).   viii, 804 p.   18s.

Based on Harrap's Standard and Shorter dictionaries, edited by J. E. Mansion.

Conciseness achieved by omitting abstruse words from *Shorter dictionary*. Number of illustrative examples reduced. Phonetic pronunciation in brackets after words that are difficult to pronounce. Double column pages. Word in bold, meaning in ordinary, examples in italic. Still perfectly legible although showing some signs of being a seventh impression. Easy to consult. Very useful single volume member of a famous family.

JAGO, R. P.   Harrap's pocket French and English dictionary.   London, Harrap, 1951 (reprinted 1964).   viii, 527 p.   9s. 6d.

Based on Harrap's Standard and Shorter dictionaries.

Contains only words likely to be met in general reading or conversation. Fewer examples than Concise dictionary.

Symbols of International Phonetic Association adopted to help with the more difficult pronunciations. Double column pages. Very clear print, especially for an eighth impression. Extremely good value. The essential words of both languages in a volume measuring $6\frac{1}{2}'' \times 4\frac{1}{2}'' \times \frac{7}{8}''$.

KOESSLER, M., and DEROCQUIGNY, J.   Les faux amis, ou Les trahisons du vocabulaire anglais (conseils aux traducteurs).   4e éd.   Paris, Vuibert, 1949.   xxviii, 390 p.

Intended for those translating from French. Arranged alphabetically under English words and idioms (*e.g.*, 'curious', 'jolly', 'journey'). Many quotations from English authors. Supplemented by J. Derocquigny's *Autres mots anglais perfides* (Paris, Vuibert, 1931, xii, 107 p.)

A comparable work, with English and French words in one alphabetical sequence and numerous examples is J. G. Anderson's *Le mot juste: a dictionary of English and French homonyms;* revised by Lewis G. Harmer (New York, Dutton, 1938. ix, 205 p.). Thanks to the single A-Z sequence, pairs of words such as 'please' and 'plaire', 'gain' and 'gagner', 'reason' and 'raison' are in juxtaposition. In these cases the English word precedes.

LINKLATER, P.   Mon premier dictionnaire français.   London, University of London Press, 1949 (reprinted 1961).   xii, 216 p.   10s. 6d.

Some 8,000 basic words with meanings in French.

Each word reproduced phonetically. Table of International Phonetic Association symbols in introduction. Illustrations on nearly every page. Used to give a meaning or to supplement a meaning where a picture is easier to understand. Single column pages with illustrations generally in right-hand margin. Attractive presentation in clear type. Designed for those who know a little French and wish to extend vocabulary by being made to think in simple French instead of English.

LITTRÉ, E.　Dictionnaire de la langue française.　Édition intégrale.
Paris, Pauvert, 1956–58.　7 v.　£32 4s.

A reprint of the great dictionary published in 1873–78 (4 v. and supplement), the supplement being here incorporated into the main sequence. As an etymological dictionary on historical principles it is particularly rich in citations from classical French literature. Its 20th-century counterpart, P. Robert's *Dictionnaire alphabétique et analogique de la langue française* (Paris, Société du Nouveau Littré, 1957–64. 6 v.) draws on more modern periods. (A new edition of Robert was begun in 1966.) The re-issued Littré, in a distinctive narrow format (5″ wide; single column) has *c.* 50,000 entry-words.

Le petit Littré (Paris, Presses Universitaires de France, 1959. 1,660 p. 50 F) is an excellent abridgement by A. Beaujean. It contains *c.* 40,000 main entries.

MANSION, J. E.　Harrap's shorter French and English dictionary.
London, Harrap, 1940 (reprinted 1963).　viii, 688, 16, 940, 11 p.
£1 17s. 6d.

Condensed from *Harrap's Standard French and English dictionary* (1954. 2 v., £7 5s.; Supplement, 1962. 21s.).

Very full treatment. New words are included in a supplement which necessitates reference to two sections for some words.

Phonetic pronunciation after each word with key to pronunciation at beginning. No illustrations. Double column pages. Word in bold, meaning in ordinary, examples in italic. Has now been reprinted 13 times and is not as easy to read as the newly set type of Cassell's. Not as up to date as Cassell's, but otherwise similar in format and comprehensiveness.

MANSION, J. E.　Harrap's standard French and English dictionary.
London, Harrap, 1962.　2 v.　£8 10s.　(v. 1, French-English.
xvi, 912, 85 p.　70s.; v 2, English-French.　xii, 1,488, 51 p.　£5).

First published 1934–39; reprinted with corrections, (1947–48. The 1962 edition includes the 1962 supplement (also published separately. 21s.) J. E. Mansion died in 1942.

The French-English part has about 60,000 main entries; the English-French half is decidedly fuller, with about 90,000 entries. Colloquialisms, technical terms (categorised) and Americanisms included. Particularly rich in idioms and sentences showing words in context. Proper names appear in the main sequences; abbreviations are noted in appendices. International phonetic alphabet used. Compounds are indented.

Still the best general two-way French and English dictionary.

MATORÉ, G.　Dictionnaire du vocabulaire essentiel: les 5,000 mots fondamentaux.　Paris, Larousse, 1963.　iv, 359 p.　22.90F.

A French-French dictionary with entry words drawn from *Petit Larousse*. Intended chiefly for educated foreigners. Words are defined succinctly, in most cases with an example of the word in context that sheds light on its sense. Less good when it defines a noun by a verb of the same family. International phonetic alphabet used.

G. Gougenheim's *Dictionnaire fondamental de la langue française* (Paris, Didier, 1959. 255 p. c. 20s.) has a basic vocabulary limited to c. 3,000 entry words (defined by less advanced words) and is very good value.

Petit Larousse. Paris, Larousse, 1959 (and reprints, e.g., 1966). viii, 1,120, xvi, 1,121–1,795, [4], 24 p. illus., maps. 56s.

First published in 1856. Previous to 1959 was criticised particularly for its out-of-date illustrations. The 1959 edition was offset-printed and the illustrations entirely modernised. The main part (p. 1–1120) is a French-French dictionary with c. 50,000 entries and precise definitions. The second part is a condensed encyclopaedia, mainly of persons and places. 73,000 entries in all; 5,130 illustrations. Included is a section "Locutions latines et étrangères" and an atlas supplement. Small but clear type. Without doubt the best single-volume combined dictionary and encyclopaedia for those with some knowledge of French.

The magnificent *Grand Larousse encyclopédique* (1960–64. 10 v. £120 the set) combines dictionary and encyclopaedia in one sequence of 450,000 entries, with 22,000 illustrations. As a dictionary it is considerably more detailed than *Petit Larousse* (e.g., compounds of 'queue' number 19, as against 7 in *Petit Larousse*). Each volume has bibliographies appended.

The *Larousse: trois volumes en couleurs* (3 v. 1965–66. 280 F) has about 110,000 entries, and 12,000 illustrations in colour.

RAT, M. Dictionnaire des locutions françaises. Paris, Larousse, 1957. xv, [1], 430 p. 1,250 fr.

Arranged alphabetically by keyword. The explanation of each expression is supported by a quotation. Includes colloquialisms. List of authors cited; index of keywords (c. 2,500).

J. O. Kettridge's *French for English idioms and figurative phrases, with many quotations from French authors* (London, Routledge, 1966. vii, 278 p. 25s.) is a re-issue of his *French idioms and figurative phrases* (2nd ed. 1949), arranged alphabetically, with profuse cross-references.

THOMAS, A. V. Dictionnaire des difficultés de la langue française. Sous la direction de M. de Toro. Paris, Larousse, 1956. xi, [1], 435 p. 995 fr.

Based on current usage. Cites as its authorities the *Dictionnaire de l'Académie française* (8e éd. Paris, Hachette, 1932–35. 2 v.), Littré, *Larousse du XXe siècle*, and French writers. Numerous examples and quotations, but citing authors only. Although intended for a French public, should be valuable to more advanced students of French in this country. Thus, the pages on genders cover such points as "Noms sur le genre desquels on peut se tromper", "Noms a double genre", and "Noms qui n'ont pas d'équivalents feminins". Pronunciation is also dealt with. Full cross-references.

VINAY, J. P., and others. Everyman's French-English, English-French dictionary, with special reference to Canada. London, Dent, 1962. xxvi, 862 p. 21s.

Prepared at the Lexicographic Research Centre, University of Montreal. French-English, p. 1–390; English-French, p. 391–862. The two sequences include proper names and abbreviations. International phonetic symbols used. Many idioms; different applications of terms are numbered and categorised. To save space, 22 symbols are used, and words of the same stem are grouped at a single entry (e.g., 'awe', 'awful', 'awfully'). The actual entry-words number 20–25,000 words in each half. Intended for the general public as well as for the school and university student. Format, type and form of entry resemble those of the *Concise Oxford dictionary*. Very good value.

WHITMARSH, W. F. H. Essential French vocabulary. London, Longmans, 1956 (reprinted 1960). vii, 141 p. 7s. 6d.

Compiled for 'O' level candidates. Part 1 has *c.* 2,000 French words, with meanings in English and classified into 90 subject groups (e.g., hotel, shops, railway travel). Part 2 provides a selective English-French vocabulary in alphabetical order.
No phonetic symbols or other guide to pronunciation. List of verbs at end. Illustrations on endpapers only. Double-column page; type clear and easy to read. Claims to be useful to those who wish to refresh or enlarge their knowledge of French vocabulary, but its chief value is as a school text-book.

Commercial and Technical Dictionaries

(a) *Commercial and Legal*

DUTTWEILER, G. Nouveau dictionnaire pratique de correspondance commerciale et privée. 4e ed. Geneva, Éditions Générales S.A., 1961. 400 p. 46s. 6d.

The main part (p. 23–289) is arranged alphabetically by key-word (*e.g.*, "Qualités d'un article"; "Différence entre le chèque et la lettre de change"), covering *c.* 2,500 entries. Dictionary of terms (French-French). p. 295–375.

DUTTWEILER, G. Les 20,000 phrases et expressions de la correspondance commerciale et privée. Geneva, Éditions Générales S.A., 1960. 432 p. 24.60 F.

The main section consists of "Texte français, avec vocabulaire allemand et anglais", – 2,337 numbered French terms and phrases, with usage illustrated in sentences. German and English equivalents are given only for the French entry-word. German and English word indexes.

KETTRIDGE, J. O. French-English and English-French dictionary of commercial and financial terms, phrases and practice. 2nd ed. London, Routledge & Kegan Paul, 1949. xii, 647 p. 40s.

French-English, p. 1–318; English-French, 325–639; separate lists of abbreviations and conventional signs, syllabification of French words (p. 324). Over 50,000 words, terms and phrases in each part, with translations and examples. A standard French and English commercial dictionary.

Beatrice C. M. Ransome's *Commercial French terms and phrases* (London, Pitman, 1965. vii, 85 p. 12s. 6d.) has been noted.

SERVOTTE, J. V. Dictionnaire commerical et financier, français-anglais, anglais-français. Verviers, Gérard, 1963. 446, [1] p. (Marabout Service). 710 fr.

French entry-words are listed in the left-hand column and English equivalents in the right-hand column on each page; numbered sub-entries in set order (*e.g.*, entry word followed by a complement, then a verb; entry word as a complement to a substantive). 'Prix' has 137 sub-entries. Over 10,000 French main entries; English index, p. 391–426. Author is Secrétaire du Président de la Kredietbank (Belgium).

Le vocabulaire baromètre dans le langage économique: dictionnaire anglais-français, by J. Delattre and G. de Vernisy (Geneva, Libraire de l'Université: Georg, 1961. 152 p.) has upwards of 1,000 main entries and includes English business jargon (*e.g.*, 'bearish', 'zoom'). Many idioms. Sponsored by École d'Interprètes, Geneva University.

DALRYMPLE, A. W. French-English dictionary of legal words and phrases. 2nd ed. London, Stevens, 1948. [v], 130 p. 21s.

About 4,000 main entries; includes many idioms. Genders and pronunciation of French terms not given. A neatly produced dictionary, with clear type. No index of English terms.

(b) *Technical*

BADER, O., and THÉRET, M. Dictionnaire de métallurgie. Paris, Eyrolles, 1961. 701 p. 68 F.

A French dictionary of metallurgy, with English equivalents for the *c.* 900 French entry-words. The rest of each entry consists of extended definition(s) and notes in French. English-word index.

BUCKSCH, H. Dictionary of civil engineering and construction machinery and equipment, English-French. Paris, Eyrolles; London, 'Contractor's Record', 1960. 419, [1] p. 65s.

BUCKSCH, H. Dictionnaire pour les travaux publics, le bâtiment et l'équipement des chantiers de construction ... français-anglais.

Paris, Eyrolles; London, 'Contractor's Record,' 1961.   547 p.   82s.

These two complementary dictionaries contain 20,000 and 25,000 main entries respectively. Terms are grouped under such entries. Differentiates between British and U.S. terminology. No illustrations.

CUSSET, F.   Vocabulaire technique, anglais-français, français-anglais: électricité, mécanique, industries extractives et connexes, métallurgie, sciences.   7e éd.   Paris, Berger-Levrault, 1965.   434 p.   c. 60s.

Revised at 4–5 year intervals. English-French, p. 5–220; French-English, p. 221–425. About 10,000 strictly technical entry-words in each part, with separately entered sub-entries (e.g., 'vitesse' – more than 50). Conversion tables appended. Compiled by a mining engineer.

DE VRIES, L.   French-English science dictionary.   3rd ed.   New York, London, McGraw-Hill, 1962.   ix, 655 p.   81s. 6d.

First published in 1940; 2nd ed., 1951. Main entries now total c. 48,000, including a supplement of more than 5,000 new terms. Has a very brief "Grammatical guide for translators". A reliable dictionary, covering both pure and applied sciences.

KING, G. G.   Dictionnaire anglais-français: électronique, physique nucléaire et sciences connexes.   Paris, Dunod, 1959.   viii, 312 p. 2,600 fr.

KING, G. G.   Dictionnaire français-anglais. . . .   Paris, Dunod, 1961. viii, 396 p.   38 F.

Each volume has c. 25,000 entry-words. Differentiates between British and U.S. terminology.

LÉPINE, P., with KRASNOFF, G. D.   Dictionnaire français-anglais, anglais-français des termes médicaux et biologiques.   Paris, Éditions Médicales Flammarion; London, Lewis, [1962?]   829 p.   63s.

French-English, p. 11–291; English-French, p. 295–829; 15 pages of numerical data and tables. Abbreviations are included in the main sequence. Intended primarily for French consumption, the French-English part having c. 20,000 main entries, as against about twice that number in the English-French half.

MALGORN, G.   Lexique technique anglais-français.   5e éd.   Paris, Gauthier-Villars, 1965.   xxxiv, 493 p.   40 F.

About 15,000 strictly technical terms, covering machine tools, mines, internal-combustion engines, aviation, electricity, wireless, shipbuilding, metallurgy, civil engineering and commerce. Genders are not stated.

The 4th edition of the companion volume, Lexique technique français-anglais, was published in 1956.

PAASCH, H. Dictionnaire anglais-français et français-anglais des termes et locutions maritimes: marine marchande. Paris, Éditions Maritimes et d'Outre-mer, 1964. 319 p. 22 F.

Based on Captain Paasch's classic *De la quille à la pomme du mât* (5th ed. 1937). About 15,000 entry-words. Many idioms.

PATTERSON, A. M. A French-English dictionary for chemists. 2nd ed. New York, Wiley, 1954. (1961 reprint). 476 p. 52s.

About 42,000 entry-words, even so omitting many terms that have the same spelling and meaning in French and English. A standard dictionary in its field.

GRAMOPHONE RECORDS

(a) *Longer courses*. The Linguaphone course of 16 records, on either 78 or 45 r.p.m. (£15 2s. 1d.) also sells on tape (two 5″ spools, 3¾ i.p.s., 2-track recording). The Berlitz Language Record course consists of 40 lessons (five 12″ 33⅓ r.p.m. records), 5 manuals, rotary verb finder and free advisory service for 6 months, at £16. The Assimil French records that accompany Chérel's *French without toil* consist of a preliminary (eight E.P. 78 r.p.m., or four 45 r.p.m. records, £6 15s.) and an advanced course (twelve E.P. 78 r.p.m. or six 45 r.p.m. records, £9 10s.), the price including the text-books. Linguaphone records accompany J. E. Travis's *Cours élémentaire* (2 parts; 10 records) and *Cours moyen* (part 1; 5 records). W. F. H. Whitmarsh's *A first French book* has three records. The Express (Oldbourne Press) 'Basic conversational French' consists of two 12″ L.P. 33⅓ r.p.m. records, plus text-book, at £5 5s. The 'Holiday enjoyment' language course (Mary Glasgow & Baker) has four 7″ 33⅓ r.p.m. records, at £7 17s. 6d., and the H.M.V. 'Learn French in record time' (43 lessons; on tape) costs £5.

(b) *Shorter courses*. In June 1964 *Which?* (p. 187–92) made an extensive survey of 13 modestly priced courses, ranging in price from £5 5s. ('Basic conversational French') to 7s. 6d. The following are included:

'French: listen and learn' (Dover: Constable): three 12″ 33⅓ r.p.m., £2 14s.

'Conversaphone': one 12″ L.P., 37s. 6d., or one 10″ L.P., 30s. 6d.; also a course for children, similarly priced.

Odhams 'Master' course: four 10″ L.P. records, £2 10s.

Odhams 'Quick' course: two 7″ L.P., 30s.

'Instant' course: two 12″ L.P. records, 70s.
'Lightning conversation' (Oriole Records): two 7″ 45 r.p.m., 29s. 9d.
'Lexiphone' (Visaphone Co.): two 7″ 45 r.p.m., 26s. 6d.
'Talking book traveller' (Methuen): one 7″ 45 r.p.m., 11s. 10d.
'Gem' course: one 7″ L.P., 9s. 2d.
French: '200 basic words' (Saga Records): one 7″ 45 r.p.m., 7s. 6d.
For beginners and holiday makers *Which?* considered the best 'buy'
to be Odhams 'Quick' course; for those with more time and money,
the 'Basic conversational French' course.

(c) *Audio-visual courses*. Harrap Audio-Visual Aids (prices on application) offer four filmstrip-and-record courses: 'Voix et images de
France' (for elementary tution at any age); 'Le français par la méthode
audio-visuelle' (Harrap-Didier Audio-Visual language course; for
tuition by the direct method); 'Parlons français' (Heath de Rochement's Audio-visual French course, for primary schools); and 'French
at home' (five L.P. records and book; prepared under the direction
of Radiodiffusion Télévision Française). Two courses, 'Bonjour line'
and 'En avant', are reviewed in *Modern languages*, v. 47, no. 4,
December 1966, p. 161–6.

BIBLIOGRAPHY

NUFFIELD FOUNDATION. Foreign Languages Teaching Materials
    Project.   French Language Information Centre.   *Audio-visual
    French courses for primary schools: an annotated bibliography*.   London,
    Nuffield Foundation: E. J. Arnold, 1964.   72 p.   8s. 6d.

NUFFIELD FOUNDATION.   *Reference library catalogue*.   [Compiled
    by A. Spicer and others].   Leeds, Nuffield ⦁Foreign Languages
    Teaching Materials Project, 1963–.

READING.   University, Institute of Education Library.   *School text-
    book collection: French*.   Reading, University of Reading, Institute
    of Education Library, 1960.

SHELLEY, H.   *French from five to fifteen: a list of French books and
    books on France for school libraries*.   London, School Library
    Association, 1962.   v, 30 p.   7s.; 8s. 6d.

3

ITALIAN

by F. S. STYCH, M.A., F.L.A.

GRAMMARS

For many years there was a need for a satisfactory, comprehensive Italian grammar for English students and one was obliged to rely on the old-fashioned Sauer-Arteaga, or an American work such as Grandgent and Wilkins (*Italian grammar*, 1915), supplemented in either case by an Italian grammar such as Fornaciari. The student working alone found himself in a better position after the appearance of Dr. K. Speight's *Teach yourself Italian* (1955), which was also adopted in some universities as a first book. Dr. D. M. White's *Italian by yourself* appeared in 1949 as a useful course for adults wishing to acquire a reading knowledge only. There was still room, however, for a large work, not too academic, equipped with full grammar notes and plenty of exercises and practice material, aimed at English students and suited to English methods of work. A competition organised by the Society for Italian Studies produced one which fulfilled these requirements reasonably in F. J. Jones's *Modern Italian grammar*, which appeared in 1962. Sharing the prize was Lennie and Grego's *Italian for you*, – a slightly more popular work, falling between Jones and Valgimigli's attractive *Living Italian* of the previous year. Public interest in Italian also produced, in the B.B.C. series of courses, the excellent little introductory course (*Italian for beginners*), with accompanying record, of Luisa Rapaccini. This has now been superseded by *Parliamo italiano*, with three books and records. Boni's *Complete English-Italian course of* 1958 and Hugo's *Italian simplified* complete the tally of sound courses at various levels now available at reasonable prices for English students working alone. Mention may also be made of the 'painless' Assimil course by A. Chérel which, to achieve its maximum effect, requires the accompanying records (see p. 64). Our section on gramophone record courses has expanded considerably since the first edition of the guide and there has appeared a number of new works and new editions while some of the old ones have gone out of print. We may perhaps particularly notice the third, considerably revised, edition of *Italian for you* and the pleasing conversational grammar *Speak Italian and know Italy*, by G. Rosa (1964).

Of the remaining grammars, it will be seen that some, – like Hall and Bartoli, the various Russo grammars and Rapaccini's *Parlo italiano* – are intended for school use and sometimes, as in the two former cases, for American schools; some, like Hossfeld's, are rather old-fashioned, while others, like Hayward, and Peruzzi, are not comprehensive, although this applies also to M. Valgimigli and the B.B.C. course; or are, for one reason or another, less suited to the needs of a beginner.

Among books which are not strictly classifiable as grammars are Rigal's *A short cut to the Italian language* and Charles Duff's *Basis and essentials of Italian*. Both of these might be found useful, the first as an introduction and the second as a handy reference book.

BONI, C. Complete English-Italian course. London, Allman, 1958. xxv, 249 p. illus., plates. 17s. 6d.

> Elementary: a complete course for beginners. 50 lessons (p. 1–197), containing grammar notes, vocabulary and exercises for translation both ways. Pronunciation is explained in p. i–xxv. Quality of *e* and *o* is marked throughout by italics for the open sound in new words and in all words of the first 25 lessons. Quality of *s* and *z* is not marked. In the vocabulary the same procedure is followed, and stress is marked with an accent, unless considered quite unnecessary. Irregular tenses of irregular verbs are listed and the auxiliaries given in full. 7 reading exercises at the end. Vocabulary: about 2,000 English words and phrases; about 2,000 Italian words, with page references for all irregular verbs and many other words likely to give difficulty. Contents list; many plates. Good use of bold type; clear and thorough presentation. Some details are relegated to footnotes.
>
> A sound grammar for class or reference use.

CAGNO, M. Collins' Cortina Italian in 20 lessons, illustrated; . . . for private study and use in schools, with . . . phonetic pronunciation. Based on the method of R. D. de la Cortina, etc. London, Collins, [1962]. 336 p. 12s. 6d.

> The first 16 lessons consists of general vocabulary, special vocabulary and dialogue. Simulated pronunciation shows stressed syllables in capitals. A reference grammar at the end is arranged by grammatical categories. Irregular tenses of irregular verbs are listed. Grammar notes to lessons them-

selves are relegated to footnotes. Vocabulary, both ways; contents list; no index.

Seems to be designed to teach a conversational rather than a reading knowledge.

CHÉREL, A. Italian without toil. Paris, Assimil; London, Pitman, 1957. viii, 407 p. 18s.

140 lessons, each consisting of short passages, often anecdotes, with English text, on the opposite page, simulated pronunciation, grammar notes, vocabulary and exercises for translation (Italian-English only), with key in the next lesson. Intended as a 5 months' self-tuition course at the rate of one lesson per day; it may be taken more quickly. Two stages of learning are envisaged, passive and active. The first 50 lessons are to be learnt 'passively' first, then gone over 'actively', while the remaining lessons are proceeded with, first passively, then actively. Grammar notes at the end include tables of verbs and pronouns. No contents or index. Stress is indicated by heavy type, but ideally the course is intended for use with records. (There is a free advisory service for purchasers of the records.) A feature of the text-book is small humorous drawings in the text.

The course is sound and comprehensive and, with some help with pronunciation, the text-book could be used without the records, although progress would probably be slower.

CIOFFARI, V. Italian review grammar and composition, with everyday idiom drill and conversation practice. Boston, Heath; London, Harrap, 1950. 308 p. illus., map. 27s. 6d.

Intended as a 4-year U.S. high-school course. 40 lessons, each with grammar notes, reading passage and exercises for translation both ways. Vocabulary, both ways. Index; contents; verb tables. Quality of *e*, *o*, *s*, *z* not marked.

DUFF, C. All purposes Italian for adults. London, English Universities Press, 1958. xvi, 376 p. illus. 16s.

Sub-title: "A comprehensive course . . . for beginners and others: for self-tuition or classes and graduated progressively to university standard." Some help from a native speaker at the outset is recommended, but some instructions on pronunciation are given. 10 lessons, each in 5 sections intended for one hour's class work per section. There are two parts: 'First principles' and 'Framework of the language'. Stress is laid on there being a minimum of made-up exercises, these being replaced by practice with 'situation material' based on passages from current Italian writing of all kinds. Stress is marked by italicised vowels in words other than *piane*. Good use of bold type. Features include jokes, cartoons, advertisements, illustrations, proverbs, a crossword puzzle and a list of Italian radio stations. Vocabulary, Italian-English only, of 2,500 words.

The accent is mainly on current Italian and the course would be of most use to those intending to travel in Italy. The book contains at least one serious grammatical error.

DUFF, C.   The basis and essentials of Italian.   London, Nelson, 1950.
x, 140 p.   8s. 6d.

Pt. 1 (p. 1–93): basic grammar, arranged by grammatical categories.
Pt. 2 (p. 96–171): essential vocabulary (Italian-English only), about 1,650
words. The total vocabulary of the book is about 2,000 words. Pages 134–40
consist of an extract from *Il Principe* as a specimen of connected prose. There
is some help with pronunciation, but further help from a native at the outset
is recommended. Quality of *e*, *o*, *s* and *z* is not marked. Stress is marked with
a grave accent or with bold capitals when very irregular. Advice on the use
of *voi* and *Lei* reflects the attitude of 1938, when the book was first issued.
Good use of sanserif bold.

A useful reference book, and cheap at the price. There is a companion
Reader at 5s.

GRANDGENT, C. H., and WILKINS, E. H.   Italian grammar.   London,
Harrap, 1915.   vi, 184 p.   21s.

Claims to be comprehensive but suited to beginners. Presence of a teacher
is assumed, especially for pronunciation. Elementary; 1–2 year course; 41
lessons (p. 97–150). Treatment is full and exceptions to rules are listed. Points
concerning historical or literary language are relegated to footnotes. Grammar, p. 1–96. Exercises include words for parsing and translation into
English, clauses and sentences for translation into Italian, sentences in both
languages for study, and vocabulary. Irregular verbs are listed and explained
by conjugation. Vocabulary: about 1,250 Italian and about 600 English
words; phrases and idioms are listed under some words. Contents; index.
Pronunciation is indicated by reference to nearest English sounds. Quality of
e and *o* is indicated throughout by accents, and stress is marked.

A good reference grammar for beginners.

HALL, R. A., and BARTOLI, C. M.   Basic conversational Italian.
New York & Toronto, Holt, 1963.   311, lxii p.   illus., maps.
42s.

Elementary textbook for class use. 40 conversations and exercises, mainly
of the substitution type. 20 "grammar units". 8 narrative selections. Supplement on phonetics and orthography and on inflexions. List of irregular verbs
includes only forms used in the book. Each conversation concerns a specific
situation (e.g. The weather; At the museum), and is based on present-day
usage. Conversations are to be learnt by heart by means of repetition and
then dramatised in class. At least half of the new words in each narrative
passage are obvious cognates of English words. Vocabularies both ways.
Attractive illustrations and layout. Expensive by English standards and
unsuitable for class use because of frequent Americanisms, e.g., 'to flunk',
'bread and fixins', 'movie (house)', 'gotten', and American outlook, e.g.,
surprise at having to buy matches. Some sounds are explained in terms
of American speech sounds. Complete recordings of the conversation drills
and pattern practice are available on tapes or records at 78s.

HAYWARD, A. L. Colloquial Italian. 2nd. ed., revised by C. McFarlane. London, Routledge, 1957. vii, 119 p. 7s. 6d.

Elementary and selective, designed to give a working knowledge of the colloquial tongue. Introductory remarks (p. 1–6) usefully outline some parallels with English. Brief pronunciation guide. Quality of *e*, *o*, *s* and *z* is not marked, nor is stress. 12 lessons: grammar notes, vocabulary and conversational material, reading passages (from lesson 7), occasional special notes. Appendix 1 contains business terms (p. 113–14). Appendix 2, reading passages from classical authors.

Could be useful to a student with a flair for languages wishing to do a 'crash course', but is too superficial for very serious study.

HILTON, N. Italiano parlato; edited by P. H. Hargreaves. London, Longmans, 1965. [7] 120 p. illus., map, plan. limp, 8s. 6d.

14 lessons on conversation for those who require a speaking knowledge only of the language. Vocabulary Italian-English only.

HUGO'S LANGUAGE INSTITUTE. Italian simplified: grammar, [etc.]. 112 p. Italian conversation simplified. 64 p. Key to the grammar. 30 p. London, the Institute, [n.d.]. sewn, 6s.; cloth, 7s. 6d.

Intended for self-instruction. Rules for pronunciation and imitated pronunciation. Quality of *e*, *o*, *s* and *z* is not shown. 'Grammar' has 18 lessons, with exercises on grammar and translation into Italian only. Comprehensive, but does not give grammatical rules where these hold also in English. More important constructions are given first, and verbs are introduced one tense at a time. Special help is given with irregular verbs. Irregular stress is shown by capitalising stressed vowel. Much use of bold type. Pages are a little full and rather daunting in appearance, but the course is sound. 'Conversation' consists of a series of sentences in both languages and would benefit by the addition of an index to topics. Principal idioms are introduced, together with expressions based on minor rules omitted from the grammar notes. Stressed vowels are printed in bold where difficulty might arise. Brief and helpful notes on correspondence, at the end. A reference list giving "every tense of every irregular verb" is available separately (*Italian verbs simplified*, 2s. 6d.).

A workmanlike course for the keen student working alone, and good value.

JACKSON, E., and LOPREATO, J. Italian made simple. Garden City, N.Y., Doubleday, 1960. 192 p. paperback, $1.

A fairly conventional grammar in a large format. Has a slight American flavour but not enough to make it unsuitable for use in this country.

JONES, F. J. A modern Italian grammar. London, University of London Press, 1962. 390 p. plates, map. 22s. 6d.

The work claims to be a complete course for beginners and a reference grammar for advanced students. It aims to deal with modern, conversational rather than literary or commercial Italian, but the Appendix has specimens of commercial letters. The main structure of Italian is expounded in the first 25 lessons, the subjunctive and other, finer points being left until later.The student should acquire an active vocabulary of 2,000 words and a passive one of 3,200. Stressed syllables of *sdrucciole* are marked in the earlier lessons and all unusual stresses are marked, either in the vocabularies to the reading exercises or in the main vocabulary at the end. The quality of *e*, *o*, *s* and *z* is not marked. Lessons consist of exposition of grammar, vocabulary and reading passages, with translation exercises into Italian only. Irregular verbs and a list of transitive verbs taking *essere* are given in an appendix. Main vocabulary: about 1,500 Italian and 1,250 English words. Contents; index; bibliography. The pages are a little full but presentation is economical and attractive.

The work shared *ex aequo* with that by Lennie and Grego the prize offered by the Society for Italian Studies for the best new Italian grammar published in this country.

LENNIE, D., and GREGO, M.   Italian for you: a practical grammar. 3rd ed.   London, Longmans, 1966.   xix, 321 p.   limp, 15s.

Intended for university and evening class students. Lessons may be split for the latter. Grammar, vocabularies, exercises, translation both ways, practice material. Lists of irregular verbs and conjugation of regular verbs and the auxiliaries, use of prepositions with verbs. Specimen letters. Contents; index. No main vocabulary. Quality of *e* and *o* marked by phonetic symbols; *s* and *z* not marked. Stressed syllables of *sdrucciole* and *bisdrucciole* marked with bold type. Treatment is full and the work is mainly directed to the more mature student.

The work shared *ex aequo* with that by Jones the prize for the best new Italian grammar published in this country, offered by the Society for Italian Studies.

The 3rd edition has been re-arranged and contains a new section on common idioms.

LENNIE, D., ed.   Selected prose passages for translation into Italian . . . with notes.   London, Longmans, 1965.   151 p.   paper, 15s.; cloth, 25s.

This book has been prepared for use with *Italian for you*, but meets a general need for a selection of this kind specially designed for students of Italian.

MCCONNELL, J.   Learn Italian quickly.   London, MacGibbon, 1960. 224 p.   15s.

Although attractively laid out, this book is so full of errors that it would be a most dangerous one to place in the hands of a beginner.

MILELLA, N. J. Italian in a nutshell. Montclair, N. J., Institute for Language Study; Garden City, N.Y., Garden City Books; London, W. H. Allen, 1959. 128 p. illus. 18s.

Elementary and selective. Based on drill with basic sentence patterns (p. 11–19). Guide to pronunciation and simulated pronunciation throughout. Conversations on a variety of useful topics (p. 20–65). Outline of grammar (p. 66–81); irregular tenses of irregular verbs. Contents; no index. Stress indicated with an accent. Vocabulary: about 2,000 Italian, 1,500 English words. Line drawings; attractive layout. The free record offered is available only in the U.S.A. Could be useful to those wishing to acquire a smattering of the language before visiting Italy, but is too slight for serious study.

MORELLI, U. Italiano ultrarapido. Corso elementare. London, Pitman, 1958. 179 p. 10s. 6d.

MORELLI, U. Italiano ultrarapido. Corso medio. London, Pitman, 1958. x, 210 p. 15s.

Mainly conversational. The *Corso medio* claims to teach a vocabulary of 4,000 words.

NEGRO, O., and HARVARD, J. Beginner's Italian: an introduction to conversational Italian. London, University of London Press, 1961. 112 p. 8s. 6d.

Brief introduction on pronunciation, stress, accents, apostrophe, intonation and capitalisation. 16 lessons, each containing a dialogue followed by material for fluency practice and grammatical explanations. Vivid line-drawings with legends begin each lesson. 14 exercises at end, involving translation both ways and grammar drill. Index to topics; grammatical categories and main tenses of a few important verbs, with good use of capitals.

Not comprehensive. Can be used alone or with a teacher. Each lesson is based on a situation and the book might make a useful "crash course" for a beginner visiting Italy at short notice.

Beginner's Italian can be followed up by:

NEGRO, O., and HARVARD, J. Conversational Italian for adults. London, University of London Press, 1964. 203 p. 7s. 6d.

This teaches spoken Italian by means of 18 lessons based on substitution drills and may be supplemented by the same authors' *Italian for pleasure* (University of London Press. 6s.). This consists of readings from operas, plays and novels, with poems, songs, anecdotes and colloquial sayings. Abbreviations. Lists of records and scores. Further explanation and advice in J. Harvard's *Teaching adults to speak a foreign language* (1961. 4s.) which serves as a teacher's book to the series.

Parliamo italiano: a course of thirty lessons for absolute beginners wishing to acquire a basic knowledge of colloquial Italian.   London, B.B.C., 1963–4.

Three books: No. 1, Texts of lessons 1–10, with vocabularies and grammatical notes; No. 2, Texts, etc. of lessons 11–20; No. 3, Texts, etc., of lessons 21–30. 2s. each. 3 12″ L.P. records, each with the basic dialogue of ten lessons. 15s. 2d. each. Produced to accompany courses on B.B.C. television.

PEI, M.   New Italian self-taught.   New York, Funk and Wagnall, 1959.   xvi, 336 p.   15s.

10 sections, 'based on Italian language phone method of linguistry', with records supplied by the publishers but probably not obtainable in this country. Simulated pronunciation.

PERUZZI, E.   Essential Italian: a practical conversation grammar for beginners.   4th ed.   Florence, Valmartina; London, Bailey, 1960. 188 p.   22s.

Not comprehensive. 24 lessons, consisting of grammar and exercises. Open and closed *e* and *o* are marked with a hook and dot respectively.

PIAZZA, S. X.   Italian in 39 steps: an easy introduction to the language, teaching the most useful words and phrases with special consideration of tourists' needs.   Kingswood, Surrey, Elliot, 1965.   126 p. tables.   7s. 6d.

Quite sound within its avowed limitations but too selective and superficial for all but tourist use.

RAPACCINI, L.   Parlo italiano.   6th ed.   Florence, Le Monnier, 1966. 236 p.   illus.   12s.

Elementary. A complete course for beginners, by direct method with a teacher. 41 lessons, each comprising a reading passage, grammar and exercises. No translation passages, but subjects are given for composition in Italian. Quality of *e, o, s* and *z*, and accentuation in words other than *piane* are marked in main vocabulary only. Vocabulary: about 2,500 Italian words and phrases only. Contents; no index. Line drawings, one coloured.

Sound and thorough. Especially suitable as a children's school text-book. Clear and attractive layout.

RIGAL, W. A.   A short cut to the Italian language.   London, Owen, 1961.   xii, 286 p.   25s.

Developed for military use, in acquiring the language quickly. Part 1 (p. 1–40): 12 lessons; grammar and essential words not cognate in the two languages. Parts 2–3 (p. 43–174, 176–244): 34 lessons on how to turn English words into Italian by means of lists of words, where only the ending is different, e.g. English abstract nouns in -*ty* often have a related Italian word in

-tà. Each lesson begins with a key-word, illustrated with a line drawing. End of lesson 2 has a short list of the main phonological consonant-changes from Latin and Greek which are similar in English and Italian. Part 4: idioms and phrases. Vocabulary (English-Italian only): about 500 words which do not correspond (p. 246–66). Verb conjugations scattered throughout the book. Stress is marked with an accent where likely to cause difficulty. Quality of *e, o, s* and *z* not marked.

The method is simple, and the book could be helpful to a student already knowing a little of the language. Although popular it is reasonably scientific. The advice to use *voi* on all occasions is now out-moded.

ROSA, G.   Speak Italian and know Italy.   London, Parrish, 1964. 512 p.   illus., map.   25s.

20 lessons with grammar, reading and conversation. Verb tables and vocabulary. Good layout and attractive presentation. Contains much information about Italy. One of the more solid of the works designed to teach mainly a knowledge of the spoken language.

ROTA, A., and CORNETT, W. N.   Hossfeld's new practical method for learning the Italian language; revised, with corrections by S. Rundle.   London, Hirschfeld, 1944.   xvi, 416, 32 p.   6s.   Key. 2s.

Complete course, intended particularly for school use. Introduction, with pronunciation, etc. (p. 3–15), 62 lessons (p. 16–289), each with grammar notes, vocabulary, translation exercises (both ways), questions on grammar, with conversation material, reading exercises with annotations to assist in their translation. The whole method is based upon reading aloud. Open *e* and *o* are indicated with a circumflex or a difference in type. Quality of *s* and *z* is not marked, nor is stress. It is assumed that the student will hear Italian spoken. First half of book (to p. 160), elementary grammar; second half (p. 162–289), syntax. Reading passages (p. 290–340); commercial correspondence (p. 341–56). Vocabulary: about 5,750 Italian words; 1,200 English words. Contents; index. Verbs listed, with irregular tenses in full, in last 32 pages. Layout rather solid, with much small type.

Treatment is thorough, but style and matter of the exercises are somewhat old-fashioned.

RUSSO, J. L.   Practical Italian grammar.   London, Harrap, 1941. xiv, 342 p. illus., map.   9s. 6d.

Elementary; a 2-year course. 50 lessons (p. 1–252). Intended for class use with a teacher. Treatment is selective; simplicity and clarity are the main aims. Lessons contain substitution and completion exercises, sentences (forming a connected passage) for translation both ways, oral drill. 14 drawings with special vocabularies are included for direct-method teaching. These are correlated with Heath's *Modern language wall charts.* Brief account of Italian geography, and the Italian passages of the last 17 lessons deal with Italian history, 1800–1914. Other contents are 5 intensive review lessons and

15 short poems. Tables of regular and irregular verbs. General vocabulary of about 1,600 Italian words and 1,500 English words. Pronunciation is treated in some detail, and phonetic symbols are used throughout to show quality of *e* and *o*. Table of contents; index.

American origin is sometimes apparent in vocabulary. More suited to class than individual use.

RUSSO, J. L.   Present day Italian.   Boston, Heath; London, Harrap, 1947.   xvi, 501 p. illus.   35s.

The plan is similar to that of *First year Italian*. 42 lessons and 7 review lessons, the whole divided into two equal halves to cover two sessions. A third section contains dialogues and letters. Appendix gives verb conjugations and a list of personal pronouns. Vocabulary: about 3,000 Italian and 2,000 English words. Contents; index to grammar. Good illustrations and large, clear type. Quality of *e* and *o* marked by phonetic symbols; voiced *s* and *z*, by italics. Stress shown by italicised vowels.

Treatment is thorough, although minor points are relegated to footnotes. Matter is interesting and should encourage a keen student working alone to follow the somewhat rapid pace of the book. Grammar questions and vocabulary drill in the review lessons and the achievement tests attached to them are searching and would provide a good check on progress.

RUSSO, J. L.   Primo corso italiano.   Boston, Heath, 1960.   xxii, 389 p.   illus.   33s. 6d.

28 lessons, consisting of pronunciation, reading, grammar notes, conversation. Uses International Phonetic Alphabet symbols for open *e* and *o*; italic *s* and *z* for sonant forms. Vocabulary both ways.

RUSSO, J. L.   Secondo corso italiano.   Boston, Heath, 1961.   xxii, 417 p.   illus.   38s. 6d.

This is a second year course similar to the *Primo corso italiano*. Both give a good deal of incidental information about Italy. These two books seem designed to replace the author's *First year Italian* and *Second year Italian*, now out of print, being similar, but rather lighter in the modern manner. A little expensive by English standards.

SPEIGHT, K.   Teach yourself Italian.   2nd ed.   London, English Universities Press, 1962.   x, 278 p.   6s.

Part 1 (p. 1–167): 30 lessons, consisting of grammar notes, vocabulary, translation both ways. Open *e* and *o* denoted by phonetic symbols; voiced *s* and *z* are dotted. Part 2 (p. 168–230): key and notes. Essentially for self-tuition. It is suggested that help with pronunciation in the early stages be obtained from a native or by listening to broadcasts. An appendix gives some help with pronunciation, accents and syllabification, lists common irregular verbs (with irregularities). Vocabulary (Italian-English only): nearly 2,000 words, showing commonly used prepositions after verbs and adjectives.

Reasonably complete and most reliable, this is still the best small grammar available and good value for money.

The companion, *Teach yourself Italian phrase book* (1954 and reprints. x, 202 p. 6s.) has guide to pronunciation, skeleton grammar, and conjugation of regular, irregular, auxiliary and reflexive verbs. The principal section consists of special vocabularies and practice material for particular subjects and situations.

SPERONI, C., and GOLINO, C. L. Basic Italian. Rev. ed. New York, Holt, 1965. xviii, 251, xlviii p. plates. 34s.

A first-year course only. 35 lessons; 9 review lessons. Grammar, vocabulary, reading passages and exercises for translation, both ways, in each lesson. Contents; index. Expensive for a first-year course.

TACCHI, A. Contemporary Italian. London, Macdonald & Evans, 1965. xvi, 320 p. 30s.

Intended primarily for use in language laboratory work but can be used with more conventional methods of teaching. 30 lessons consisting of grammar, exercises and readings. Covers some irregular verbs. Vocabulary.

TACCHI, A., and COLLIER, A. D. Italian for schools, with bilingual lessons and short stories. London, Tiranti, 1961. 404 p. sewn, 12s. 6d.; cloth, 18s.

Three sections: grammar (30 lessons); irregular verbs; short stories. Vocabulary, both ways. Assumes the presence of a teacher. Nothing about pronunciation and use of accents; very little about stress. Only the bare bones of grammatical rules. According to *The incorporated linguist* (v. 1, no. 2, April 1962, p. 57) the text bristles with errors.

TASSINARI, G. Brush up your Italian. 7th ed. London, Dent, 1965. 109 p. illus. 10s. 6d.

The main part of the book consists of 57 conversations, with English on one page and Italian facing it, in a variety of different situations, such as in various shops, with the doctor. The last 20 pages contain useful information such as the numbers, diminutive and other terminations, openings and endings for letters, paragraphs on wine, cheese and other food. This edition claims to be completely revised, but the old drawings, with their 1930-ish fashions, have been retained. Not in any sense a grammar but quite a useful handbook for travellers or tourists who already have some knowledge of the language.

VALGIMIGLI, M. Living Italian. London, University of London Press, 1961. 254 p. illus., map. 13s. 6d.

Intended for students working alone or at evening classes. 30 lessons, in three equal sections, with a revision test at the end of each section. Elementary; to cover one year's work. Lessons consist of grammar, vocabulary, reading passage and exercises, including translation both ways. Quality of *e*, *o*, *s* and *z* not marked. Accentuated syllables are marked by an italic vowel, except in *piane*. Vocabulary: about 1,350 Italian and 1,500 English words. Tables of auxiliary, regular and irregular verbs. Features include map, line illustrations, puzzles, word games. Sections 2 and 3 are concerned with a 'Journey to Italy', with accent on travel in the vocabulary and short description of places. Layout is clear and attractive.

Very suitable for adult beginners, especially those wishing to acquire the language for travel purposes.

DICTIONARIES

The number of works in our dictionary section is now much enlarged by the decision to remove the price-limit and by the inclusion of monolingual dictionaries in this edition. Among the bilingual dictionaries which stand out at various levels for the general reader are Cassell's at 36s., Purves's at 12s. 6d., and *Mondadori's pocket dictionary* at 3s. 6d. A library of any pretensions will need the *Cambridge Italian dictionary*, at £8 10s. for the first volume, and may well choose the Hazon Garzanti bilingual dictionary to supplement this and to supply a good English-Italian dictionary. Among monolingual dictionaries we may single out the excellent Migliorini, at about £3 5s., the large Garzanti dictionary, at about £3 10s., and the new edition of Zingarelli, at about £3 15s. Large libraries will doubtless be buying the great Battaglia dictionary if they have responsibility for Italian material and will also need the DEI with its supplements.

Of the smaller dictionaries, the small Spinelli and Pulford have very small print, while Mazzoli, and Meller and Mazzucato are not always accurate in the equivalents which they give for English words. Enenkel and McLaughlin is now considerably out of date, not having been revised since 1912 and, in view of its small size and the brevity of its definitions, it is dear at 50s. Among monolingual dictionaries *Il mio primo Palazzi* is an attractive work for small children but rather expensive at about £2.

The following points are worthy of consideration in selecting an Italian dictionary:

1. Accuracy (particularly in bilingual dictionaries).
2. Number of entries.
3. Extent of entries, i.e., words and phrases, words with compounds, derivatives, etc., *versus* single word entries.

4. Modernity (Italian is especially rich in words and expressions reflecting a way of life which is passing and, like most modern languages, is acquiring new terms daily).

5. Amount of help given with pronunciation, especially quality of vowels and sibilants.

6. Amount of help given with stress (Italian lacks the written accents of, for example, Spanish).

7. Presence of verb tables.

8. Legibility *versus* portability.

9. Price.

BILINGUAL DICTIONARIES

BORGOGNI, M. Novissimo vocabolario inglese e italiano. Rome, Casa Editrice Poliglotta, [n.d.] 2 v. in 1. 556, 592 p. 40s.

About 50,000 words each way. English proper names and abbreviations. Obviously designed for use by Italians.

EDGREN, H., and others. Italian and English dictionary, with pronunciation and brief etymologies. London, Bell; New York, Holt, 1901. ix, 576, 452 p. $7.50; 60s. (Apparently only the American edition is still in print.)

Italian-English about 18,000 main headings; English-Italian about 18,000. Pronunciation and stress very fully indicated, including palatalised or hard *c* and *g*, by a variety of diacritical marks. Geographical and personal names, both ways. English irregular verbs. Marks words obsolete when the dictionary was published. A useful work in spite of its age. Slightly American in its usage but spellings are English.

GLENDENING, P. J. T. Beyond the dictionary in Italian. London, Cassell, 1963. 159 p. 15s.

On similar lines to Gerrard and Heras' *Beyond the dictionary in Spanish* (see p. 55). Sections: Miscellaneous notes (on pronunciation, etc.), p. 8–17. – Italian-English dictionary (idioms, etc.; 'niente' and 'non so' – each have a half-page of small type, single column), p. 19–110. – Special vocabularies ('False friends': Disconcerting genders: Cars, etc.), p. 111–44. – English-Italian index. Well produced; particularly good for those with some knowledge of the language who want to get away from "classroom" Italian to something more lively and colloquial.

Another guide to colloquial usage is the new work by C. Pekelis: *Dictionary of colorful Italian idioms*. (New York, Braziller, 1965. 226 p. illus. $5).

GUALTIERI, F. M. Dizionario inglese moderno. Milan, Trevisini, [n.d.] 1,383 p. illus., col. pl. o.p.

About 60,000 words Italian-English; 50,000 English-Italian. Weights and
measures. English proper names, abbreviations and irregular verbs. Mainly
for use by Italians.

HAZON, M. Dizionario inglese-italiano, italiano-inglese. Milan,
Garzanti, 1961. x, 2,092 p. £7.

English-Italian, p. 1–1,018; Italian-English, p. 1,047–2,081. About 55,000
and 65,000 main headings respectively. Abbreviations both ways. Italian
proper names in main sequence. English proper names, weights and measures,
verbal constructions, etc. Doubtless intended primarily for Italians but very
good for use in this country. Up-to-date. Indicates stress, using grave and
acute accents for open and closed *e* and *o* respectively. Does not mark *s* and *z*.
Glazed bookmark with International Phonetic Alphabet and other symbols
used. The I.P.A. is used for English pronunciation.

HAZON, M. Nuovo Hazon Garzanti dizionario inglese-italiano,
italiano-inglese. Milan, Garzanti, [1960]. 1,700 p. 32 p. of keyed
illus. L 6,000; *c.* 70*s.*

A smaller version of the above, with about 45,000 words each way. The
Garzanti comprehensive dictionary, also edited by Hazon and published in
New York by McGraw-Hill in 1963, has 2,099 p. and costs £6 15*s.* 6*d.*,
although it claims only 21,000 entries. It would therefore seem to be relatively
much dearer than the large dictionary mentioned above.

HOARE, A. A short Italian dictionary. Cambridge, University Press,
1926 (and reprints). 2 v., ea. 25*s*; 2 v. in 1. 45*s.*

V. 1 (Italian-English) is abridged from the author's larger work; v. 2 is an
expansion of the English-Italian vocabulary appended to that work. Contains
about 18,000 words in each language as main entries, with many inflected and
compound forms, phrases and idioms within the articles. Open and close *e*
and *o* are marked with grave and acute accents respectively; voiced *s* and *z*,
with a superior dot. Accented syllables are given an acute accent 'where it
seems desirable'; this causes no confusion with the closed vowel markings.
V. 1 has a note by Professor Grandgent on the development of the language.
Notes on verbs likely to cause difficulty and all verbs in -*ire*; tables of
irregular verbs. V. 2 has a table of words which may be followed by an
infinitive, showing use of prepositions to translate English 'to', a valuable
feature.

The content is rather literary for the general student and a little old-
fashioned. A number of words and expressions are included which are not
common outside Tuscany and some modern words are naturally lacking.
The standard is high, however, and the volume of information compressed
into the work is astonishing. Probably the best short dictionary for the reader
who wishes to read the Italian classics.

The large Hoare dictionary (2nd ed. 1925) is now out of print, the Italian-
English part having been superseded by the *Cambridge Italian dictionary* v. 1.

Lysle's Italian dictionary, Italian-English, English-Italian; based on the two-volume Lysle dictionary by Prof. Agostino Severino, with a commercial supplement by Prof. Lora Lamia Gualtieri. New ed. with an addenda. London, Allen and Unwin, 1955. xviii, 644, 755, 192, 80 p. 37s. 6d.

Italian-English (p. 1–644): about 28,000 words and phrases; English-Italian (p. 1–755): about 40,000 words. Both include proper names. The commercial supplement has 4,000 words and phrases in the Italian-English section (p. 1–109); 3,300, in the English-Italian (p. 111–87). The supplement of newer words has 2,500 in the Italian-English (p. 1–51); 1,000 in the English-Italian (p. 53–80).

The work is fairly up to date but seems to be intended for Italian rather than English users, as it contains a list of English irregular verbs and a folding table of English sounds. There is also a list of English and American abbreviations.

Not to be confused with the larger work, which is a major dictionary: Lysle-Gualtieri. *Nuovo dizionario moderno delle lingue italiana e inglese.* Ed. riv. e aggiornata con aggiunta di un supplemento commerciale della Prof. Lamia Gualtieri (Turin, Casanova, 1950–58, 2 v. v. 1: *Inglese-italiano.* Ed. riv. 1950 [x], 2,069, [1], 132 p. L.3,200. v. 2: *Italiano-inglese*, 1958. [x], 958, [1], 191 p. L.2,000).

ORLANDI, G. Dizionario italiano-inglese e inglese-italiano: voci dell'uso corrente e familiare e della lingua classica; termini commerciali, scientifici, tecnici; americanismi; voci del gergo. Milan, Signorelli; London, Bailey, 1963. 2,130 p. £5 8s.

About 100,000 words Italian-English; 50,000 English-Italian. No pronunciation, except open and closed *o* indicated by grave and acute accents respectively. A handy, reliable one-volume dictionary.

ORLANDI, G. Il 'piccolo' Orlandi: edizione minore del 'Dizionario italiano-inglese, inglese-italiano' di G. Orlandi. Milan, Signorelli, 1965. xvi, 576, 1,170 p. 55s.

Italian-English section (590 p.): about 32,000 words and phrases; English-Italian (810 p.): about 40,000. Stress is marked with a grave accent. Italian pronunciation is not shown and quality of *e, o, s* and *z* is not marked. Reasonably up to date.

Evidently intended for Italian rather than English students.

PURVES, J. A dictionary of modern Italian: Italian-English, English-Italian. London, Routledge, 1953. xxviii, 833 p. 12s. 6d.

Introductory guide to pronunciation; paradigms of regular and auxiliary verbs; irregularities of irregular verbs; also, English irregular verbs. Italian-English section contains words and phrases listed under 14,500 main headings.

English-Italian section has a list of proper names and lists words and phrases under 13,500 main headings.

A very good small dictionary; reasonably up to date and good value for money.

REBORA, P., and others. Cassell's Italian-English, English-Italian dictionary, 5th ed. London, Cassell, 1965. xxi, 1,096 p. 36s.

Italian-English section (p. 1–571): about 55,000 words and phrases; English-Italian section (p. 573–1,079): about 40,000 words and phrases, with pronunciation indicated in the International Phonetic Alphabet. Appendices (p. 1,081–1,094) to both parts, containing neologisms, Americanisms and new and additional meanings of words already included. From the 3rd ed. onwards "realistic measures of simplification" have been adopted with regard to Italian pronunciation. The distinction in quality of *e, o, s* and *z* is no longer marked where there is "no possible ambiguity". In practice difference of vowel sound is indicated in, e.g., *pésca, pèsca* but not in *aréna, arèna* (or *tócco, tòcco,* in spite of this being quoted as an example in the preface). In the case of non-*piane* the word is repeated in squares with the stressed vowel capitalised. Older words, many synonyms and variant spellings are omitted. Not all *faux amis* and traps have been avoided.

A good up-to-date dictionary for less academic purposes. It has been better received by Italian than English critics. Good value for money.

REYNOLDS, B. The Cambridge Italian dictionary. Vol. 1 Italian-English. Cambridge, University Press, 1962. xxxi, 900 p. £8 10s.

Based on Hoare but always gives English equivalents, not definitions. Inclusive but words are qualified as colloquial, figurative, poetic, etc., and obsolete words are marked. Words peculiar to Tuscany are noted. Proper names are included. Some local names, e.g., of fishes, have been omitted. Entries are in two columns under 45,000 to 50,000 main headings in a similar way to those in Hoare, i.e., with many inflected and compound forms, phrases and idioms within the articles. Some hard-pressed translators have complained of difficulty in finding the exact phrase required in the longer entries because of lack of type variation, but the dictionary is now indispensable for serious work. Special subject fields have been covered by specialists. Stress is marked and so are stressed, closed *e* and *o,* sonant *s* and *z,* and *g* before *li,* where it is to be pronounced as in English. Abbreviations, verb conjugations and the use of prepositions with verbs are given in separate tables.

SPINELLI, N. Dizionario italiano-inglese, inglese-italiano. 3a. ed. interamente rifatta. Turin, Società Editrice Internazionale; London, Bailey, 1955. £17.

V. 1: Italian-English (vi, 682 p.) about 40,000 words; v. 2: English-Italian (vi, 685–1,532 p.) about 55,000 words. Marks stress of Italian words but gives pronunciation of English words only. Geographical and proper names both ways and English abbreviations. Very expensive in comparison with other works which give more information. Despite its claim to be 'interamente rifatta', the 3rd edition shows few changes or additions to the 2nd ed., published 25 years previously.

SPINELLI, N. Piccolo dizionario italiano–inglese e inglese–italiano, ecc. Turin, Società Editrice Internazionale, [1946 ?] (and reprints, e.g. 1958). 2 v. (602, 595 p.) 18s.

> V. 1, English–Italian: about 5,000 main headings, under which appear many compounds and derivatives. V. 2, Italian–English, similarly arranged: about 5,500 main headings. Includes proper, geographical and mythological names. Very small print.
> There is also a Spinelli school dictionary: *Dizionario scolastico* (3rd en. 1959, vi, 1,955 p. L. 5,500).

TEDESCHI, A., and others. Mondadori's pocket Italian–English, English–Italian dictionary. New York, Pocket Books, 1959. xxxiv, 271, xii, 305 p. 3s. 6d.

> Italian–English section: about 25,000 words and phrases; English–Italian: about 30,000. Gives notions of pronunciation; verb tables.
> Up to date and excellent value at the price.

Other Bilingual Dictionaries

ENENKEL, A., and McLAUGHLIN, J. New dictionary of the English and Italian languages. New York, McKay, 1912. viii, 519, vi, 533 p. 50s.

> English–Italian section: about 45,000 words; Italian–English: about 30,000. Simulated pronunciation. Brief entries under each word. Not revised for over 50 years.

HALL, R. A. The Italian vest pocket dictionary: Italian–English, English–Italian. London & Edinburgh, Oliver and Boyd, 1962. 318 p. 5s.

> Italian–English section (p. 5–149): about 12,000 words; English–Italian (p. 153–318): about 15,000. Brief guide to pronunciation.

Hugo's Italian–English, English–Italian dictionary. London, Hugo's Language Institute, [n.d.]. xvi, 622 p. 5s.

> Italian–English section (p. 1–320): about 11,000 words; English–Italian (p. 321–622): about 9,000. Simulated pronunciation.

MAY, I.   Collins' Italian gem dictionary: Italian-English, English-Italian.   London, Collins, 1954.   xvi, 622 p.   4s. 6d.

> Italian-English (p. 1–320): about 11,500 words; English-Italian (p. 321–622): about 9,000. Includes notions of grammar and verb tables. Geographical names included. Simulated pronunciation.

MAZZOLI, A. M.   Dizionario italiano-inglese, inglese-italiano   Bologna, Capitol, 1961.   377 p.   (Holl's series).   10s. 6d.

> Italian-English section (p. 49-184): about 10,000 words; English-Italian (p. 235–377): about 11,000. Lists of Christian and geographical names. Grammar notes and brief pronunciation guide to both parts. Conversational phrases on various topics; verb lists. Quality of *e, o, s* and *z* not indicated. Definitions of Italian words better than those of English words.

MELLER, L., and MAZZUCATO, F.   English-Italian pronouncing dictionary, etc.   London, Pordes, 1963.   [vi], 410 p.   12s. 6d.

> Italian-English (161 p.): about 10,000 words; English-Italian (p. 169–410): about 16,000 words. Includes geographical and proper names; brief guide to pronunciation. The definitions of the Italian words are better than those of English ones.

Methuen's Universal dictionary, English-Italian, Italian-English.   15th ed.   London, Methuen, 1959.   384 p.   3s. 6d.

> English-Italian section (p. 1–196): about 6,500 words; Italian-English (p. 197–384): about 5,000.

MURRAY, L.   Dizionario tascabile, inglese-italiano, italiano-inglese, ecc.   Florence, Monsalvato, 1946.   379 p.   6s.

> English-Italian (p. 11-198): about 7,500 words; Italian-English (p. 203–370): about 7,000 words. Simulated pronunciation. Poor paper.

PULFORD, J.   Pocket Italian-English, English-Italian dictionary.   London, Bailey Bros. & Swinfen, 1960.   xix. 783, xxxv, 660 p.   18s.

> Simulated English pronunciation; no Italian pronunciation. Quality of *e, o, s* and *z* not indicated. Verb tables. Very small print.

MONOLINGUAL DICTIONARIES

BATTAGLIA, S.   Grande dizionario della lingua italiana.   Turin, UTET, [1961–].   (in progress).   £14 9s. 6d. per v.

> Has reached v. 4: Dah-Duu. A very large, well-produced, scholarly dictionary, of similar type to the N.E.D., but the quotations are not dated. Cumulative fascicules, of which those to v. 1-4 had appeared by 1966, are, however, giving precise references to the authors cited. Etymologies are given and the dictionary covers some dialect words. It incorporates work by

research teams at Florence and Padua. The work is intended to be in 8 vols. including an index.

BATTISTI, C., and ALESSIO, G. Dizionario etimologico italiano. Florence, Barbèra, 1948–1957. 5 v. £22.

Published under the auspices of the Istituto di Glottologia of the University of Florence and usually cited as DEI. Gives etymology, date of introduction into the language, definition, variants and parallels or cognates in other languages. Includes many technical terms, for which alone it is most useful, and dialect words. A series of *Aggiunte e retrodatazioni* began publication in 1964 and has reached the word *fatica*.

Duden italiano, dizionario figurato. 2nd rev. and enl. ed. Novara, Istituto Geografico De Agostini; London, Harrap, 1964. 672, 134 p. 8 pl. 32s.

This was originally based on the German *Duden* and published in Mannheim by the Bibliographisches Institut. It follows the well-known Duden principle of illustrating words pictorially instead of defining them. 25,000 words and drawings are included. Covers such subjects as mythology but excludes abstract terms, which cannot well be illustrated. Alphabetical index. Very useful for technical subjects.

Dizionario Garzanti della lingua italiana. Milan, Garzanti, 1965. xvi, 1,990 p. 1,500 illus. 55 tables. L.5,800; £3 10s.

Includes about 60,000 entries. Contributions by over 60 specialists. Etymologies. Many of the figures have numbered details with key. The tables group together words with related meanings. Marks stress of non-*piane* or *tronche* and *e* and *o* with grave or acute accent, sonant *s* with *f*, sonant *z* with *ʒ*.

A smaller dictionary, published with the same title in 1963, is intended for school use. It has 994 p. 1,300 illus. and contains 42,000 entries. There are supplements for Italian proper names, place names of Italy and correct usage. It uses the same pronunciation system as the larger work and is edited by M. Hazon. The price in this country is £1 and although the book is a paperback it is not dear at this price.

GABRIELLI, A. Dizionario linguistico moderno: guida pratica per scrivere e parlar bene. Milan, Mondadori, 1961. 1,179 p. L.4,000 54s. 6d.

Suggests equivalents for foreign words imported into the language and for unnecessary neologisms. Marks open or closed quality of *e* and *o* with an accent and gives rules for surd or sonant *s*. The Florentine and Roman pronunciations are indicated for many words with *z*. Bibliography.

Part 1 gives grammatical rules and difficult constructions. Neologisms, foreign and barbarous words with suggested replacements. Dialect forms. Stylistic rules. Metrical rules and forms. Etymology. Pronunciation of common foreign words.

Part 2. Dictionary with spelling and pronunciation but no definitions. proper names. Geographical adjectives. Feminine and plural forms. Comparative forms. Verb tables. Use of *essere* and *avere*. Difficult constructions, including many not usually covered.

MELZI, G. B. Il novissimo Melzi: dizionario enciclopedico italiano in due parti, linguistica-scientifica. Milan, Vallardi, 1965. 2 v. col. pl., illus., maps, plans. £5 10s.

Comparable with the *Petit Larousse*, this has now run through nearly forty editions. V. 1 is a dictionary containing 33,000 words; v. 2 an encyclopedia with short articles arranged like a dictionary.

MIGLIORINI, B. Vocabolario della lingua italiana. Turin, Paravia, 1965. xvi, 1,640 p. 40 pl. L.5,500; c. 65s.

A new edition of Migliorini's 1945 revision of Giulio Cappuccini's dictionary of 1911. Includes new, technical and foreign words. Gives etymologies, going back beyond the classical languages where necessary. References to synonyms and words of similar meaning. Abundant examples of use. Notes on fields in which words are appropriate and on stylistic nuances. Probably the most scholarly one-volume dictionary.

PALAZZI, F. Novissimo dizionario della lingua italiana. 2nd ed. Milan, Ceschina; London, Bailey, 1959. 1,406 p. 8 col. pl. 41 illus. 90s.

60,000 entries arranged in three columns. Includes etymology, phraseology and synonyms. Appendix with proper names, abbreviations, geographical adjectives.

Il piccolo Palazzi of 900 p. (2 columns) has 3 appendices: foreign words, signs and abbreviations, phonetics. 1,200 lire, about 15s.

Il mio primo Palazzi contains 2,000 words, each one illustrated. The illustrations are grouped together, 10 to a colour plate. 3,500 lire, about 40s.

ZINGARELLI, N. Vocabolario della lingua italiana. 9th ed. Bologna, Zanichelli, 1965. xvi, 1,845 p. illus. L.6,400; £4 13s. 6d.

Edited by Giovanni Balducci. Gives symbols to show subject field. Abbreviations and acronyms. Appendix of foreign words and neologisms and technical words. About 28,000 main headings arranged in two columns and with ½″ to 6″ of phrases and derivatives under each heading. Indicates stress, using grave and acute accents for open and closed *e* and *o*. Uses diacritical marks for sonant *s* and *z*.

Technical Dictionaries

DENTI, R. Dizionario tecnico, italiano-inglese, inglese-italiano. 6. ed. megliorata ed aumentata. Milan, Hoepli, 1965. xiv, 1,307 p. 70s.

First published 1950; 4th ed. 1958. Italian-English, p. 1–515 (stress and pronunciation not shown); English-Italian, p. 517–1,233, giving gender of Italian words. Technical terms are categorised, e.g. '(auto)', and '(aereo)'. Appendices, p. 1,237–1,307: technical abbreviations (outdated); conversion factors; tables of British and American measures and metric equivalents; table of elements. The two parts have about 35,000 and 50,000 entries respectively.

An excellent translating dictionary, compounds and extensions of entries being indented and easy to refer to.

GATTO, S. Dizionario tecnico scientifico illustrato, italiano-inglese, inglese-italiano . . . Milan, Ceschina, 1960. xxii, [1], 1,381 p., illus. (London, Bailey Bros. & Swinfen 54s.).

English-Italian (pronunciation of English given), p. 1–824; Italian-English, p. 827–1,381. Terms are categorised; separate entries for compounds; references from second part of compound words (e.g. 'brake', see also 'air-'). About 75,000 and 60,000 entries in the two parts, respectively. Very small illustrations, about one per page. Bibliography of 40 items, p. vii–viii.

MAROLLI, G. Dizionario tecnico, inglese-italiano, italiano-inglese. 8. ed. riveduta e ampliata. Florence, Le Monnier, 1963. xxii, [1], 4, 1,621 p. illus. c. £12.

First published 1946. English-Italian, p. 1–899; Italian-English, p. 905–1,578. Stress is shown, but not genders. Technical terms are categorised. The two parts have about 30,000 and 20,000 entries respectively. A feature is the appendix of 38 folding outline drawings (e.g., of an atomic power station, with 91 keyed parts). Conversion and other tables, p. 1,580–1,621. The layout is less good then in Denti, which is a better bargain.

Among monolingual technical dictionaries may be mentioned R. Leonardi's *Dizionario illustrato delle scienze pure e applicate* (2nd rev. ed. Milan, Hoepli. 1950–1952. 2v. illus. diagrs., bibliography); the *Dizionario d'ingegneria*, edited by E. Perucca (Turin, UTET, 1951–56. 5 v. illus. with 2,200 diagrs., some of them large, folding ones), and *Dizionario delle scienze: definizione e analisi dei termini usati nella chimica, fisica e matematica*. Versione italiana ed. Ornella Coletti (Milan, Martello, 1957), which is a translation of the Penguin *Dictionary of science*, by E. B. Uvarov and R. R. Chapman. The second volume (*Parte scientifica: dizionario enciclopedico*) of *Il novissimo Melzi*, mentioned above, is devoted to the arts and sciences.

Commercial Dictionaries

MOTTA, G. Dizionario commerciale, inglese-italiano, italiano-inglese: economia – legge – finanza. Milan, Signorelli, 1961. x, [1], 1,051 p. 68s.

English-Italian, p. 1–515; Italian-English, p. 519–1,051 ('account': 2½ cols.;

'stock': 2 cols.; 'mercato': 1⅔ cols.). Stress of Italian words not shown; English terms are categorised; many idioms and compounds. Clearly intended primarily for Italian users. About 30,000 entries in all, fairly equally divided.

SPINELLI, N. Dizionario commerciale: italiano-inglese, inglese-italiano. Terminologia commerciale, contabile, economica, finanziaria, giuridica. Ed. 1957 con un 'Appendice' a cura del Prof. Dott. Guiseppe Motta. Turin, Lattes, 1957 (reprinted 1961). vii, 464, 683, 138 p. (London, Bailey Bros. & Swinfen. 48s.).

First published 1917. Italian-English, p. 1–464; English-Italian, p. 1–683; supplement, both ways, of 138 p. About 12,000 and 17,000 entries respectively in the main parts. Stress of Italian words is not shown. 'Account': 4 cols.; 'mercato': 2 cols.

GRAMOPHONE RECORDS

(a) *Longer courses.* An essential accompaniment to Chérel's *Italian without toil* is the Assimil 20-lesson preliminary and advanced course on discs (twenty 10" 78 r.p.m. or ten 7" 45 r.p.m. records, including the grammar, at £14). A little more expensive is the Linguaphone 16-record course on 45 r.p.m. and 78 r.p.m. (£15 2s. 1d.), also available on tape, – two 5" spools 3¾ i.p.s. (2-track recording).

Berlitz Language Record Courses (sole concessionnaires, Berlitz Language Records, 40, Parkgate Road, London, S.W.11) publish a very good course at about the same price (£16) consisting of 40 lessons on five 12" 33⅓ r.p.m. records, 5 manuals, a rotary verb finder and a free advisory service which is valid for six months following the date of purchase. The records and manuals are not normally sold separately but in certain cases additional sets of manuals (with verb finder), up to a maximum of twelve sets per complete course, may be supplied at £5 5s. per set of manuals. Each record has four easily distinguished tracks on each side, each track corresponding to a lesson, which represents a 'chapter' in a continuous story covering the various stages of a journey to Italy, shopping, a visit from the doctor, a social call, sightseeing, and so forth, as well as such varied topics as 'In the office,' 'A marriage proposal,' 'Military life,' 'A car accident,' 'The professions' and 'A legal consultation'. The 32 speakers are native experts and several of the lessons introduce regional accents and dialect. The manuals, which are illustrated, are designed to lie flat. The text gives the dialogue on the record with a translation underneath and notes on grammar and points requiring special clarification on the opposite page. There is an exercise to each lesson. The records include local sound effects and there is music in the breaks between lessons. Very good points in favour of this course are the large number of speakers and the 12″ sized records. The Express (Oldbourne Press) 'Basic conversational Italian' course consists of two 12″ L.P. 33⅓ r.p.m. records, plus text-book, at £5 5s. (The text-book of the same title, by Martin and Ciatti, 1959 (reprinted 1963; 40 lessons) is sold separately.)

(b) *Shorter courses.* In June 1964 *Which?* (p. 187–92) made an extensive survey of 13 modestly priced courses, ranging in price from £5 5s. ('Basic conversational Italian') to 7s. 6d. The following are included:

'Italian: listen and learn' (Dover: Constable): three 12″ 33⅓ r.p.m., £2 14s.

'Conversaphone': one 12″ L.P., 37s. 6d., or one 10″ L.P., 30s. 6d.; also a course for children, similarly priced.

Odhams 'Master' course: four 10″ L.P. records, £2 10s.

Odhams 'Quick' course: two 7″ L.P., 30s.

'Instant' course: two 12″ L.P. records, 70s.

'Lightning conversation' (Oriole Records): two 7″ 45 r.p.m., 29s. 9d.

'Lexiphone' (Visaphone Co.): two 7″ 45 r.p.m., 26s. 6d.

'Talking book traveller' (Methuen): one 7″ 45 r.p.m., 11s. 10d.

'Gem' course: one 7″ L.P., 9s. 2d.

Italian: '200 basic words' (Saga Records): one 7″ 45 r.p.m., 7s. 6d.

For beginners and holiday makers *Which?* considered the best 'buy' to be Odhams 'Quick' course; for those with more time and money, the 'Basic conversational Italian'.

The current B.B.C. course has been mentioned in the Grammars section above.

Two new sets of records appeared in 1965 for the use of Italians:

TAGLIAVINI, C. La corretta pronuncia italiana. Corso discografico di fonetica e ortoepia italiana. Bologna, Casa Editrice Libreria Capital/Dischi C.E.B. L.30,000 (c. £17).

52 lessons on 26 records (33 r.p.m.) and a book of 360 p. which includes diagrams, palatograms and radiographs for each lesson. The records include examples of regional pronunciation and 800 examples of errors.

A more 'popular' work is:

FIORELLI, P. Corso di pronunzia italiana. Padua, R.A.D.A.R.,
1965. L.18,000 (c. £10 10s.).

28 lessons on 14 records with a book with accents and diacritical marks.
The pronunciation is that used in the *Dizionario enciclopedico* of the Istituto
dell'Enciclopedia Italiana (1955–63) and to be used in a new dictionary to be
published by RAI under Fiorelli's editorship. There are 7 speakers and
examples are given of pronunciations to be avoided. Notes, tables and
indexes.

4

SPANISH

by A. J. Walford, M.A., PH.D., F.L.A., in consultation with G. H. Green, B.A., H. Lennox-Kay, A.I.L., and W. W. Timms, M.A.

GRAMMARS

In an article entitled "Two hundred years of Spanish grammars", J. R. Jump[1] traces the development of Spanish grammars published in this country from the earliest, dated 1725 (*A short and compendious method of learning to speak, read and write the English and Spanish languages*), to *Spanish through pictures*, by I. A. Richards and others (New York, Pocket Books, Inc., 1950). This last uses the visual method and is written entirely in Spanish, apart from the pronunciation notes.

The forerunner of the orthodox Spanish grammar appeared in 1858, – *A new practical and easy method of learning the Spanish language, after the system of T. Ahn*, by F. F. Moritz Foerster. This grammar provided a pattern that has since become familiar: chapters, each with a word list, notes on grammatical points, passages for translation, each way, with an alphabetical vocabulary and list of useful phrases appended. To obviate the need for a reader as well as a grammar, reading passages were later included, as well as exercises other than translations.

Early in the twentieth century came a boon for the student without a teacher, – the provision of a grammar with a key to the exercises. The Direct Method of language teaching introduced in the inter-World War years threw out a challenge to authors and publishers of grammars. Audio-visual methods provided an answer: the grammar or course-book supported by recordings (gramophone and, tape), films and the profusely illustrated text-book, with graduated vocabulary and skilful use of diagrams, drawings, photographs and maps, not to mention crossword puzzles, and songs, with music.

Spanish is spoken by some 150 million people, ranking after Chinese, English, Russian and Hindi among the world's languages. In Britain, however, it is taught in schools as, possibly, a third language or as an

[1] *Modern languages*, v. 42, no. 1, March 1961, p. 24–26.

alternative to German for those who wish to take up commerce. "Considering its great literature and its widespread use in commerce no modern language has received less attention than Spanish. There are few text-books that satisfy modern ideas of teaching. . . ." So wrote two officials of the Institute of Linguists[1] in 1931. The situation has improved a little since then. Spain has become a major attraction for tourists, and adults are increasingly taking up the language, if only to gain a smattering. The 1950s saw a fairly large output of grammars and course books.

The standard Spanish reference grammars are generally recognised as those by Ramsey, Ramsden, and Harmer and Norton.

BARLOW, J. W. Basic Spanish. London, Bell, 1951. xii, 208 p. maps. 8s. 6d.

> 25 lessons, each with reading passage, questions, exercises and vocabulary. Vocabulary, each way, p. 171–92. Index to grammar.

CASTILLO, J. L. Universal Spanish grammar. London, Harrap, 1964. 320 p. 16s.

> 20 lessons, each with vocabulary, grammar notes and exercises, including passages for reading. Appendices on irregular verbs and finer points of grammar; vocabulary, each way, and index to grammar. Praised in *Modern languages* (v. 46, no. 1, March 1965, p. 45) for dealing with first things first: the familiar form of address is not mentioned until the student is well over halfway through the course; the perfect tense appears in lesson 5, and by lesson 8 students are familiar with all past tenses. Well suited to grammar-school students and adult beginners.

CHÉREL, A. Spanish without toil. Paris, Assimil (available from Pitman's Correspondence College, Farncombe, Godalming, Surrey), [c. 1930?]. viii, 373 p. illus. 18s.

> 112 lessons, each consisting of short Spanish passages with English translation, notes on grammar, vocabulary and exercises each way. An admirable self-tutor, the Spanish text being enlivened by humorous drawings and keys being provided to exercises. Simulated pronunciation. No contents; no index to grammar.
>
> An extensive gramophone record course in two parts, preliminary and advanced, is available with this grammar (see p. 87).

CLARK, A. C., and WILLIAMS, W. O. A modern Spanish course. London, Hirschfeld, 1932. 2 v. (pt. 1, reprinted with corrections, 1948; pt. 2. 2nd ed., rev. 1936). illus. pt. 1, 3s. 6d.; pt. 2, o.p.

---

[1] *A guide to the study of foreign languages and foreign shorthand*, by A. C. Elliott and R. Stafford (1931), p. 31.

Pt. 1 (xiv, 184 p.): consists of 20 lessons: vocabulary, readings, coversational phrases; drill and exercises. Everyday vocabulary, each way, equivalents only, p. 165–84. Follows the style of A. C. Clark's *A modern French course*, aiming to assist users to acquire a large vocabulary quickly.

Pt. 2: 20 lessons, including notes on the subjunctive. Vocabulary, each way, equivalents only, p. 132–56. No index to grammar.

COESTER, A. A Spanish grammar, with practical introductory lessons. Rev. ed. London, Ginn, 1955. vi, 346 p. illus., maps. o.p.

First published 1912. This revision seems to be a reprint of the 1917 edition, which has similar pagination. Pt. 1: 22 introductory lessons; pt. 2: Systematic accidence and syntax (18 chapters); 3 appendices. Lessons include drill and exercises. Vocabulary, each way, 297–340. Good use of bold type.

The index to grammar and many examples of usage make this a handy reference grammar.

CORTINA, R. D. de la. Collins' Cortina Spanish in 20 lessons. London, Collins, 1964. 384 p. illus. 12s. 6d.

The first Collins Cortina edition, based on the 153rd Cortina edition (New York, Cortina). Each of the 20 lessons consists of vocabulary and conversational exercises, using "a new system of simplified phonetic pronunciation". Grammar is relegated to footnotes. According to the *Times literary supplement* (no. 3,270, 29 October 1964, p. 985) the translations are mostly in stilted, outdated English and the line-drawings are unattractive. Reference grammar, p. 206–336; vocabulary, each way. Intended both for class use and as a self-tutor.

DEAN, E. L., and ROBERTS, M. C. M. Nos ponemos en camino. London, Harrap, 1958 (and reprints). 225 p. illus. 8s.

For third-form beginners and for those who start the language earlier. 20 lessons: vocabulary, grammar and a variety of exercises. Vocabulary, p. 199–225.

DEAN, E. L., and ROBERTS, M. C. M. Seguimos adelante. London, Harrap, 1957. 288 p. illus. 9s.

20 lessons: reading matter, questions, grammar, numerous exercises; attractively illustrated; good use of bold type. Vocabulary, each way, p. 259–85. No index to grammar. For grammar school pupils in their pre-G.C.E. year.

DORADO, C. M., and LAGUNA, M. F. de. Primeras lecciones de español. London, Ginn, 1949 (and reprints). xxvi, [1], 223 p. 7s. 9d.

84 short lessons, using Direct Method, for young beginners. The original
edition (1934) was written for North American students, and is here adjusted.
Lesson consists of oral practice; reading matter; exercises and drill; vocabulary
and phrases; questions. Irregular verbs, p. 185–90; Spanish-English vocabulary, p. 193–223. No index to grammar.

DORADO, C. M., and LAGUNA, M. F. de.   Segundas lecciones de
español.   London, Ginn, 1949 (and reprints).   313 p. illus.   9s. 3d.

64 lessons; for third and fourth years of study. Original U.S. edition, 1934.
Vocabulary, each way, p. 251–313. No index to grammar.

DUFF, C.   All purposes Spanish for adults.   London, English Universities Press, 1957.   296 p.   o.p.

Pt. 1: first principles (85 p.); pt. 2: full explanation of grammar. The
student is encouraged to use the language in real-life situations and is introduced to the Spanish classics. Accent is on Spanish passages ,with translations.
No vocabulary, but a list of 3,500 Spanish words is appended. For strong-
willed students only.

FITZGIBBON, J. P.   El español práctico.   London, Harrap, 1964.
viii, 338 p.   illus.   18s.

53 lessons, with enough material for a two-year Spanish course, at least.
Since keys are given to all exercises, it can also be used as a self-tutor. According to *Modern languages* (v. 45, no. 3, September 1964, p. 127) the course
provides up-to-date, idiomatic Spanish, and has interesting material on
Spain and the Spanish way of life. Reading passages are all in dialogue form;
delightful illustrations by Goñi.
A set of four 10″ records covers all reading passages.

GREENFIELD, E. V.   Outline of Spanish grammar.   New York,
Barnes & Noble; London, Constable, 1942 (and reprints, e.g., 1960).
5–236 p.   (College outline series). $1.

36 'unitary' lessons, each on one topic only, with vocabulary, grammar,
exercises and oral drill. Goes up to past perfect subjunctive. Verbs, p. 169–204
(conjugation of each verb occupies one page). Vocabulary, each way, p.
205–24 (only about 600 words); index to grammar.

GURRIN, T. E.   Hossfeld's new practical method for learning the
Spanish language.   4th ed., rev. and enl. by F. de Arteaga.   London,
Hirschfeld, 1945 (and reprints).   xvi, 340, 59, 32 p.   6s.   Key. 2s.

62 lessons: general observations, vocabulary, exercises, questions, conversation; reading exercises. Spanish passages appended; 32 p. on Spanish
verbs. Vocabulary, each way, 59 p. Index to grammar. Poor typography;
small type.

HARMER, L. C., and NORTON, F. J.   A manual of modern Spanish.
2nd ed.   London, University Tutorial Press, 1957.   xii, 623 p.
17s. 6d.

First published 1935. This edition, with the same pagination, has revised
text, to accord with the new rules for the use of the written accent, laid down
by the Spanish Academy in 1952.

44 lessons. The verb receives full treatment in chapters 20–36 (p. 160–387);
chapter 44: 'Order of words'. Exercises: sentences each way. Appendix:
conjugation of verbs; gender of nouns. A feature: the many examples drawn
from classical and contemporary Spanish writers (about 200 alone for
chapter 30, 'The infinitive (continued)'). Spanish-English vocabulary (p.
549–98): about 5,000 words; words in round brackets may be read as
extensions (explanations, if in italics) of the English translation; those in
square brackets may be read as alternatives to the preceding word. English-
Spanish vocabulary (p. 599–611): about 1,000 words; includes references to
chapters and paragraphs of the text. Index to grammar; cross-references in
text. Good use of bold type.

Very full and sound, but said to be difficult to find points in. Only 1½
pages on pronunciation.

HILL, B. J. W.   A Spanish course.   London, E. Arnold, 1952 (and
reprints).   391 p. illus.   14s. 6d.

45 lessons, with exercises, drill and connected passages for translation.
Vocabulary, each way, p. 336–88. Good use of bold type. Index to grammar.
Covers rather more than the requirements of G.C.E. "Primarily for those
who take up Spanish at the age of sixteen or a little later" (*Preface*), although
younger and older students are also catered for, it is claimed.

HILLS, E. C., and FORD, J. D. M.   Heath's practical Spanish grammar.
London, Harrap, 1920 (and reprints, e.g. 1961).   x, 340 p.   7s. 6d.

34 lessons. Parts to each lesson: 1. Inflections and syntax, and Spanish-
English exercise; English-Spanish exercises. 2. Inflections and syntax, with
much oral drill; exercises, each way. The verb, with an alphabetical list of
verbs, p. 184–242. Vocabulary, each way; index to grammar. Alternative
exercises, p. 293–340.

A complete course for grammar schools.

HILLS, E. C., and FORD, J. D. M.   New first Spanish course.   New
ed., prepared with the collaboration of Guillermo Rivera.   Boston,
Heath, 1942 (and reprints, e.g. 1961).   viii, 318 p.   (Heath's Modern
Language series).   7s. 6d.

A complete revision of *First Spanish course* (first published 1917; new ed.,
1925), with smaller vocabulary. 49 lessons, plus 5 revision lessons. Adequate
exercises and drill. Appendix: the verb. Vocabulary each way, p. 288–308

(the Spanish vocabulary comprises the active vocabulary used in the lessons).
Index to grammar.

Suitable for senior beginners.

HUGHES, J.   Modern Spanish for adults.   London, Dent, 1954–57.
2 v. (156; 320 p.).   4s. 9d.; 8s. 9d.

A text-book much used in adult classes. Pt. 1 has 21 lessons, going up to the
imperfect indicative. Pt. 2 has 24 lessons. Vocabulary, each way, p. 277–310;
index to grammar.

HUGO'S LANGUAGE INSTITUTE.   Spanish simplified: an easy & rapid
self-instructor.   Standard edition, enl. and rev.   London, the
Institute, [n.d.].   90 p.   Key; Spanish conversation simplified.   58 p.
7s. 6d.

Sub-title: "Grammar, exercises and vocabularies, with the pronunciation
exactly imitated". 26 lessons; vocabulary, p. 92–96.

KELLY, B.   Spanish today.   London, Ginn, [1965].   2 v. (336 p.;
288 p.).   illus.   12s. 6d.; 11s. 6d.

Intended for adults and for those who begin the study of Spanish in the
later stage of their school career. Each book has only 10 lengthy chapters,
with revision sections. Book 1 has interesting readings, with plenty of
dialogue; vocabulary; grammar; exercises; vocabulary, each way; index to
grammar. In Book 2 the large helpings of grammar and page after page of
exercises are relieved by amusing line drawings and lively, interesting
material reminiscent of *Heute Abend*, states *Modern languages* (v. 45, no. 1,
March 1964, p. 43). Book 2 also has vocabulary each way and index to
grammar. Quite adequate for 'O' level.

LESTER, H., and TERRÁDEZ, V.   Essential Spanish.   3rd ed.   London,
University of London Press, 1960.   9s. 6d.

First published 1953. "Intended for use by pupils in the 3rd or 4th year of
the study of Spanish." Sufficient material for a whole year's work in preparation for G.C.E. 'O' level, including the type of question found in that
examination. Sections: 1. Passages for comprehension and translation
(Spanish prose and poetry). 2. Free compostion. 3. Summary of grammar
(p. 86–167). 4. Translation into Spanish (sentences and prose passages).
Vocabulary, each way, p. 206–54. No index to grammar; no key. Small type.

A sound guide to style for advanced study, with notes on Spanish pronunciation and accentuation. For fifth forms in grammar schools.

LITTLEWOOD, R. P.   Living Spanish.   London, University of London
Press, 1949 (and reprints, e.g., 1962).   320 p. illus.   9s. 6d.

Author is Head of the Department of Modern Languages, Leicester College of Technology and Commerce. "Intended primarily for students in commercial and technical institutions and for private students preparing for the more elementary examinations of such bodies as the Royal Society of Arts or the Institute of Linguists. It is equally suitable for older students in secondary schools." Illustrates modern usage through the medium of descriptive passages to notes. 25 chapters, plus 5 recapitulations. Vocabulary, each way, p. 262–320. Exercises: questions, drill, exercises each way. Very sparing use of bold type. No index to grammar.

LITTEWOOD, R. P. Further living Spanish. London, University of London Press, [1965]. 384 p. illus., map. 13s. 6d.

Whereas *Living Spanish* is for the beginner, this second book is mainly suitable for 'A' level candidates and students, and would also be valuable for first-year university students, especially in the revision of grammar that occupies the second half. "One of the best grammars I have come across", states the reviewer in *The incorporated linguist* (v. 5, no. 4, October 1966, p. 120–1). The first half consists of 32 chapters: readings plus notes, grammar exercises and translations involving points of grammar that cause difficulty or confusion. Chapters 1–17 have as their theme general topics or Spanish background, but chapters 18–32 enterprisingly concentrate on aspects of Latin America. Incorporates the latest Academy pronouncements on grammar and spelling. Vocabularies each way; no index to grammar.

LÓPEZ-MORILLAS, J. New Spanish self-taught; the quick, practical way to reading, writing, speaking, understanding. Rev. ed. New York, Funk & Wagnalls, 1959. xix [1], 340 p. (Language phone series). $3.50.

A revision of the 1945 edition. Uses the sentence, not the word, as the basis for learning Spanish. Ten parts, pt. 10 being the grammar (p. 223–329). Simulated pronunciation. Spanish-English vocabulary only (p. 330–7); index to grammar. Gramophone records are available.

LYON, J. E. Pitfalls of Spanish vocabulary. London, Harrap, 1961. 120 p. 9s. 6d.

Author is Spanish Master, Birkenhead School. Aims "to provide the student with a readily accessible list of Spanish words which vary in meaning or usage from their apparent English equivalents" (*Preface*). Alphabetical list with examples, p. 11–114 (e.g. *formal; simpatía*: ea. ¾ p.) index to about 350 English words, p. 115–17; 74 authors quoted in the text. p. 119–20.

McSPADDEN, G. E. An introduction to Spanish usage: basic elements of Spanish and principles of their use. New York & Toronto, Oxford University Press, 1956. xv, [1], 267 p. 30s.

24 lessons; verb tables. Vocabulary, each way, with notes and references, p. 227–59; index to grammar. "A functional presentation of Spanish linguistic practice, combined with features of an exercise book and a guide to conversation" (*Preface*).

MARKARIAN, R. H. M., and MOORE, S.   Vamos a hablar español. 2nd ed. London, University Tutorial Press, 1963. vi, 41 p. illus. 4s. 9d.

A first book in oral Spanish, intended to help students to think in Spanish from an early stage (e.g., after one term of Spanish). 10 sections, each with illustration, reading passage, short conversation (based on the reading), 3 sets of questions, and a list of useful words and idioms. Rather large page; clear print.

PACKER, P. W., and DEAN, E. L.   A comprehensive Spanish course for first examination. New ed., rev. London, Harrap, 1961 (i.e., 1962). 226 p. 8s.

For G.C.E. 'O' level and equivalent examinations year. Pt. 1. Each section contains a Spanish passage and questions in Spanish; English, for translation into Spanish; Subjects for free composition. 35 sections. Pt. 2: Grammar section, with exercises (19 sections). 3. Verbs (14 sections). Appendix: School Certificate examination questions. Vocabulary, each way, p. 180–224. No index to grammar. Attractively produced; clear type.

PEERS, E. A.   A skeleton Spanish grammar. 3rd ed. London, Blackie, 1937. xvi, 181 p. o.p.   Key to exercises. o.p.

First published 1917. "Elementary grammar for adolescent and adult beginners and for use in schools as 1 or 2-year course" (*Note to the 3rd ed.*).
Contents: 49 concise lessons, with introduction on the sounds of the Spanish language (p. 1–69) and appendices; exercises on the lessons: reading, conversation, sentences (into Spanish); additional reading selections, in verse; pronunciation exercises; phonetic transcription of lessons 1–3, 9–11. Vocabulary, each way, p. 153–81.
A compact, well-arranged manual for reference and self-study (with the *Key*), as well as a class book.

PITTARO, J. M., and GREEN, A.   Beginner's Spanish. Boston, Heath, 1932. xvi, 501, 30 p. illus., maps. (Heath's Modern language series). 25s.

56 lessons. "Designed to meet the needs of the beginner in an elementary course comprising two to four terms" (*Preface*). Ten of the lessons are devoted to the subjunctive. Plenty of exercises, drill, questions and conversation. Vocabulary, each way, p. 457–96. Index to grammar.
A comprehensive course.

QUINLAN, P. M. H., and COMPTON, W. V. Español rápido; edited by P. H. Hargreaves. London, Leonard Hill, 1966. ix, 169 p. illus. 14s. 6d.

An attractively produced paperback that aims at teaching Spanish to mature beginners. Pt. 1 introduces the elements of Spanish, each of the 20 lessons consisting of pronunciation exercise, reading passage, vocabulary, grammar and exercises (Spanish into English only). Pt. 2 (test papers, 2 series) provides intensive work for those who progress more quickly than is normal or who wish to have supplementary revision exercises. The end-vocabulary consists of c. 1,000 words, Spanish-English only; index to grammar.

RAMSDEN, H. An essential course in modern Spanish. London, Harrap, 1951. 416 p. 15s.

The author was Lecturer in Spanish at the University of Manchester. 25 lessons, plus 8 review and development sections. "For University students who offer Spanish as one of their Intermediate subjects" (*Preface*). Plenty of drill and exercises; verb tables; key to exercises. Vocabulary, each way, p. 371–413. Index to grammar. Good typography; good use of bold type.

Highly recommended; easy to use. Used as a model for Willis's *An essential course in modern Portuguese* (q.v.).

RAMSEY, M. M. A Spanish grammar. A textbook of modern Spanish, as now written and spoken in Castile and the Spanish American Republics; revised by Robert K. Spaulding. New York, Holt, 1956. xix, [1], 692, xvii p. 60s.

First published 1894. *A Spanish grammar* (London, Bell, 1902, vii, 610 p.) differs from the above in that it includes many exercises and vocabulary each way, p. 527–603. To that extent it is not superseded.

The 1956 ed. has four parts: 1. Orthography and pronunciation; 2. Preliminary lessons (1–20). Forms and uses (p. 23–672). Appendices: Spanish forms of address; Social and epistolary usages; Derivative geographical adjectives. A bibliography of 'useful works of reference' and index to grammar precede. Features are the several thousand examples of idioms. Lesson vocabularies (only essential vocabulary, based on the findings of V. García Hoz and Hayward Keniston), but no general vocabulary or exercises.

The authoritative Spanish grammar; a major reference book. A complete and thorough course, as it must be for students who wish to reach G.C.E. 'A' level in 8 months.

REAL ACADEMIA ESPAÑOLA. Gramática de la lengua española. Nueva ed., reformada, de 1931, y apendice con las nuevas normas de prosodia y ortografía declaradas de aplicación preceptiva desde 1.° de enero de 1959. Madrid, Espasa-Calpe, 1959. 542 p. c. 15s.

First published 1879. Four parts: Analogía (p. 9–151). – Sintaxis (p. 153–445). – Prosodia (p. 447–66). – Ortografía (p. 467–91). This last part includes a list of the most commonly met abbreviations in Spanish, p. 491–94. Appendix: Catálogo de voces de escritura dudosa, p. 495–515. Analytical subject index (p. 517–34); contents list. Copious examples.

The authority on current usage. This 1959 edition consists of the 1931 edition plus the new appendix.

RESNICK, S. Essential Spanish grammar. London, Hodder & Stoughton, 1959. 127 p. 5s.

A self-tutor, for acquiring fluency in simple everyday conversation, for those who have learned no formal grammar. Grammar notes are graduated, so that the familiar form of address does not appear until half-way through. Examples for each rule. No exercises. List of c. 2,400 cognates (English–Spanish). p. 80–110. The English glossary of grammatical terms could well have come at the beginning of the book. Index to grammar.

SCARR, J. R. Present-day Spanish. Oxford, Pergamon Press, 1966. v. 1. 219 p. 10s. 6d.; 21s.

20 lessons on orthodox lines, each containing a reading passage, lengthy vocabulary and full grammar notes (which should precede the reading matter) and an abundance of exercises in forbiddingly small print. Formal translation from English starts with lesson 1. The reviewer in *Modern languages* (v. 47, no. 3, September 1966, p. 132) praises the early treatment of the past definite and considers the course quite suitable, in the hands of a good teacher, for grammar-school classes – "but languages are now studied in other kinds of schools".

SHOEMAKER, W. H. Spanish minimum. Boston, Heath, 1953. xi, 160 p. maps. 20s.

20 lessons and 4 *repasos*. "A one-semester course for beginners" (*Preface*). Plenty of exercises and drill. Lessons consist of vocabulary, a Spanish passage, grammar and exercises. Appendices on verb and pronouns. Vocabulary, each way, p. 135–58; index to grammar. Good range of type.

TIMMS, W. W. A first Spanish book. Longmans, 1957 (2nd impression, with corrections, 1960). x, 190 p. illus. o.p.

15 lessons. For class use; A lively oral approach. This and the *A second Spanish book* (see below) aim at presenting material for the first two years of a three-year study of Spanish for G.C.E. 'O' level. Plenty of useful and interesting exercises (about 12 per lesson) and drill. Topical Spanish-English vocabulary only. Good use of bold type.

TIMMS, W. W. A second Spanish book. London, Longmans, 1958 (and reprints). 238 p. illus. o.p.

12 lessons. Plenty of exercises and drill. Vocabulary, each way. A well-planned course.

TIMMS, W. W., and PULGAR, M.   A simpler Spanish course, for first examinations.   London, Longmans, 1962.   viii, 326 p.   9s. 6d. Teachers' book.   7s. 6d.

"To help those who are in their First Examination year" (*Introduction*). Contents: 1. Spanish passages for comprehension, translation and précis (50 passages), p. 1–59; 2. Sentences and exercises on the grammar, p. 60–93; 3. English prose passages for translation into Spanish (60 passages, with notes), p. 94–132; 4. Summaries and subjects for free compositions, p. 133–38; 5. Summaries of stories for aural tests, p. 139–48; 6. Outlines of grammar, p. 149–248. Copious examples. Attractive clear type. Appendices, on verbs, etc. Vocabulary, each way.

Examples and prose extracts make this ideal for use with a native tutor, or by consulting the key.

TRAVIS, J. E., and others.   Principios de español.   New and rev. ed. London, Harrap, 1956–59 (and reprints).   2 v. (190, 224 p.).   illus. o.p.

First published 1935–36. For class use; plenty of reading matter, exercises and drill in each lesson. Vocabulary, each way (Book 1, p. 162–90; Book 2, p. 186–224).

TURK, L. H., and ALLEN, E. M.   El español al día.   3rd ed.   Boston, Heath; London, Harrap, 1963–64.   2 v.   36s., 35s.   Teacher's manual and key.   9s. 6d.

Sumptuously produced, with coloured illustrations and maps. Attractive layout, with a variety of exercises and drill. Book 1 consists of 45 lessons (dialogue; vocabulary; questions on dialogue; grammar; exercises). Gramophone records (six 7" 33⅓ r.p.m.) are available with book 1, and tape with book 2.

VALENTÍ, H., and others.   ¡Vamos a ver!   Let's look at Spanish. London, B.B.C., 1966.   176 p.   illus.   6s.

20 lessons for beginners on B.B.C. TV. Includes a note on pronunciation and intonation, and a well-arranged select glossary. 2 companion 12" L.P. discs are available at 19s. 3d. each. An admirable tourist's vade mecum to modern everyday life and situations in Spain.

WALTON, L. B.   Spanish by yourself: a quick course in reading for adult beginners and others.   London, Bell, 1951.   vi, [1], 214 p. maps.   o.p.

Author was Head of the Department of Hispanic Studies in the University of Edinburgh. Pt. 1: 1. Alphabet; pronunciation. 2. Synopsis of grammar (Section 1. p. 11–58). 3. Passages for reading (Group A). Part 2: 4. Synopsis of grammar (Section 2, p. 95–146). Word lists (Group B). Passages for reading. Vocabulary.

WILSON, N. S.   Teach yourself Spanish.   London, English Universities Press, 1938.   242 p.   (Teach yourself language series).   6s.

30 lessons. An elementary self-tutor, leading up to the subjunctive. Exercises: sentences each way, working up to connected passages; key. Table of irregular verbs. Vocabulary, each way, p. 224–42.

Continued by L. D. Collier's *Teach yourself everyday Spanish* (London, English Universities Press, 1957, 232 p., 6s.). This comprises 20 lessons, with key to exercises. Connected passages; no vocabulary.

Commercial Correspondence

MACDONALD, G. R.   Manual of Spanish commercial correspondence. 5th ed.   London, Pitman, 1940.   xii, 348 p.   12s. 6d.

21 chapters; contains an extensive and varied selection of commercial letters in Spanish and in English, with graduated footnotes explaining commercial terms and expressions. The English-Spanish vocabulary is full and particularly helpful ('way' and 'take' : one column apiece) and with the Spanish-English vocabulary occupies p. 186–225. Technical vocabulary and list of Spanish verbs follow.

Special Aspects of Grammar

Notes on Spanish pronunciation & accentuation, by H. Lester and V. Terrádez (London, University of London Press, 1953. 32 p. o.p.) incorporates some of the recent changes authorised by the Spanish Academy and includes reading exercises. H. Lester is also joint author of the practical *Conversaciones espanolas*, with Ariza Almeida (London, University of London Press, 1961. 160 p. o.p.). This covers topics likely to arise when an English visitor goes to Spain for the first time. Ideal for practising phrasing and intonation of spoken Spanish, it is rather advanced in language and very idiomatic. E. Kucera's *Learn Spanish with me: libro del turista inglés* (Barcelona, Kucera, 1954. 144 p. illus. 4s. 6d.) is an illustrated booklet which covers everyday contingencies. *Teach yourself Spanish phrasebook*, by W. W. Timms and M. Pulgar (London, English Universities Press, 1954, 250 p., 6s.), gives a fuller treatment, with chapters on Spanish life and a fairly full supporting grammar. Manuel Seco's *Diccionario de dudas y dificultades de la lengua española* (3. ed. Madrid, Aguilar, 1965, xx, 516 p. illus., tables) consists of a dictionary (including tables of verb conjugations), a synthesis of Spanish grammar and sections on abbreviations, signs and the latest rulings of the Spanish Academy, plus a short bibliography.

GENERAL DICTIONARIES

General criteria for foreign-language dictionaries have been stated in chapter 1; they include: accuracy, number of entries,[1] up to dateness, provision of aids to pronunciation and stress, inclusion of verb tables, legibility plus portability, and a reasonable price.

Two further qualities, at least, must be looked for in Spanish-and-English dictionaries:

1. Inclusion and indication, preferably by country, of Hispanic American vocabulary. British and U.S. usages also need to be differentiated.
2. Differentiation between various meanings of the same Spanish word.

BENEDETTO, U. di, and others. Nuevo diccionario general inglés-español; [and] New comprehensive Spanish-English dictionary. Madrid, E.D.A.F.E., 1966. 2 v. in 1. liv, [1], 1,495 p.; li, [1], 1,300 p. 152s. 6d.

About 100,000 entry-words in each part. Includes Latin American words and expressions and some technical terms but no abbreviations. Intended primarily for those whose native tongue is Spanish (e.g., pronunciation is given only for English entry-words). Terms are categorised and applications numbered. A lengthy synopsis of grammar precedes each part. Clear, sanserif type; thumb index.

CUYÁS, ANTONIO. Appleton's revised English-Spanish and Spanish-English dictionary. 4th ed., rev. and enl. by Lewis E. Brett and Helen S. Eaton. New York, Appleton-Century-Crofts, 1953 (and reprints, e.g. 1961). xxxii, 697, xvii, 575 p. 65s.; $7.50 (with thumb index, $8.50).

First published 1903. Sub-title: "containing more than one hundred and twenty thousand principal and subsidiary terms, with idioms and technical usages." Major different applications of terms are enumerated, using bold Roman figures; others are categorised; superior to Cassell's dictionary in this, as in some other aspects. Pronunciation is simulated only of English entry-words. Each half has appendices of geographical, proper and pet names, as well as abbreviations. Good for Americanisms.

One of the biggest and best of the one-volume two-way dictionaries. A student's edition is also available.

[1] This needs qualification. Margaret Raventós, in the introduction to her *A modern Spanish dictionary* (q.v.) states that word-counting is "not an acceptable criterion by which to judge the expressive power of any language". In some dictionaries, again, compounds of a word may be given separate entries; in others, they may be run-on, sub-entries. This invalidates word-counting except as a very rough check.

CUYÁS, ARTURO Y ANTONIO.   Gran diccionario Cuyás, inglés-español,
español-inglés.   Nueva ed., corregida y aumentada por Mauricio
Bohigas y Rosell.   Barcelona, Hymsa, 1960.   xxxvi, [1], 810, [1],
748 p.   52s. 6d.

First published 1928. About 70,000 main entries, including geographical
and proper names, in each half. Includes many technical terms, as well as
Spanish phrases, idioms and proverbs. Different meanings of Spanish words
are separated by double upright strokes. Pronunciation of English words is
given, plus pronunciation of more difficult Spanish words. Spanish American
words are indicated as '(Amer.)'. Summary of grammar precedes each half.
Bears no apparent relation to the Appleton Cuyás, and is fuller.

Diccionario manual Sopena; enciclopédico e ilustrado.   Barcelona,
Sopena, 1962.   2 v.   2,320, cxxxiv p.   c. 60s.

A medium-sized Sopena encyclopaedic dictionary, in between the
Diccionario la fuente (for school use) and the *Diccionario enciclopédico ilustrado*
(3 v.). 100,000 entry-words, combining language dictionary and encyclopaedia in one sequence (A-H, I-Z). 6,240 clear if small text illustrations à la
Petit Larousse, 94 full-page illustrations, 16 colour plates and 91 maps (7 in
colour). Illustrations helpfully group objects (e.g., 'viviendas'; 'flores';
'oceanografia' [submarine life]), and shows keyed parts (e.g., the horse : 51).
Appended, on tinted paper, is a compendium of Spanish grammar.

Duden español.   Diccionario por la imagen.   Mannheim, Bibliographisches Institut; London, Harrap, 1963.   672, 111, 128 p.   38s.

Uniform with the *Grosse Duden, Duden français* and *English Duden*. Two
main parts: (a) 368 illustrations, grouped by subject, on verso pages, with
numbered Spanish terms on pages facing; (b) Spanish and English indexes
to the 25,000 terms. Clear line-drawings and a few illustrations in colour.
A valuable visual aid.

GILLHOFF, G. A., and MORALES, P.   Black's Spanish dictionary.
London, Black, 1963 (i.e., 1964).   xii, 1,261 p.   illus.   42s.

Originally published by Crowell, New York, 1963. Designed for the
student, businessman and tourist rather than the university graduate. 80,000
entry-words, including Latin American. Appendices include outlines of
grammar, lists of abbreviations and numerals. The reviewer in *Modern
languages* (v. 45, no. 4, December 1964, p. 168) finds this dictionary no
improvement on existing compilations: it has many omissions (its chief
defect) and it tends towards the take-it-or-leave-it, word-for-word translation.

MARTÍNEZ AMADOR, E. M.   Standard Spanish-English dictionary,
and Diccionario inglés-español.   4. ed.   Barcelona, Sopena; London,
Bailey Bros. & Swinfen, 1958 (and reprints, e.g. 1965).   2 v.   72s.

First published 1946; 3rd ed. 1957. The 4th ed. (2,166 p.) is the first to appear in 2 volumes, each with over 60,000 main entries. Simulated pronunciation is given of English, but not of Spanish, entry-words. Different applications of terms are categorised, sub-entries in italics. Gives entries for past participles. Includes Spanish-American words, designated, e.g., '(Amer.)' or '(Cuba)'. Particularly rich in idioms and synonyms. Appendices: Geographical names; proper names; abbreviations; metric equivalents. One of the best two-way dictionaries.

The smaller *Diccionario manual Amador, inglés-español y español-inglés* (Barcelona, Sopena, 1962, 1,263, [3] p. 30s) is good value for money. Each half has some 50,000 entries, including colloquialisms and technical terms. Pronunciation of English entry-words only; summary of grammar in each part.

Nuevo pequeño Larousse ilustrado. Diccionario enciclopédico... Paris, Larousse, 1951 (and reprints, e.g. 1963). viii, 1,520 p. illus., maps. 54s.

Diccionario, p. 1–1,008; Algo de ortología española, p. 1,009–16; Locuciones latinas y extranjeras, p. 1,017–48; Enciclopédia (history, geography, biography), p. 1,049–520. Based on the French *Petit Larousse*, but not on the 1959 edition, with its modernised layout and clearer illustrations. The dictionary section is particularly useful, with its many synonyms, for the more advanced student and translator. 6,000 line drawings; 200 plates; 70 maps. Small type.

Pequeño Larousse ilustrado... (Buenos Aires and Paris, Larousse, 1964. viii, 1,663 p. illus., maps. *c.* 70s.) is the much-needed modernised version of the preceding item. 60,000 entries; 5,000 black-and-white and 75 coloured illus.; 100 maps.

Diccionario escolar ilustrado, by M. de Toro (Paris, Larousse, 1950, 1,084 p., 30s.) is a shortened version, adapted for school use.

Vox. Diccionario general ilustrado de la lengua española (2. ed., corregido y notablemente ampliado por D. Samuel Gili Gaya. Barcelona, Spes, 1961 (reimpressión corregida). xxxix, 1,814 p. *c.* 75s.) has clearer but fewer illustrations than the *Nuevo pequeño Larousse ilustrado*. Appendices of geographical names, Latin and foreign sayings.

PEERS, E. A., and others. Cassell's Spanish dictionary. London, Cassell, 1959 (and reprints, e.g., 1966, called '4th edition'). xiv, [1], 1,477 p. 36s.

Spanish-English, p. 1–790; English-Spanish, p. 795–1,445. About 70,000 main entries to each half, including geographical names. Appendices: Spanish verbs; common abbreviations (Spanish; English); English geographical names; tables of weights and measures. Includes Central and South American variants, indicating country. Categorises special applications of terms, but less clearly than does the Appleton Cuyás, and fails to distinguish between suggested translations, especially in the English-Spanish part;

italics for sub-entries. Good for idioms. Phonetic pronunciation is given only for English entries. Good typography and attractive appearance of page.

"For their English-Spanish translations school pupils and university undergraduates will probably prefer the dictionary by M. H. Raventós", states the review in *Modern languages* (v. 41, no. 2, June 1960, p. 81–82).

RAVENTÓS, M. H.   A modern Spanish dictionary.   London, English Universities Press, 1953.   xx, 494, [5], 495–1,230, [6] p.   45s.

Author was Special Lecturer in Spanish in the University of Manchester. Spanish-English, p. 1–494 (27,000 entries); English-Spanish, p. 495–1,230 (32,000 entries). Grammatical introductions precede each half; appendices of geographical and proper names, abbreviations, weights and measures, and currency (Spanish-English only). Many idioms. Includes U.S. terms. Omits highly specialised technical terms and Spanish-American usage, unless adopted by present-day Castilians or where justified on literary grounds. Good use of bold type for sub-entries.

Intended to meet the needs of English students of Spanish and as such is warmly recommended.

An unabridged reprint (*Modern Spanish-English, English-Spanish dictionary.* London, E.U.P., 1963. 15s.) is rather unfairly criticised (*The incorporated linguist,* January 1966, v. 5, no. 1, p. 24–25) for failure to keep with the times. Excellent value at 15s.

REAL ACADEMIA ESPAÑOLA.   Diccionario manual e ilustrado de la lengua española.   2. ed.   Madrid, Espasa-Calpe, 1950.   xi, 1,572 p. illus.   36s. 6d.

Based on the 16th and 17th editions of the Spanish Academy's *Diccionario de la lengua española* (18th ed. Madrid, Espasa-Calpe, 1956, xxiii, [1], 1,370 p. 625 pesetas; c. 112s.), the standard authority on current usage, and acts as a corrective to the larger work by including new words, including Spanish-American terms (designated by country). Gives many examples of usage. Line drawings, about two per page. Very good value at the price.

SMITH, C. C., and others.   Langenscheidt's Standard dictionary of the English and Spanish languages.   London, Hodder & Stoughton, 1966.   561 p.   25s.

English-Spanish, p. 17–533 (c. 15,000 main entries); Spanish-English, p. 17–474 (c. 14,000 main entries); appendices on proper nouns, abbreviations, weights and measures, etc. A dumpy volume, with a smallish page. Helpful features: International phonetic alphabet in both parts; syllabification; categorised nouns, as well as 21 graphic symbols; genders given; good use of bold. Lengthy entries (e.g., 'Water:' 1 column) are divided up. The writing of Spanish words has been governed by the *Nuevas normas* issued by the Academy in 1952 and revised in 1959. A reliable small dictionary for desk use.

VELÁSQUEZ DE LA CADENA, M., and others. New revised Velásquez Spanish and English dictionary. Newly revised by Ida Navarro Hinojosa. Chicago & New York, Follett, 1960 (and reprints, e.g., 1962). 696, [2], 780 p. 60s.; $7.50 (with thumb-index, 68s.; $8.50).

First published 1852. Spanish-English, p. 19–690; English-Spanish, p. 15–766. Each half has appendices of geographical terms, abbreviations, weights and measures, and currency. Grammatical introduction to each half. Different meanings of words are numbered; different applications are categorised. Simulated pronunciation of words in each half. Many idioms and illustrative phrases. Well balanced. According to the *Preface*, particular attention has been paid to the terms and idioms commonly used in Spanish America and the United States. About 60,000 in the Spanish-English half; 70,000, in the English-Spanish half. 3 columns; small but clear type.

Well used, and recommended for general purposes.

VOX: diccionario ilustrado inglés-español, español-inglés. Barcelona, Bibliograf, S.A., 1964. xxxi, 1,419 p. 400 pesetas (*c.* 50s.).

English-Spanish, p. 1–779 (*c.* 60,000 main entries); Spanish-English, p. 791–1,419, on buff-tinted paper (*c.* 50,000 entry-words); appendices on proper names, abbreviations. Numbered meanings under entry-words. Helpful boxed grammatical notes (e.g., on 'posesivo', 'gerundio'). American English terms are asterisked in the Spanish-English part.

WILLIAMS, E. B. Holt Spanish and English dictionary. Diccionario inglés y español. New York & London, Holt, 1955. xi, 621, xli, 605 p. 48s.; $7.70 (with thumb-index, 56s.; $8.50).

About 115,000 separate entries, almost equally divided: English-Spanish, 621 p.; Spanish-English, 605 p. Gives phonetic pronunciation for English entries, but not for Spanish. There is also a summary of English grammar, but not of Spanish. Vocabulary claims to cover peninsular and Spanish-American Spanish, British and American English. Bold type for sub-entries; different meanings of terms are categorised.

Recommended as a good all-round dictionary. While conceding that Martínez Amador is much richer in ideas, and Raventós, more careful in distinguishing differences, the reviewer in *Modern languages* (v. 38, no. 3, September 1957, p. 118) states that Williams, "as a practical guide of contemporary language, especially the scientific and technical, is very good".

Other General Dictionaries

The English edition of *Phrase and sentence dictionary of spoken Spanish* (New York, Dover, 1958; London, Constable, 1959. 513 p. 14s.) has the title *Dictionary of spoken Spanish*. It covers both languages, each way, and is a practical guide, with a good appendix covering daily contingencies. H. Keniston's *A standard list of Spanish words and idioms* (Boston, Heath; London, Harrap, 1941. xiv, 108 p. 14s. 6d.) is a revision of his *Basic list* of 1933. T. Folley's more recent *A dictionary of Spanish idioms and colloquialisms* (London, Blackie, 1965. [vii], 68 p. 8s. 6d.) is a selection of the most current expressions met in everyday speech and in the works of contemporary writers; c. 1,400 entries. E. B. Williams' *Diccionario del idioma español* (New York, Pocket Books, Inc., 1959. 469 p. 50cs.) has 35,000 entries and is good value for the money.

G. H. Calvert's *Dictionary of the Spanish and English languages* (London, Routledge & Kegan Paul, 1956 (and reprints, e.g. 1962), xv, 516 p. 12s. 6d.) is useful within the limits of its size. It is fairly up to date and pays special attention to Spanish irregular verbs. The paperbacked edition of *The University of Chicago Spanish dictionary . . .*, by C. Castillo and O. F. Bond, with the assistance of Barbara M. García (New York, Pocket Books, Inc.; Oadby, Leics., Thorpe & Porter, 1953. xxxvi, 226, xvi, 251 p. 3s. 6d.) has about 15,00 entries in each half, with appendices of idioms, irregular verbs, numerals, etc. Although J. G. Fucilla's *Concise Spanish dictionary, Spanish-English and English-Spanish* (London, Harrap, 1948 (and reprints, e.g. 1961), viii, 306, 332 p., 26s.) is slightly larger (about 50–60,000 entires in all, including geographical and proper names), and gives genders of Spanish nouns in both halves, it gives strings of undifferentiated alternative meanings and is not recommended. Based on it is *A practical Spanish and English dictionary*, by I. A. Hinojosa and C. Toral, revised under the editorial supervision of Emilio C. Lefort (Chicago, Follett; London, Harrap, 1955. 238, 272, 18 p. 16s.).

A. L. Dupays' *Essential Spanish vocabulary* (London, Longmans, 1965, xi, 120 p. 7s. 6d.) provides a classified list of c. 3,000 words that are considered essential for first examinations. It also has full tables of verbs (irregular, radical changing and consonant changing) and an English-Spanish reference vocabulary. In his *A classified Spanish vocabulary* (London, Harrap, 1964. 231 p. 12s. 6d.), G. J. G. Cheyne also provides a classified list, in 14 sections and many sub-sections, of c. 8,000 words, for undergraduates and other advanced students and teachers. Recently coined words are included.

Pocket dictionaries, generally, have the faults of their size: they rarely give more than word-for-word equivalents and they lack appendices on irregular verbs, etc. They include *Methuen's* (Langenscheidt's) *Universal dictionary, Spanish-English, English-Spanish* (London, Methuen, [n.d.], 463 p. 3s. 6d.; *Hugo's Spanish-English, English-Spanish dictionary* (London, Hugo's Language Institute, [n.d.], xvi, 622 p. 6s.); W. B. Wells' *Dictionary of the Spanish and English languages* (London, Eyre & Spottiswoode, 1949. ix, 874 p. 5s. 6d.); *Vocabulario Cuyás. Vocabulario español-inglés, inglés-español* (4. ed. Barcelona, Hymsa, 1958, 640 p. 6s. 6d.; and *Diccionario inglés-español, español-inglés*, by E. Serrano Mesa and J. M. Calder (3. ed. Madrid, MAYFE. 640 p. 8s.).

Special mention must be made of *Beyond the dictionary in Spanish: a handbook of colloquial usage*, by A. B. Gerrard and J. de Heras Heras (London, Cassell, 1953. 160 p. 10s. 6d.), which aims to bridge the gap, for the Englishman, "between the written word, as acquired from grammar books, and the living Spanish as spoken by a native" (*Preface*). Contents: Miscellaneous notes (pronunciation, accent, diminutives, etc.); Spanish-English dictionary, with commentary (p. 17–117); Special vocabularies, particularly well drawn up (p. 118–43): 'false friends' (excellently done); disconcerting genders; topics (e.g. cars, domestic appurtenances, food, music, office appurtenances, telephones); English-Spanish cross-reference index.

Technical and Commercial Dictionaries

Special Spanish and English dictionaries are numerous. A handy list is available in the *Canning House Library Bulletin*, no. 48, February 1962, "Portuguese and Spanish special dictionaries". This is a six-page folder, listing some 70 items, with notes, in some cases, on subject coverage. Some of the best-known are the following:

Castilla's Spanish and English technical dictionary. 3rd ed. London, Routledge & Kegan Paul, 1958. 2 v. £14.

V. 1, English-Spanish (xi, 1,611 p.; *c.* 150,000 main entries); v. 2, Spanish-English (1,137 p.; *c.* 120,000 main entries). Original Spanish title: *Diccionario politécnico de las lenguas española e inglésa* (Madrid, Ediciones Castilla S.A.). Concentrates on engineering technology, excluding terms in physical, chemical and biological sciences except where these are of importance to engineers and technologists. In comprehensiveness second only to Sell (which also finds room for proper names, abbreviations, etc.), and not over-priced, comparatively.

Chambers diccionario tecnológico, español-inglés, ingles-español . . .
dirigido por C. F. Tweeney y L. E. C. Hughes. La traducción
española . . . dirigida por Carlos Botet. Barcelona, Omega, 1952.
[xv], 1,227, 287 p.   c. 80s.

   Basically a Spanish translation of *Chambers's Technical dictionary* (which
defines and categories *c.* 60,000 scientific and technical terms). Spanish terms
are explained in Spanish, but the entries in the main sequence (p. 1–1,227)
include English translation of entry-words, and an English-Spanish dictionary
of equivalents is appended.

GOLDBERG, M.   Spanish-English chemical and medical dictionary.
New York, McGraw-Hill, 1952.   viii, 609 p. $17.50.

GOLDBERG, M.   English-Spanish chemical and medical dictionary.
New York, McGraw-Hill, 1947.   ix, 692 p. $15.

   The two volumes contain about 30,000 and 35,000 entry-words respectively, with definitions following the equivalents in each case.

MACDONALD, G. R.   Spanish-English and English-Spanish commercial dictionary.   5th ed., rev. and enl.   London, Pitman, 1944
(and reprints, e.g. 1960).   950 p.   30s.

   First published 1915. About 25,000 terms in each part. Well spoken of.
The only sizeable Spanish and English commercial dictionary in print,
though it needs updating.

ROBB, L. A.   Engineers' dictionary, Spanish-English and English-
Spanish.   2nd ed.   New York, Wiley; London, Chapman &
Hall, 1949 (and reprints, e.g., 1965).   xvi, 664 p. $15; 105s.

   First published 1944. Spanish-English, p. 3–324; English-Spanish, p.
327–664. Each part has about 30,000 entry-words, with equivalents. Clear
typography. Needs updating.

SELL, L. L.   English-Spanish comprehensive technical dictionary . . .
New York, London, McGraw-Hill, 1944.   xii, 1,478 p. $35; £14.
Section 2.   1959.   [3], 1,079 p. $35; £14.

SELL, L. L.   Español-inglés diccionario técnico completísimo . . .
New York, International Dictionary Co., 1949.   xi, 1,706 p.   £16.

   Very detailed and bulky. The three volumes claim to contain 525,000,
400,000 and 700,000 technical terms, but these figures are arrived at by
counting entry-words and equivalents as well. Covers Spanish terms in Latin
American countries and differentiates between British English and American
English. Rather forbidding layout, entries being set solid.

SELL, L. Spanish-English comprehensive specialists' dictionary for insurance, finance, law, labor, politics, business. New York, McKay, 1957. xi, 650 p. o.p.

Claims to contain more than 135,000 entry-words and equivalents; lists of abbreviations, p. 643–60. The corresponding English-Spanish volume, also out of print, was published in 1955 (New York, International Dictionary Co. 535 p.).

GRAMOPHONE RECORDS

Two Linguaphone courses cover Castilian Spanish and Spanish-American Spanish, each on sixteen L.P. 45 or 78 r.p.m., £15 2s. 6d. Instruction books are included. The Castilian course is also on tape (two 5″ spools 3¾ i.p.s., 2-track recording). Odhams 'Master' course, – four 10″ L.P.s, with dictionary and instruction manual – costs £12 10s. The Assimil 20-lesson preliminary and advanced course (twenty 10″ 78 r.p.m. or ten 7″ 45 r.p.m. records, £14) is designed to accompany Chérel's *Spanish without toil.* J. P. Fitzgibbon's *El español práctico* is similarly supported by four 10″ 33⅓ r.p.m., *c.* £6 17s. 2d. The excellent 'Express' Basic conversational Spanish course (Oldbourne Press), consisting of two 12″ L.P. 33⅓ r.p.m. records, plus textbook, £5 5s., is also available on tape. The Interpret (Daily Mail/Visaphone Co.) course is on three 7″ 33⅓ r.p.m., £3 19s. 6d., or on tape, £4 15s. 6d., and has an accompanying booklet with vocabulary. The Heath de Rochement Audio-visual Spanish course, "Una aventura española" (price on application to Harrap, Audio-Visual Aids,) is advertised as a complete introductory course for the primary school. It consists of nineteen 15-minute 16-mm. films in black and white, with supplementary material.

Of the cheaper and more limited courses, Odhams' Quick (Odhams Press – two 7″ 33⅓ r.p.m. records and books) – is recommended, at 30s. The Dover 'Listen and learn' language records – three 12″ 33⅓ r.p.m. records and manual – costs 58s. Conversa-phone issue a single-disc course ('CX': 12″ L.P., 37s. 6d.; 'C'9 10″ L.P., 30s. 6d.), as well as a course for children, similarly priced. Other courses on the market are: the 'Instant' (two 12″, 70s.); 'Lightning' conversation (Oriole Records) (two 7″ 45 r.p.m., plus booklet, at 29s. 9d.); Lexiphone (Visaphone Co.) (two 7″ 33⅓ r.p.m., plus books, 26s. 6d., or on tape, 38s. 6d.), 'Gem' (one 7″, 9s. 2d.): 'Rainbow' Spanish without tears (one 7" 33⅓ r.p.m., plus pamphlet, 8s. 6d.), and 'Spanish: 200 basic words' (Saga Records) (one 7" 45 r.p.m., 7s. 6d.). The single 12" L.P. 33⅓ r.p.m. Hugophone disc (29s. 6d.) aims to be "an advanced help to pronunciation" and not a language course. Two 12" L.P. discs, each 19s. 3d., accompany the Valentí grammar (q.v.).

An evaluation of 13 of the cheaper courses on discs (12 of them covered Spanish) was made in *Which?*, June 1964 (p. 187–92). The Odhams' Quick Spanish was recommended as the best buy; for those with more time and money to spend on a longer course, Basic Conversational Spanish course was ranked first.

A number of disc courses are available from the U.S.A., some for use in conjunction with grammars (e.g., those by López-Morillas, and by Twik and Allen), but these may provide pronunciation difficulties for the British user.

5

PORTUGUESE

by A. J. WALFORD, M.A., PH.D., F.L.A., in consultation with G. H. GREEN, B.A., H. LENNOX-KAY, A.I.L., Dr. L. S. REBÊLO and MARIA DA SILVA

GRAMMARS

There are comparatively few Portuguese grammars and even fewer are published in Britain and are in print. For this reason J. Dunn's standard grammar has been included, although it is out of print, and so, too, have a number of grammars published in Portugal or even Spain. Portuguese as spoken in Brazil is covered by the grammars of Rossi and Cuesta, Hills and Ford, and, more recently, Willis are the grammars currently used in classes.

BARKER, J. W. Teach yourself Portuguese. New ed., edited and revised by L. Stringer. London, English Universities Press, 1962 (and reprints, e.g., 1965). 196 p. 7s. 6d.

First published 1945. Author was Lecturer in Portuguese in the University of Cambridge. 28 lessons: exercises; sentences, each way; conversation and reading; some correspondence. Matters of special difficulty, such as the personal infinitive, pronoun object and sequence of tenses, are dealt with very fully. Tables of verbs, p. 163–76. Vocabulary, Portuguese-English only, p. 177–190. Short bibliography, p. 161–2.

DUFF, C. The basis and essentials of Portuguese, and reader. London, Nelson, for the Orthological Institute, 1944. xii, [1], 160 p. 8s. 6d.

3 parts: 1. The basis of grammar (p. 1–83). 2. The essential vocabulary (p. 86–112, consisting largely of an alphabet of about 2,000 Portuguese words). 3. Extracts for reading. No simulated pronunciation. Good use of bold type.

DUNN, J. A grammar of the Portuguese language. London, Nutt, 1930. xi, 669 p. o.p.

First published 1928 (Washington, National Capital Press). Author was Professor of Celtic in the Catholic University of America.

24 chapters. Aims "to provide a rather complete descriptive grammar. . . . It contains all the grammar needed by the ordinary student of modern Portuguese and, in addition, enough of the obsolete forms to enable him to read the poets of the classic period" (*Preface*). Many examples; no exercises; no vocabulary. 300 Portuguese proverbs, p. 620–30; abbreviations, p. 631–5. Italics are used for Portuguese words. Brazilian, dialect and colloquial usages are added when necessary. Detailed, analytical index to grammar.

A reference grammar still well thought of.

HILLS, E. C., FORD, J. D. M., and COUTINHO, J. de S. Portuguese grammar. 2nd ed., revised by L. G. Moffat. Boston, Heath; London, Harrap, 1944. x, 352 p. illus., map. 37*s*. 6*d*.; $5.

49 lessons and 10 revision lessons; detailed review exercises and drill. Vocabulary, each way (with simulated pronunciation for Portuguese entry-words), p. 319–49. Conjugation of verbs, p. 235–80; list of irregular verbs, p. 282–5. Appendix: Pronunciation and phonetics of Portuguese, p. 287–318. Helpful on the personal infinitive (one of the touchstones of the quality of a Portuguese grammar). Good index to grammar.

A reliable reference grammar and course book. The revised edition introduces no fundamental changes but it does point out variant Brazilian usage.

HUGO'S LANGUAGE INSTITUTE. Portuguese simplified: an easy & rapid self-instructor. Standard ed., rev. and re-written. London, the Institute, [*c.* 1961]. xii, 164 p. 6*s*.

Part 1: 17 lessons, with exercises each way; practical exercises; verbs; 'other rules'. Part 2: Exercises on preceding rules; irregular verbs; progressive reading. Simulated pronunciation; no key or vocabulary.

PEI, M., and PRISTA, A. R. Getting along in Portuguese. New York, Harper, 1958. viii, [3], 238 p. map. (The Holiday magazine language series). $2.50.

Parts: 1. The Portuguese language. 2. Phrases (with simulated pronunciation; 24 sections, covering such topics as passport, customs, baggage, directions and signs). 3. Grammatical outline, p. 141–65. Vocabulary, each way, p. 166–238 (only the English entry-words are given simulated pronunciation). No exercises or index to grammar. Essentially for the tourist, not the student.

PEREIRA TAVARES, J. Gramática portuguesa. 2.° ciclo dos liceus. Lisbon, Livraria Sá da Costa, 1960. 272 p.

Parts 1. Fonetica. 2. Morfologia. 3. Sintaxe. Many examples from classical and contemporary authors. Index to grammar.

Other Portuguese grammars published in Portugal or Brazil: *Gramática portuguêsa em esquemas* (Curitiba (Brazil), 1943); *Gramática sintética da lingua portuguêsa; para o ensino secundário,* by Cândido de Figereido (Lisbon,

Livaria Classica Eda., 1948); and N. M. de Almeida's *Gramática metódica da lingua portuguêsa* (São Paulo, Saraiva, 1960. 544 p. $2), "a well-organized, reasonably complete grammar of written Portuguese" (*MLA Selective list of materials*, p. 73).

An up-to-date and recommended Portuguese grammar for Spanish-speaking people is *Gramática portuguêsa*, by P. V. Cuesta (Madrid, Editorial Gredos, 1962).

ROSSI, P. C.   Portuguese, the language of Brazil.   New York, Holt, Rinehart, Winston, 1945.   377, lxxxv p.   40s.; $5.

A general reference grammar. Reading passages, with phonetic transcription; realistic dialogues. Appendices on modern spelling and accentuation are particularly clear and complete. Vocabulary each way; index to grammar.

SÁ PEREIRA, M. de L.   Brazilian Portuguese grammar.   Boston, Heath, 1948.   403 p. illus., maps.   15s.

"Primarily intended for students of Portuguese interested in Brazil" (*Preface*). 35 lessons: Vocabulary; grammar; reading, with questions. Each lesson comprises two 50-minute periods. Exercises cover drill, translation, reading and questions. Essentially for class-room work. Many examples of usage, making it valuable also as a reference grammar. Includes 'Phonetic introduction and transcription', by Robert A. Hall, jr. Portuguese English vocabulary, with phonetic pronunciation, p. 347–400.

The author was Research Director for Portuguese Studies, Barnard College, Columbia University.

Another Brazilian-Portuguese grammar is *Brazilian Portuguese, from thought to word*, by Frederick B. Agard and others (Princeton U.P., 1944. xvii, 277 p. 40s.).

THOMAS, F.   Hossfeld's new practical method for learning the Portuguese language.   Rev. ed.   London, Hirschfeld, 1950.   xii, 332, 18 p.   7s. 6d.   Key. 1949.   2s.

Previously published 1941. Revised in conformity with the official Portuguese orthography, by Professor Gabriel J. Teixeira. Grammar, p. 1–262; 56 exercises. Lengthy passages for translation into English. Many lists of special (e.g., commercial) words and phrases; guide to irregular verbs; proverbs; slang; Brazilianisms. No vocabulary.

WILLIAMS, E. B., and PESSOA, M.   Cortina's conversational Brazilian-Portuguese, intended for self-study and for use in schools.   2nd rev. ed.   New York, Cortina, 1960.   vi, 186 p. $2.95; 25s.

14 lessons, each with vocabulary, dialogues, passages (with translation), questions and exercises. Grammar, p. 133–73. Brief Portuguese-English vocabulary, p. 174–86, combined with an index to the grammar.

Edwin B. Williams, who is Professor of Romance Languages at the University of Pennsylvania, has also compiled *An Introductory Portuguese grammar, with exercises and vocabulary* (New York, Crofts; London, Harrap, 1942. 174 p. o.p.; old orthography) and a rather similar *First Brazilian grammar* (New York, Appleton; London, Bailey Bros. & Swinfen, 1944. 294 p. 28s.), but neither is considered adequate.

WILLIS, R. C.   An essential course in modern Portuguese.   London, Harrap, 1965.   529 p.   27s. 6d.

Author is lecturer in Portuguese, University of Manchester. 40 lessons, each consisting of grammar, voabulary and exercises. A detailed grammar that aims to meet a long-standing demand: "the need for an adult, reasonably detailed and up-to-date teaching grammar of the Portuguese language" (*Preface*). As such, it is intended primarily for first-year university students with no previous knowledge of Portuguese. Modelled on Ramsden's *Essential course in modern Spanish* (q.v.). Appendix I. Regular verb tables; II. The Portuguese of Brazil. Vocabularies each year, p. 451–524. Index to grammar. Good use of bold type.

Commercial Grammar

CORNETT, W. N.   Portuguese commercial correspondence and technicalities, etc., revised in conformity with the official Portuguese orthography, by Professor Gabriel J. Teixeira.   Rev. ed.   London, Hirschfeld, 1949.   vi, [1], 176 p.   5s.

First published 1905. 28 topics, from 'opening phrases', 'closing phrases', 'abbreviations', 'circulars', 'offers' to 'commercial documents', 'money, weights and measures' and 'commercial products'. Gives examples of letters, usually in Portuguese, forms of accounts and commercial documents, as well as vocabularies.

Special Aspects of Grammar

For the spoken language, *Spoken Portuguese: basic course*, by Margarida F. Reno and V. Cioffari (Boston, Heath, 1945. x, 512 p. $4.75. *Key*, $2) is thought highly of by the Modern Language Association of America (*MLA Selective list*, p. 70). It is supported by 24 twelve-inch 78 r.p.m. records ($61). Many examples of dialogues are given in *Hossfeld's English and Portuguese dialogues for travellers and students*, by W. N. Cornett (London, Hirschfeld. 1941. 351 p. 2s. 6d.). It contains classified sections, a list of proverbs, an alphabetical vocabulary, and a table of weights and measures.

The *B-P frasograf*, by Rosalind Ashe and Albert Avigdor (New York, Ungar, 1944. 200 p. 13*s.* 6*d.*) is a dictionary of phrases, idiomatic expressions and conversational language, with a Portuguese-English index. E. Kucera's *Learn Portuguese with me: English-Portuguese phrasebook* (Barcelona, Kucera, 1954. 144 p. 4*s.* 6*d.*) is cheap, and has illustrated vocabularies and phonetic pronunciation of Portuguese words. There is also a useful *Brazilian Portuguese idiom list*, by C. B. Brown and H. L. Shane (Nashville, Tenn., Vanderbilt University Press, 1951. 118 p. $2).

For advanced students of Portuguese, *Glossário crítico de dificuldades do idioma português* (1947. 622, [1] p.) and *Problemas da linguagem e do estilo*, both by Vasco Botelho de Amaral (Oporto, Livraria Simões Lopes) can be recommended.

GENERAL DICTIONARIES

ALBINO FERREIRA, J.   Dicionário inglês-português, português-inglês. Nova ed., revista e melhorada pelo Dr. Armando de Morais.   Edição escolar. Oporto, Barreira, 1952–54 (and reprints).   2 v. in 1.   58*s.*

Previous edition (2 v.) 1933–42. A standard dictionary, the two halves being almost equal in length (English-Portuguese, 1954. 886 p.; Portuguese-English, 1952. 896 p.), with about 60,000 entries in each. Brazilian and technical terms are included. 'A': 1 col.; 'Haver': ⅓ col.; 'Mal': ⅔ col.; 'Subir': 18 lines.

Published in two editions: edição grande and edição escolar. Only the latter seems to be exported.

COSTA, J. A. DA, and SAMPAIO E. MELO, A. DE.   Dicionário de língua portuguesa ortoépico, ortográfico e etimológico. Elaborado em rigorosa conformidade com as bases do Acordo ortográfico luso-brasileiro de 1945.   Oporto, Porto Editora, [195–?]. viii, 1,465 p. illus.   *c.* 35*s.*

As a one-volume dictionary published in Portugal, considered to be the best of its kind (Modern Language Association of America, *Selective list*, p. 71).

For Brazilian Portuguese there is *Novo dicionario brasileiro Melhoramentos, ilustrado* (2. ed. revista. Organização geral: Adalberto Prado e Silva. São Paulo, Edicões Melhoramentos, 1964. 4 v.).

HOUAISS, A., and AVERY, C. B.   The new Appleton dictionary of the English and Portuguese languages.   New York, Appleton-Century-Crafts: Meredith, 1964.   xx, 636, xx, 665 p. $11.75.

English-Portuguese, p. 1–624, plus appendices on abbreviations, weights and measures; Portuguese-English, p. 1–631, plus appendices on abbreviations and verbs. About 60,000 entry words, with International Phonetic alphabet pronunciation, in each part. "The emphasis is on Portuguese as it is written and spoken in Brazil." Where equivalents do not exist, explanations and definitions of the English word is given. Cross-references from Portuguese verbs to verb tables.

PIETSCHKE, F. Novo Michaelis. Dicionário ilustrado. São Paulo, Edições Melhoramentos; Wiesbaden, Brockhaus, 1958–61 (and reprints). 2 v. illus. ea. 78s.

V. 1, *Inglês-Português* (sub-title: "Based on material selected from the original Michaelis dictionary, and completely reorganised, revised and enlarged by the Lexicographic Staff of Edições Melhoramentos, under the direction of Fritz Pietschke"), 1958. xxxii, 1,123 p.; v. 2, *Português-Inglês*, 1961, li, 1,320 p. About 60,000 entries in each volume. The English-Portuguese volume is considered by the Modern Language Association of America to be by far the best dictionary in the market (*MLA Selective list*, p. 71). Cover title: "Brockhaus picture dictionary."

Not so many illustrations as in *Sprach-Brockhaus*, nor are they particularly well drawn; keyed parts (e.g. 'Electric bell'). Includes technical terms and many idioms. 'A': ¼ col.; 'Haver': ½ col.; 'Mal': ⅓ col.; 'Subir': ½ col. Appendix: proper names; common abbreviations; weights and measures. Includes Brazilian terms; no pronunciation. Covers both British and American English. Clear, small sanserif type.

OLIVEIRA, M. M. TEIXEIRA DE. Dicionário moderno português-inglês. Revisto por Colin M. Bowker, Margaret P. Bowker e Gloria Gusmão de Morais. Lisbon, Gomes & Rodrigues, 1954. 1,304 p. 40s.

One of the fullest Portuguese-English dictionaries and particularly rich in idioms. 'A': ⅓ col.; 'Haver': ¾ col.; 'Mal': 1 col.; 'Subir': ½ col. Appendix of proper names.

SÉQUIER, J. DE. Dicionário prático ilustrado. O pequeno Larousse português. Novo dicionário enciclopédico luso-brasileiro. Ed. actualizada e aumentada por José Lello e Edgar Lello. Oporto, Lello & Irmao, 1959. 1,966 p. illus. *c.* 60s. (3. ed. 1964. 1,966 p. 136 escudos, *c.* 35s.).

First published 1927. Modelled on the *Nouveau petit Larousse illustré* (1952), with its dictionary of words and idioms followed by a list of sayings in Latin and other languages, and a biographical, geographical and historical encyclopaedia. Several thousand illustrations, 125 plates and 115 maps. Covers both Brazilian and Portuguese usage. Spelling conforms to the rulings of the Acordo Ortográfico Luso-Brasileiro of 1945.

TAYLOR, J. L. A Portuguese-English dictionary. Stanford, Cal., Stanford University Press, 1958; London, Harrap, 1959. xx, [1], 655, [7] p. 75s.

Author is Brazilian born and Lecturer in Hispanic American Studies, Stanford University. About 65,000 entries, including many Brazilianisms, scientific and technical terms, and colloquialisms, as well as abbreviations. Many equivalents; bold type for sub-entries. 'A': 3½ cols.; 'Haver': ⅞ col.; 'Mal': ½ col.; 'Subir': 9 lines. Lengthy bibliography, p. xvii–xviii. Appendix: verbs, Categorises different meanings; no guide to pronunciation. English is spelt in the U.S. fashion.

Rather expensive but well thought of for its accuracy and scope.

Dicionário da linguagem corrente de inglês-português, by M. I. Anacleto (Lisbon, Livraria Sá da Costa, 1956. lxix, [1], 496, [1] p.) includes many idioms and has appendices of familiar similes, proverbs, classical idioms, foreign expressions, abbreviations, proper names, etc., but typography is poor. *Modern Portuguese-English, English-Portuguese dictionary*, by E. L. Richardson and others (London, Harrap, 1944 (and reprints), 347 p. 15s.) has only about 15,000 entries in each half and does not differentiate sufficiently between meanings, although it does have notes on the new orthography and on pronunciation. Syllabification of Portuguese entry-words is given in the Portuguese-English part.

For the tourist there are various cheap pocket dictionaries: the *Dicionário inglês-português* (1956, xxvii, 381 p.) and *Portuguese-English dictionary* by Hygino Aliandro (New York, Pocket Books, Inc., ea. 5s.); *Methuen's* (Langenscheidt's) *Universal dictionary, Portuguese-English, English-Portuguese* (London, Methuen, [n.d.]. 382 p. 3s. 6d.; and *LEP's bilingual English-Portuguese and Portuguese-English dictionary*, by F. J. Silva Ramos and J. L. Campos (São Paulo, LEP; London, Bailey Bros. & Swinfen, 1959. 16, 366, 269 p. 10s. 6d.).

Technical and Commercial Dictionaries

Most of the general technical dictionaries are either English-Portuguese (e.g. Fürstenau, E. E. *Dicionário de têrmos técnicos*. 2. ed. Rio de Janeiro, Carneiro, 1948. 514 p.; and L. L. Sell's *English-Portuguese comprehensive technical dictionary* (New York, McGraw-Hill, 1953. 1,168 p. £14), which claims to have Portuguese definitions of over 500,000 English technical words and expressions (we still await the Portuguese-English volume of Sell)); or else they are polyglot (e.g. the six-language *Dicionario técnico poliglota;* or F. J. Buecken's *Vocabulário técnico: português-inglês-francês-alemão.* 3 ed. São Paulo, Edições Melhoramentos; London, Bailey & Swinfen, [1958]. *c.* 1,012 p. *c.* 72*s.*). The *Canning House Library Bulletin,* no. 48, February 1962, "Portuguese and Spanish special dictionaries", already referred to (p. 56), lists 28 Portuguese special dictionaries, with notes on some of them.

A fairly recent commercial dictionary is M. M. Netto's *Vocabulário de intercâmbio comercial; português-inglês, inglês-português, com um apêndice contendo abreviaturas comerciais, pêsos e medidas, sistema monetário, modelos de cartas comerciais,* etc. (Rio de Janeiro, Editôria Civilização Brasileira, [1961]. 251 p.).

GRAMOPHONE RECORDS

There are few Portuguese language courses on discs. Reno and Cioffari's *Spoken Portuguese* (see p. 61) is supported by 24 twelve-inch 78 r.p.m. records ($61). The Linguaphone course is on sixteen L.P. 45 r.p.m. records, at £21 8s. 1d. The Dover 'Listen and learn' course, distributed in Britain by Constable, consists of three 12″ 33⅓ r.p.m. records, plus instruction manual, at 58s. The Conversaphone short 'C' language course runs to one 10″ L.P. gramophone record, plus instruction manual, at 30s. 6d.

6

GERMAN

by GERTRUD SEIDMANN, M.A.

The years since the first edition of this *Guide* appeared (1964) have seen a veritable revolution in the approach to language teaching in the schools. In particular, the all-comprehensive grammar-course books are tending to give way to audio-visual and audio-lingual courses (see p. 111), as in schools, school examinations (the C.S.E.) and the world at large, greater oral fluency is demanded.

GRAMMAR COURSES

Traditionally, these have been designed with the demands of fairly academic courses and public examinations in mind. They are usually planned to take beginners in 2, 3 or 4 years to G.C.E. 'O' level which, in the case of German, requires a thorough knowledge of all the basic grammar combined with a limited vocabulary relating to a young person's daily life at home and in school. This type of course usually also includes some descriptive material on daily life or travel and holidays in Germany or German-speaking countries.

In method, they usually progress through a number of 'lessons', each consisting of grammatical instruction, exercises, and reading material that is normally designed to exhibit the grammatical features discussed.

The following list also contains courses specially designed for evening-classes or the adult home-learner: these mostly follow similar patterns.

If the user of this annotated list will keep the foregoing remarks in mind, he will find that the notes on each grammar or course-book stress its distinguishing features rather than those it has in common with most or all of the others.

'Gothic', black-letter or *Fraktur* type is no longer used in contemporary Germany. It will, therefore, only be of interest to those who may wish to turn to older editions of books and journals.

ADAMS, Sir J.   Teach yourself German . . .; completely rev. and enl. by S. W. Wells.   London, English Universities Press, 1938.   x, 11–195 p.   6s.

A grammar of the most traditional type, disguised as a self-tutor by the simple addition of a key to the grammar exercises that form the bulk of the book. The 30 lessons contain 75 such exercises. Grammar is far too detailed, giving too much emphasis to minor points, but it is well explained. There are far too many words to be learnt with each lesson, nor are they chosen with any regard to frequency or practical use; no end-vocabularies. A helpful chapter on letter-writing. Guide to alphabet, written and printed declensions and verbs. There are many better self-tutors.

ASHER, J. A.   The framework of German.   London, Harrap, 1963. 56 p.   4s.

A *very* rapid gallop through 'the essential minimum' of German grammar in 10 chapters (e.g., 5: weak verbs, all tenses indicative, and *haben*) and even translation passages with each. Verb list, vocabulary, index. More likely to teach *about* the language than teach the language.

ANDERSON, W. E.   Aufenthalt in Deutschland.   London, Harrap, 1949.   2 v.   illus.   ea. 6s. 6d.

A concentrated cram course, 2 years to 'O' level. Reading matter sparse, rather boyish, but remarkably well done, considering that it consists of the maximum number of piled-on grammatical examples. Weak on the perfect tense. Needs supplementing by a reader.

ANDERSON, W. E.   Das schöne Deutschland.   London, Harrap, 1956. 2 v.   illus.   ea. 7s.

A book mainly for adult courses, evincing a rather split mind: reading matter (lavish) is firmly and somewhat boringly geared to travel abroad, while the grammar build-up proceeds on traditional lines (the student does not learn to wash until v. 2). Each volume has 20 lessons. V. 1 had a 2nd edition in 1960; v. 2 includes songs. Photographic illustrations.

BERGER, E. W., and BERGER, D.   New German self-taught.   New York, Funk and Wagnalls, 1959.   xix, 389 p. $1.95.

Mainly dialogue matter, with facing translations and footnote explanations of the grammar involved. Stress laid on sentence building. Fairly old-fashioned in content; later readings are difficult. Gothic type, for most part. Outline of grammar at end. Not recommended.

BETTERIDGE, H. T., and HORNE, J.   A rapid German course.   London, Macmillan, 1960.   xiv, 302 p.   12s. 6d.

A book designed for adult students with a primary interest in reading German. 25 graded lessons, each consisting of grammatical introduction, reading passage, exercises and word-list. These are preceded by a chapter containing a guide to pronunciation and hints on the etymological relation between German and English words, and followed by a detailed grammatical synopsis and advanced reading passages. No end-vocabulary; each lesson contains its own, which the student is expected to master. But there is an index, with lesson locations, to important words, and an index to the grammar.

BITHELL, J., and DUNSTAN, A. C. A modern German course. 2nd ed. London, Methuen, 1952. viii, 180 p. 6s.

For adults. After a grammatical introduction (to p. 43), the contents consist of texts for reading. These, from No. 6 onwards, are from German authors, – supposed to be readings on history, geography, etc. – but the overwhelming flavour of Nazi doctrine, with ample excerpts on 'Race and Folk' and prominent Nazi authors, makes the book seem dated rather than 'modern'. The present selection was obviously compiled before the war.

BUCKLEY, R. W. Living German. 2nd ed. London, University of London Press, 1960. 317 p. 11s. 6d.

A graded school-course to intermediate stage in 45 lessons. Distinguishing features: lessons 23–28 add no new grammar, but consist of dialogues and descriptive passages relating to travel. From the 23rd lesson onwards all German matter is in Gothic type. There is a guide to pronunciation and a grammatical summary of 46 pages. German-English end-vocabulary only. Pleasantly illustrated.

BURKHARD, O. C. Sprechen Sie Deutsch! London, Harrap, 1935. xxi, 235 p. o.p.

25 lessons. Old fashioned; Gothic print. Grammar progress too fast. Not recommended.

CHÉREL, A. German without toil. Paris, Assimil, 1957. viii, 387 p. 18s.

A German course consisting of dialogues, with translations facing, in 126 lessons (to p. 361), with grammatical explanations and pronunciation at foot of page. Each lesson is followed by a brief exercise. Grammatical summary of 26 p. No vocabulary lists. Amusing illustrations. This is a handbook to accompany records (see p. 114) but can be used on its own. With or without records, can be recommended as a self-tutor, as these dialogues aim to give snatches of 'real speech' from the very beginning (they are *not* model dialogues for use in hotels, shops, etc.) and to teach the grammar inductively. After learning by heart a number of these dialogues, the learner will possess a stock of phrases. He may then like to turn to a more conventional grammar if he wishes to have its solid backing.

DICKINS, E. P. German for advanced students. London, Oxford University Press, 1963. xv, 320 p. 20s.

This book is designed to lead students from 'O' to 'A' level. It concentrates on language work, its first part ingeniously trying to combine 18 sections of grammatical revision and elucidation of finer points with a study in depth of 18 vocabulary topics, through readings from German sources followed by made-up proses and composition topics. Part 2 contains passages in both languages for translation, as also German poems, and an extended reference section; part 3, more difficult translation passages and German prose and poetry for commentary; grammar index. There is a wealth of good material here from which almost any sixth-form teacher will be able to make his own selection; home-learners will find the first part particularly useful, although they should be warned that notes to proses, particularly, are fallible and could do with revision.

DORING, P. F.   Colloquial German.   2nd rev. ed.   London, Routledge & Kegan Paul, 1950 (reprinted 1960).   224 p.   6s.

Title is misleading. Pt. 1: 36 chapters on German grammar, explanations being followed by sentences with facing translation. A good point: word families and idioms. Contains reading passages from German authors. No index to grammar, no word lists, and needs to be supplemented with a dictionary. Pt. 2 (from p. 170): bilingual reading matter from pleasingly varied sources, including verse, cookery recipes and practical advice. Suitable for self-tuition, but has maddening omissions.

DUFF, C., and FREUND, R.   Basis and essentials of German.   3rd rev. ed.   London, Nelson, 1945.   xiv, 113 p.   6s.

Begins with a brief summary of grammar; the different type-faces used add to the difficulties of assimilation. This is followed by lists of 'essential' words, grouped according to grammatical category (nouns, verbs, etc.). There are two samples of German writing, with facing translation. The grammar is scrappy and badly set out, though the word lists could be useful for those who can memorise separate units. Not recommended.

DUFF, C., and STAMFORD, I.   German for adults.   London, English Universities Press, 1957.   xvi, 17–375 p.   16s.   Rev. ed. 1966.   6s.

The authors recommend this book "for all uses and all learners", but its approach raises the gravest doubts. It is divided into 10 lessons, each attempting to cover an enormous amount of vocabulary and grammar. The first 'lesson' – over 40 pages in length – contains a choice collection of howlers both in the grammatical terminology, the paradigms, and the illustrative sentences. Printer's errors and further howlers abound in subsequent lessons, though in the later part there are some German passages from native authors, with translations. Virtually the only good point is a guide it includes to dictionaries and reading material. There is a list of 3,000 basic words.

EICHINGER, H., GRINVALDS, M., and BARTON, E. German once a week. Edited by P. H. Hargreaves. Oxford, Blackwell, 1963–65. v. 1. iii, 127 p. 7s. 6d. v. 2. vi, 130 p. 7s. 6d.

Designed for evening classes, this course nevertheless follows entirely conventional lines, with a grammar core to each lesson, around which a reading-piece is artificially constructed. The grammatical progression is not designed on grounds of frequency or practical usefulness (no summary), but the topics of v. 1 are quite sensibly angled for the potential tourist. The reading matter of v. 2 – to which such essentials as subordinate clauses and the perfect tense are relegated – differs not at all from that of the conventional school-book.

FENN, R. W., and FANGL, W. Ich lerne Deutsch. London, Harrap, 1954–59. 3 v. 6s.; 7s. 6d.; 8s. 6d.

A course for schools, 2 years to 'O' level. V. 1: 28 lessons. The reading matter is in dialogue form throughout (not necessarily natural dialogue material). Set in Gothic. Contains songs with music notation. V. 2: 24 lessons.

FREUDENBERGER, M., and KELBER, M. Heute und Morgen. London, Ginn, 1955. 4 v. 7s. 6d.; 10s.; 10s. 6d.; 11s. 6d.

V. 1–2 consist substantially of the material in M. Kelber's *Heute Abend I* (q.v.), adapted for school use by division into 24 and 26 chapters respectively, with additional material and more lavish (and delightful) illustrations. V. 3–4 are by M. Freudenberger. V. 3 contains newly chosen excerpts on "children in German literature", with original material. It is also designed to provide a bridge to *Heute Abend II*, and goes beyond 'O' level, but does not advance so rapidly. V. 4 contains 26 lessons, with original reading matter, of contemporary interest; the grammatical part has information on the subtler points, rather miscellaneously arranged; a third section contains interesting introductions to, and brief excerpts from, German authors in 19 sections. There are re-translation exercises and a full vocabulary, each way. Interesting for background study and wider reading. A useful book, suitable for adults and in schools where a longish course does not call for unrelieved cramming. The new material contains unidiomatic matter.

GREATWOOD, E. A. School German course. 2nd ed. London, University Tutorial Press, 1959. 390 p. 11s.

A full basic course, to 'O' level; 65 chapters. The grammar is well explained but there is no summary; reading matter fallible, but on topics of adult interest. Vocabularies for each lesson are grouped at end of book. 90 pages of supplementary exercises, including questions on stories. End-vocabulary, German-English only, with chapter references. Suitable for school use, but containing more than one year's work; and for adults looking for a sensible approach.

GRETTON, G. H., and GRETTON, W.   German by yourself.   London, Bell, 1960.   viii, 271 p.   12s. 6d.

Begins with introduction to grammar, then introduces reading matter with marginal vocabulary notes (p. 48–78). This is followed by more difficult selections, partly in Gothic type, and a section "Aus deutscher Geschichte" (p. 104–62), in which there is a heavy over-emphasis on Nazi Germany. The introductory map of Germany is also out of date. Not recommended.

GRIESBACH, N., and SCHULZ, D.   Deutsche Sprachlehre für Ausländer Grundstufe.   14th rev. ed.   Munich, Max Hueber Verlag, 1962. 2 v.   ea. DM 5.90.

An immensely thorough course, written for adults, primarily those attending the courses for foreigners at the various branches of the Goethe-Institut. V. 1 has 16, v. 2, 15 very full lessons, each containing a great deal of reading matter and exhaustive exercises to drive home each point. Grammatical explanations are very well set out, but written throughout in German, and thus not accessible to foreign readers without a teacher. These two volumes contain a mass of information on present-day Germany and its background, and the reading texts are very well written. If anything, the grammar covers too much ground too rapidly for the 'ordinary learner'. Glossaries and keys are published separately, but the books are hardly suitable for self-tuition, though very suitable for adult classes. A curious feature is the re-thinking on German sentence structure which has evidently taken place, and which has led to some rather intricately designed tables, although in practice they still leave the German verb where it was. Highly recommended.

The previous edition, in 1 v., with English grammar, glossary and key, plus records, is available at DM 42.

HARVARD, J.   Beginner's German: an introduction to conversational German.   London, University of London Press, 1960.   111 p. 4s. 6d.

For sixth form or adult beginners. Consists mainly of simple dialogues in 16 lessons, with grammatical explanations and exercises; the fluency exercises based on substitution tables, with facing English text, deserve praise. No end-vocabularies, but a brief index to grammar and some basic words. Help with reading is given by footnotes. Suitable for conversation practice, but material is rather meagre to stand alone. Records are available.

HARVARD, J.   Conversational German: a course for adults.   London, University of London Press, 1961.   160 p.   9s. 6d.

18 lessons (to p. 87), consisting of conversational material on the usual practical topics (travel plans, etc.). Guidance on letter-writing; brief exercises; grammar appendix, p. 88–143. Fluency exercises are a notable feature. Not for beginners. Useful for evening classes, second year.

HUEBENER, T., and NEWMARK, H.   A first course in German.   New York, Heath, 1952.   456 p.   32s.

—, — A second course in German.   New York, Heath, 1952. 415 p.   32s. 6d.

The first book consists of 30, the second of 24 lessons. Well-produced, with ample reading material. Gothic as well as Roman type is used throughout.

HUGO'S LANGUAGE INSTITUTE.   How to speak German in three months without a master.   London, the Institute, [n.d.].   128, 64, 38 p. 6s.; 7s. 6d.

This consists of *Hugo's German grammar*, *German conversation* and *Key to German grammar* bound together and separately paginated. Each of the 26 lessons in the first part consist of grammar notes followed by an exercise of unconnected English sentences for translation to exemplify these, with occasional 'conversational practice', i.e. German sentences to illustrate a point, set in Gothic type. A 5-page English-German words list of 'selected words' and 15 pages of further grammar points follow. The second part comprises unconnected German sentences, in Gothic, with translation facing, plus sundry idioms. Approach and material hopelessly old-fashioned. Not recommended.

ONES, H. C. H.   Points to watch in 'O' level German.   London, Heinemann, 1962.   54 p.   3s.

... Or rather, points to watch in 'O' level German prose composition. Quite a useful little *aide-mémoire* on the commonest stumbling-blocks, though not very well organised.

KELBER, MAGDA.   Heute Abend.   London, Ginn, 1938–48.   2 v. (v. 1. Rev. ed., 1955.   xvi, 304 p.   9s.;   v. 2.   viii, 472 p.   16s.).

V. 1 (1st ed. 1938) has long been the outstanding beginners' book for evening classes and in schools for older beginners. It is notably well written, with plenty of humour and very authentic in feeling. Besides the usual features, each of the 20 lessons contains a song with music notation. Much of the reading matter is in easily memorised, simple rhyming couplets. Well illustrated. The 1955 edition is re-set in Roman type, but pronunciation guide is used in conjunction with Gothic alphabet. Full vocabulary, each way. This volume covers basic 'O' level requirements. Highly recommended.

V. 2 (20 lessons) is set in Gothic. The reading passages contain very varied and intellectually more taxing material, including adaptations and excerpts from German literature, with notes on the authors, and more advanced grammar instructions. For ordinary mortals the pace might be too fast immediately after the conclusion of v. 1. Post 'O' level stage; suitable for advanced adults or students taking German "for interest" in the sixth form without attempting 'A' level. Recommended.

KELLETT, F.   Advanced modern German.   London, University of London Press, 1964.   446 p.   25s.

This book contains several independent sections: a reference grammar containing much elementary material, a section of 70 English proses, with good notes on vocabulary and idiom, but little reference to section 1, 80 well-chosen German passages, 42 poems, with good questions, and 15 essay-subjects and outlines.

LANGE, EVA C.   Collins' Cortina German in 20 lessons.   London & Glasgow, Collins, 1962.   360 p.   12s. 6d.

16 lessons, in which vocabulary is followed by German dialogue passage on left-hand page, with English translation and aids to pronunciation (not International Phonetic Alphabet) facing. Grammar and idiom are explained at foot of page and notes refer to grammar section (p. 190 ff.), which also contains verb lists, German proverbs, business-letter forms and German alphabet. Idioms are featured. Last 4 lessons consist of more extended dialogues, conversations being strictly limited to practical topics. Vocabulary, each way. Of limited suitability for self-tuition.

LAW, M. H.   How to read German: a short cut for non-linguists.   London, Hutchinson Educational, 1964.   252 p.   11s. 6d.; 18s.

This is an excellent introduction to German for those to whom reading is the main aim. The author uses only genuine – and often entertaining – German texts from a variety of contemporary sources, including the press. By this means he gradually introduces the reader to the distinguishing features of German, as well as a nicely varied vocabulary. Greatly superior to the narrowly-based, and not more efficient, 'introductions to scientific German' and all such. Highly recommended.

MACE, J.   Build up your German.   London, Harrap, 1963.   167 p. 8s.

Ten extracts from German writers (Schiller to Vicki Baum) serve as pegs for a study of vocabulary, idiom and grammar 'constructions'. Ingenious, with many useful nuggets, but should have been rigorously edited. Fine in the hands of a native teacher. Advanced.

MACPHERSON, A. S., JONES, H. C. H., and others.   Deutsches Leben. London, Ginn, 1931–39.   3 v. illus.   o.p.   2nd ed.   v. 3.   1965. 9s. 6d.

This course has run through several editions, thanks to its thoroughness and, perhaps, to the conservatism of teachers, and the absence of an equally thorough and reliable rival. V. 1 (31 chapters and 4 extra reading passages) has an introductory section on pronunciation and thereafter favours the Direct Method exclusively. Each reading passage is followed by German word list only (German-English vocabulary at end) and grammar is explained in German (grammar summary, with English explanations, in Appendix).

Old-fashioned and somewhat childish in contents and appearance, but it covers most basic topics. Vocabulary load is heavy.

The new v. 2 (1961, 20 lessons) abandons the Direct Method: large chunks of reading matter with an enormous vocabulary spread, but well written and thoroughly modern in tone, are followed by bilingual vocabulary lists. Final two lessons are in Gothic (no alphabet provided). Brief end-vocabulary, each way. Text, while vocabulary is thoroughly up to date, seems over-full of technical vocabulary, slang, etc. Grammar, too, goes beyond 'O' level requirements.

V. 3 contains 17 lessons and 10 extra reading passages, and grammar reference section. As in other volumes, one feels that the authors' main interest lies in the grammatical framework; the reading-matter, though well written, is a rag-bag of stories and miscellaneous 'background' material.

MARE, M. Bergauf! London, Metheun, 1950. 152 p. illus. 7s. 6d.

— Am Gipfel. London, Methuen, 1954. xii, 226 p. illus. 9s. 6d.

Two volumes, to School Certificate level. The reading passages are of a pleasing, rather childish, but very German flavour and they have a connecting thread running through them. There are also excerpts from fairy tales (rather more difficult than the original stories). Printed in Roman. The second book has literary extracts, also in Roman, though the later chapters are in Gothic. Chapters are followed by brief, German only, word lists: brief end-vocabulary. V. 2 includes 5 picture stories; both volumes include songs.

NICHOLSON, J. A. Praktisches Deutsch. London, Harrap, 1958–60. 2 v. illus. 8s. 6d.; 11s. 6d.

A middle-of-the-way-method course, with fairly lavish reading material of oddly uneven quality (some good chapters on the contemporary scene and a comparison between English and German life, interspersed with stories of dolls and boring descriptions). Some unidiomatic German creeps in where examples to illustrate grammar rules are piled on. Perfect tense is misconstrued. Some types of exercises good, others bad. No grammar summary in Book 1 (23 lessons); re-translation exercises together at end; poor illustrations. Book 2: 19 lessons, 3 set in Gothic; part 2: grammar summary. Appendices contain songs and passages for translation.

ORTON, E. Auf Deutsch, bitte! London, Harrap, 1959–63. 2 v. 7s.; 8s.

V. 1 (142 p.) is a 'non-academic' course in 16 lessons, plus 4 revision lessons; recommendable for young non- or pre-examination pupils. Lessons are interspersed with German reading material. Contains "Spike's German diary", in English, – an alert boy's impressions of German life. V. 2, by E. Orton and B. Hunt has 15 chapters of conventional school course. Idiomatic, but not a suitable follow-up to v. 1; too difficult for stream 6.

OTTO, E.   Elementary German grammar; revised by F. R. Mattis.
Method Gaspey-Otto Sauer. 16th rev. ed. Heildelberg, Groos,
1962. viii, 216 p. 12s. 6d. Key, by D. M. Mennie. 39 p. 4s.

50 lessons, according to the 'grammatical method'. Explanation of
grammar (very detailed, noting all exceptions); bilingual word lists, with
phonetic transcription; sentences and short reading-passages in German, with
translation exercises into German. Brief vocabulary, each way; list of 'very
common words' and Gothic alphabet. The *Key* contains translations of all
German and English passages.

Far from elementary; weighted by immense amount of grammar and
vocabulary. Quite old-fashioned (the reading material is reminiscent of the
age of Bismarck) and very thorough. Not recommended.

PFEFFER, J. A.   German review grammar. Boston, Heath, 1196.
xii, 270 p. illus. 26s. 8d.

Elementary to intermediate. 24 chapters of grammar, systematically
presented and explained in English, and backed by exercises. These latter
are intended for revision and continuation after elementary course, but would
be suitable for mature beginner, as the book is progressive in difficulty. Each
chapter has well-written, lengthy reading material, adult in tone and of
contemporary interest, followed by questions, conversation and sentences
illustrating idiomatic usage. Recommended.

RIVERS, J.   A new German course. London, Macmillan, 1931–36.
2 v. ea. 6s. 6d.

27 and 20 lessons respectively; major part of reading is in Gothic. Old-
fashioned and rather difficult. Not recommended.

ROSENBERG, J.   How to speak German. London, Nicholson &
Watson, 1939. xii, 207 p. illus. (Living languages). o.p.

25 lessons (with pronunciation guide), each consisting of simple German
sentences with translation, followed by explanation of grammar and conversation practice sentences. Substitution tables are used for sentence building.
No index or vocabulary. Could be of use as self-tutor.

RUSSON, A., and RUSSON, L. J.   A first German book. London,
Longmans Green, 1959. xv, 219 p. illus. 8s.

—, —   A second German book. London, Longmans, Green, 1961.
vii, 272 p. illus. 8s. 6d.

A 2-volume 'O' level course for schools. V. 1 (18 lessons) includes brief
guide to pronunciation. Much of the early reading matter is in the question-
and-answer form suitable for a 'direct method' lesson; later reading matter has
descriptive passages on Germany and Austria. Grammar progression fast;
grammar explanations in each chapter are in English. Grammar summary

(accidence only), very restricted, but index to grammar refers back to lessons. Chapter vocabularies; idiomatic phrases are listed. Brief end-vocabulary, each way. Rather dry.

V. 2 (14 lessons) follows the same pattern. Features: extended reading matter, informative on German background; each lesson concludes with poem or extract from German writer, mostly contemporary. Course vocabulary is somewhat beyond elementary 'O' level stage. Poor illustrations. Unidiomatic matter in both volumes.

Russon, A., and L. J. Advanced German course. London, Longmans Green & Co., 1965. xiv, 426 p. 19s. Key to prose passages. 96 p. 12s.

The initial 'grammar and syntax' (sic) section of 118 p. contains the 'rules' (some questionable) and points relevant to the 120 English prose passages for translation which follow; bi-lingual vocabularies at end: the *Key* demonstrates all too clearly the fallibility of both. This massive compendium further provides 125 essay titles, 45 German prose passages and 40 poems or verse extracts for translation (no apparatus for these sections except end-vocabulary). There are also 41 German prose and 39 verse passages 'for comment and appreciation'. These are well chosen and grouped, and the authors provide four excellent examples of the form such essays might take; but no other assistance, in comment- or question-form, on individual passages.

Russon, A., and Russon, L. J. Simpler German course for first examinations. London, Longmans Green, 1955. xii, 313 p. 11s.

A shorter course than the *Complete German course*, and similar in pattern, but with somewhat lowered sights. Grammar section is filed down to more basic topics, but the principle of lists is retained. Proses are graduated from the very simple upwards. Translations are a little simpler but not more modern; the first 25 are in Roman script. More appropriate to present 'O' level.

Russon, L. J. Complete German course for first examinations. London, Longmans, Green, 1948. xvi. 369 p. 12s.

Not a graduated course, but essentially a reference grammar going rather beyond basic requirements, followed by a section of practice exercises. 50 annotated and 10 non-annotated passages for translation into German, 50 topics for free composition, 30 with outlines, 50 pages from German authors (Gothic type) for translation or comprehension (questions appended in both languages) of rather higher than 'O' level standard, 25 'outlines' to help with reproductions, 40 poems with questions attached, vocabulary each way, and index to grammar.

Thorough but parts are disparate: proses are all of same standard, rather simple; translation passages and poems are very demanding in vocabulary, grammar section thorough but containing long lists of nouns, adjectives, etc., under each heading. Suitable for cramming, selectively used.

SALAMÉ, S. J. W. Deutsch für Dich. London, Faber & Faber, 1965. 2 v. illus. ea. 9s. 6d.

This nicely illustrated course has lesson vocabularies grouped together at end and very simple grammar notes in German. Texts are in outstandingly up-to-date German (about schoolchildren in Freiburg and their life), but progession, particularly in vocabulary, is much too fast for beginners; and yet the teacher will have to fill in a good many of the 'basic' topics. Great quantities of reading-matter. Some of the not very exciting 'stories' stretch over several chapters each. Will be found too taxing for all but the most bookish.

SAVIGNY, W. B. Advanced German. Oxford, Pergamon Press, 1965. xiii, 146 p. 15s. ;25s.

This book consists almost entirely of unannotated texts (30 each for translation from German and English), 30 essay titles, and, on the literery side, a selection of poetry and prose for interpretation and discussion. Neither selection nor such advice as has been included inspire much confidence.

SAVIGNY, W. B. A sixth-form German course. London, Harrap, 1962. 274 p. 11s. 6d.

Rather over-titled, as this book only offers instructions in a limited field. It consists of a grammar-section obviously geared to remedy faults frequently met with, revision exercises, and prose passages for translation from English and German. Not enough help is given with these, though, and most teachers will find there is not enough variety in the selection. There are 45 essay topics, and 10 poems 'for appreciation'.

SAVIGNY, W. B., and MITCHELL, W. C. Frisch auf! A German course for the 'O' level examination. London, Harrap, 1959. 236 p. 8s.

Very much a school-examination cramming book. Contains grammar section, including vocabulary lists: followed by well-designed practice sentences; 'O' level-type proses, for which vocabulary lists only are given – not enough help without a teacher, and with no direct reference to grammar section. 50 German prose extracts, unfortunately practically all adapted minor 19th-century writers, 20 anecdotes, pictures (amateurishly drawn) and topics for essay-writing, 25 poems 'for comprehension' (again rather poorly selected). Two-way vocabulary list.

SCHLIMBACH, A. Kinder lernen Deutsch. Munich, Max Hueber, 1964. 263 p. DM 9.80; 11.80.

Colourful and varied primer designed for the teaching of German to young children from German families living abroad. As largely oral acquaintance with the language is presumed, this book is not suitable for foreign beginners, but may offer ideas to teachers of young children.

STEINBERG, S. H.   A one-year German course.   London, Macmillan, 1939.   vii, 199 p.   8s.

This book covers basic grammar in 59 lessons. It is peculiarly old-fashioned in that it contains almost no reading material in German; each lesson consists of grammar explanation with examples, followed by an exercise consisting of a brief English prose passage for translation into German, which contains examples of the grammar point in question.

STOPP, F. J.   A manual of modern German.   London, University Tutorial Press, 1957.   xv, 619 p.   27s. 6d.

A massive work of scholarship; a graduated course and descriptive and reference grammar in one, from beginning to advanced stage. Pt. 1 (p. 1–351) covers all major grammar points except the Subjunctive which, together with more detailed treatment of selected topics, is reserved for Pt. 2.

Pt. 1, preceded by introduction on sounds and spelling rules, has 43 chapters, each containing a number of grammar rules and examples, and exercises consisting mainly of sentence translations, both ways, illustrating these. Then follows a two-way word list relating to exercises. Pt. 2 (chapters 44–66) continues and refines on the material in Pt. 1, covers the subjunctive and deals exhaustively with idiomatic use of prepositions. No further word lists; then follow appendices on subtler points, a list of strong and irregular verbs, a list of English grammar terms, with German translations, an index of prepositions referring to the text, a synoptic table of 15 common prepositions, and a separate index of grammatical categories and German words with special grammatical connotations. The grammar points dealt with are numbered consecutively 1–553, with cross-references. Exhaustive and scholarly, the work is difficult for the learner to use with profit, unless backed by considerable linguistic scholarship and experience.

STRINGER, L.   Teach yourself: a first German.   London, English Universities Press, 1966.   xii, 180 p.   8s. 6d.

Much more lively than the older 'Teach yourself' book, by Sir J. Adams (q.v.). Agreeably illustrated and provided with brief but up-to-date reading-matter with each of its 30 sections, this book still presents a stiff, because so brief, guided tour to a lot of German grammar and vocabulary. Key and short German-English vocabulary included. Might do for a quick revision course, as grammar is ingeniously explained and each point has brief exercise.

SUTCLIFFE, K. E.   Fahrt ins Blaue. A German course for schools. London, Bell, 1960–61.   2 v.   7s. 6d.; 8s. 6d.

A course on the usual lines, but bristling with errors.

TAENI, R., and CLYNE, M. G. Efficient German. Melbourne, Macmillan, 1965. 260 p. 28s. 6d.

Not likely to be noticeably more efficient than other courses of instruction, this book has poor reading-texts and indifferent grammatical explanations, with far too much material crammed into each lesson. It does, however, provide a great quantity of drill exercises.

TUDOR, L., and HEYDORN, M. H. G. Deutsches Land und deutsches Volk. London & Glasgow, Blackie, 1956–59. 3 v. o.p.

This attractive-looking course is very disappointing. In v. 1) especially, the reading passages are both exceptionally boring and also written in a particularly stilted and quite unidiomatic way (although a native German shares the responsibility). On the score of method and progression v. 1 is often odd, e.g. reflexive and 'compound verbs' are left to v. 2, so that the simple actions of daily life such as getting up and washing are held over rather long. Pupils experience difficulty in reading by themselves, as vocabularies are incomplete. 20 lessons. V. 2 is better written and has more interesting information, but contains vast lists of often technical vocabulary, before even the basic grammar is mastered. 20 lessons. V. 3 contains 15 well-illustrated reading passages on the German background, with essays and essay-outlines. There are extracts from German writers, 12 poems and 19 additional reading passages. With none of these is any help given, not even a vocabulary list: a dictionary must be used. Grammar summary is confused. Printed and written Gothic alphabet.

TYRER, A. K. A programmed German grammar. London, Methuen, 1965. Part I. 228 p. 12s. 6d. Part II. 160 p. 12s. 6d.

A linear programme in book form, this is the first in the field, but commendable more for revision than for beginners' use, for although it is ingenious in explaining grammatical terminology, when it comes to examples the result is less helpful.

WEBER, W. E. The intelligent student's guide to modern German. London, Pitman, 1957 (rev. reprint of 1944 ed.). ix, 404 p. 15s.

81 lessons in 4 parts. A very ingeniously written book that explains German grammar and builds up the student's vocabulary by analysing, in sections, the text of a German story of the 19th century (Gerstäcker's Germelshausen). There is an index to grammar and vocabulary. The German text is printed in Gothic. Useful only for intending readers of the classics.

WINTER, H. N. Fluency in German. London, Longmans Green, 1964. 2 v. ea. 124 p. 10s. 6d.

Contains hundreds of exercises on German grammar and vocabulary, suitable for accompanying any course or grammar book. Full indexes precede and 2-way vocabularies are appended, but no key; hence not for the home-learner.

AUDIO-VISUAL, AUDIO-LINGUAL
AND RELATED COURSE MATERIAL

The major breakthrough in language-teaching method in the last few years has been the replacement of the course-book (which might, or might not, be accompanied by recorded spoken material, but which was primarily for *reading*) by the spoken word in recorded form (which might, or might not, be accompanied by a printed text and/or pictorial material).

By *audio-visual* material we usually understand a combination of speech on tape or record with visuals in the form of slides or film-strip; there may be accompanying students' and/or teachers' handbooks containing the text and/or reproductions of the visuals.

By *audio-lingual* we understand material which is primarily designed to be heard and studied in its recorded form: this is usually accompanied by a printed text.

We are including in this section also related books and courses in which the pictorial element plays a large part.

A-V Courses

BURGDORF, I., and others. Deutsch durch die audio-visuelle Methode. London, Harrap. 2 parts. Part I: Book 18s., 25 film strips, £18 10s., 50 tapes, £87 10s. Part 2: 25 film strips, £18 10s., 50 tapes, £82 10s.

  The two parts of this course are designed for an adult audience which is introduced to conversational German by means of quite amusing scenes based on the life of a number of characters, depicted in cartoon-form on the visuals in film-strips and the accompanying books.

DAVIDSON, R., and others. Los! London, Mary Glasgow and Baker, 1964. 3-year A-V course (3rd year in preparation). Teacher's set (records, scripts and notes), per year, £3. Class set (20 pupils), per year, £7 10s.

  Principally designed for primary-school beginners, this course, with its simple, but brightly recorded speech material interspersed with jolly music, and its illustrated work-books and opportunities for acting and model-making, may be found of interest with secondary-age children, too.

GRIESBACH, H., and SCHULZ, D. Ich spreche Deutsch. Audio-visual editor, G. Murjahn. Munich, Hueber, 1966. Book. illus. 105 p. 440 slides. 4 tapes (90 mins.). 4 language laboratory practice tapes (218 mins.) and text. Teacher's manual. German-English glossary.

Designed for adults, this course exploits 25 situations of daily life in family, at leisure and at work. Grammatical structures are drilled in exercises. The linguistic content is thorough but the text is rather humourless and the visuals, with their rather tortuous conventional sign-language (reproduced in the book), are poor.

PECK, A., and others. The Nuffield A-V German course for schools. Tapes, filmstrips, map, flash-cards, reading-books, slides.

At the time of going to press still in a very thorough testing-phase. This course, aimed at 11 to 13-year-old beginners, is based on the life of the young people of Cadolzburg.

RUSSELL, C. V. Audio-visual German. Oxford, Pergamon Press. 10 filmstrips and 5 tapes. Parts 1, 2 and 3 ea. £65. 3 students' books, ea. 5s.; teacher's handbook, 10s. 6d.

A school course, at the time of writing still at the try-out stage. On the evidence of the first student's book not so much an exploitation of the new techniques and an exploration of the spoken language as a traditional grammar-progression course using visual and audio aids. Visuals outstandingly attractive.

A-L Course and Material

Audio-lingual drills: German. Oxford, Recorded Aids, 1966. G 1–10, ea. 30s. (tape and booklet). Extra booklets, 9s. per dozen.

So far available: separate tapes of Stack-type structure-drills on various conjunctions and prepositions.

CREESE, K. J. H., and GREEN, P. S. German: a structural approach. Edinburgh, Oliver & Boyd, 1966. Pre-reading book, 6s. Tapes (set of 3), £6. V. 1, 15s. Tapes (set of 35), £70. Teacher's manual, 15s.

An audio-lingual course for the class-room, preceded by an audio-visual ('pre-reading') introduction to German sounds and a few simple structures. In spite of its superficial air of modernity, and its stress on listening to the language (and learning great chunks of material by heart), the approach is basically old-fashioned and the texts dull and poorly recorded. The best feature is the exercise-material of the type recommended by E. M. Stack ('The language laboratory and modern language teaching'), but this can hardly be used on its own.

EISNER, O. Z., and CUNLIFFE, W. G. Advanced conversational German. Edinburgh, Oliver & Boyd, 1966. 160 p. 15s. Tapes, £65 per set of 32.

Aimed at producing fluent speakers, to assist budding interpreters and translators, the 26 sections of this book provide dialogue and tape-recorder-exercise material on a variety of topics of contemporary interest. Explanatory glossary and idiomatic translation of main texts provided.

LAVY, G. J. W. Language Laboratory pattern drills in German. London, Pitman, 1966. Book, 20s. Tapes, £70.

Stack-type drills on German accidence and syntax. Of limited use only, as points dealt with are restricted and vocabulary used may not be found suitable.

Pictorial and similar Course Material

Ina und Udo. London, Harrap, 1965. 108 p. 22s.

Delightfully illustrated multi-coloured reading primer for German primary schools offers stimulating possibilities for use with young beginners.

JEWRY, K. Deutsch in Bild und Wort. London, Harrap, 1966. 150 p. Tapes available per lesson, at £5 5s.

30 lessons of adult and practical interest, ranging from 'The office' to motoring, shopping, sport, etc. Not for beginners, but systematic grammar revision. Large black-and-white illustration with bilingual vocabulary list, questions, reading-text, and grammar explanations with each topic.

JONES, B. Lustiges Lernen. London, University of London Press, 1965–66. 2 v. 7s. 6d.; 12s. 6d.

These large-size books in facsimile typescript are lavishly illustrated with often very funny cartoon-type and other drawings by Barry Cummings; v. 2, also with many large-size photographs of Germany. *Lesestücke*, grammatical paradigms, sparse exercises. The books are handsome to look at and make a lively impression, although basically of the standard type.

KESSLER, H. Deutsch für Ausländer. Königswinter, Verlag für Sprachmethodik. 3 v., ea. 11s. 6d. Wall charts and pictures, £4 15s. Tapes, £5 10s.

This course, designed for the teaching of the language to foreigners in Germany, built up entirely on a question-and-answer method, has been found useful for evening classes in this country.

MADRIGAL, M., and HALPERT, I. D. See it and say it in German. New York, New American Library, 1962. 256 p. (Signet language book). 50 cents.

Paperback; 10 lessons. Illustrated sentences, question-and-answer exercises (with key), and explanations of grammar. German-English word list at end. Does not go very far, but could be used as a beginner's course. Records are available ($3.95).

RICHARDS, I. A., and others.   German through pictures.   New York,
Washington Square Press, [n.d.].   254 p.   6s. 6d.

> Very elementary but ingenious paperback. Help with pronunciation and
> alphabet. The book contains a selection of very simple sentences, mostly in
> present and future tenses, with a very little past tense, supposed to be self-
> explanatory with their drawings. No two-way vocabulary, but an index to
> words used. Most people will want to use a small dictionary with it.

GRAMOPHONE RECORDS

The Assimil course accompanying Chérel's *German without toil* (see p.
67) consists of a preliminary course (eight 78 r.p.m. E.P. or four
45 r.p.m. records, £6 15s.) and an advanced course (twelve 78 r.p.m.
or six 45 r.p.m. records, £9 10s.). Other text-books supplemented by
gramophone records are J. Harvard's *Beginner's German* (see p. 70)
and the American *See it and say it in German*, by M. Madrigal and I. D.
Halpert (see p. 72). The Linguaphone course is on 16 records (78 or
45 r.p.m.) at £15 2s. 1d., and also on tape (two 5″ spools, 3¾ i.p.s.,
2-track recording). Conversa-phone has a one 12″ L.P. (37s. 6d.) or
10″ L.P. (30s. 6d.) course.

The Express (*Daily Express*) course on basic conversational German
consists of two 12″ L.P. 33⅓ r.p.m. records costing, with text-book,
£5 5s. Hugophone's single 12″ L.P. 33⅓ r.p.m. record (29s. 6d.) is not
a language course, but an advanced help to pronunciation. Other
courses: Odham's 'Master' (four 10″ L.P. £12 4s.) and 'Quick' (two
7″ L.P. 30s.); 'Instant' (two 12″ L.P. 70s.); and 'Gem' (one 7″ L.P.,
9s. 2d.). The Visaphon Interpret German course, for beginners onwards, consists of 3 records, with booklets.

Grammar Courses for Scientists

ANDERSON, W. E.   German for the technologist.   London, Harrap,
1960.   293 p.   16s.

> 21 lessons, plus 4 revision interchapters, cover the grammar (German
> passage; vocabulary; grammar; exercises). Pt. 2 consists of readings in
> chemistry, physics, textiles, electrical and mechanical engineering, with notes
> and German-English vocabulary. Ingeniously written course on traditional
> lines, with reading matter and grammar tailored to the needs of the scientist.
> No index to grammar, but fairly full contents list.

BARKER, M. L.   Basic German for science students.   5th ed.   Edinburgh, Oliver & Boyd, 1956.   x, 164 p.   o.p.

Pt. 1: basic grammar, taught deductively from simple readings from *Genesis*, with the aid of footnotes; followed by simple general-science passages with vocabulary in footnotes. Pt. 2: readings in various sciences. German-English vocabulary (28 p.). Test papers for translation.

BITHELL, J., and DUNSTAN, A. C. A German course for science students. 8th ed. London, Methuen, 1953. viii, 198 p. o.p.

Grammar section is followed by readings on mathematics and seven other sciences, with full vocabulary. Some additional passages.

BUCKLEY, R. W. Essential German for science students. London, University of London Press, 1954. 256 p. 8s. 6d.

26 lessons on German grammar (not with the science student particularly in mind), followed by 32 passages, with vocabulary of readings primarily in chemistry and physics. Grammar summary and German-English vocabulary.

CUNNINGHAM, A. F. Science student's guide to the German language. London, Oxford University Press, 1958. xii, 186 p. 15s.

Pt. 1 contains a descriptive grammar in 19 chapters – very full and well beyond reading requirements. Hints on use of dictionary, and brief list of dictionaries. Pt. 2 contains 10 passages of readings apiece in chemistry, geography, mathematics, engineering, bacteriology and physics. No help given, by way of either vocabulary or notes. Index to grammar.

EATON, R. S., JACKSON, H. S., and BUXTON, C. R. German for the scientist. 2nd ed. London, English Universities Press, 1966. vi, 286 p. 15s.

91 passages on physics, mathematics, engineering, chemistry and bio-chemistry, introduced by well-written reference grammar, laying suitable stress on likely points of difficulty. Full end-vocabulary. First 7 extracts helpfully annotated, though users may be puzzled by painful misprint in introduction (p. 106).

EICHNER, H., and HEIN, H. Reading German for scientists. London, Chapman and Hall, 1959. xi, 207 p. 30s.

40 chapters, introducing the grammar, with reading exercises; followed by readings in chemistry and physics, with footnotes. Gothic alphabet given. Brief two-way vocabulary; index. Recommended.

HORNE, J. A streamlined course in scientific German. London, Pitman, 1960. x, 130 p. 15s.

Pt. 1 (primarily for beginner): 21 chapters on grammar, up to subjunctive (p. 4–47), with additional reading passages. Pt. 2: note on scientific transla-tions, followed by 63 extracts for translation in 9 branches of science and technology, plus economics and sociology. Vocabulary for pt. 2, p. 127–30; but a good German dictionary is indispensable.

MOFFATT, C. W. P. A science German course; revised by J. Horne and H. T. Betteridge. 6th ed. London, University Tutorial Press, 1961. 338 p. 12s. 6d.

In 3 parts: grammar and vocabulary, followed by simple readings and in pt. 3, by readings in the various sciences. German-English vocabulary, p. 287–336; brief index to grammar. Includes a list of scientific abbreviations and a pronunciation guide.

RADCLIFFE, S. Learn scientific German, London, Harrap, 1961. 345 p. 21s.

Section 1: 21 lessons on grammar, with exercises and translation practice (p. 19–139). Section 2: 'The technique of translation', includes an unannotated list of general and scientific German dictionaries. Section 3: passages for translation in chemistry, physics, medicine, engineering, zoology, botany, geology, geography. A dictionary is essential, since the appended select vocabulary covers section 1 only. Key to exercises (lessons 1–20); index to grammar.

REFERENCE GRAMMARS

ATKINS, H. G. A skeleton German grammar. Rev. ed., by M. O'C. Walshe. London & Glasgow, Blackie, 1957. viii, 87 p. o.p.
Brief but clear; contains an amazing amount of valuable material; both accurate and in line with modern linguistic scholarship. Recommended.

CLARKE, F. A German grammar for revision and reference. London, Bell, 1962 (reprint of 1936 ed.). 234 p. 7s.
Set in Gothic type throughout. No exercises.

CURME, G. O. A grammar of the German language. Rev. ed. New York, Ungar, 1952. 623 p. $9.50.
The standard large reference-work in the English language, with detailed indexes, of German words and suffixes and of subjects. Recommended.

GREBE, P. Duden Grammatik der deutschen Gegenwartssprache. Völlig neu bearb. Mannheim, Bibliographisches Institut, 1959. 699 p. (London, Bailey Bros. & Swinfen, 25s.). (Der grosse Duden, Bd. 4).
An authoritative grammar in 1,308 sections, with many examples of usage. Words and subject indexes, p. 631–699.

GRIESBACH, N., and SCHULZ, D.   Grammatik der deutschen Sprache. Munich, Max Hueber Verlag, 1960.   450 p.   DM 14.80.

A very sound monolingual German reference book. Recommended.

JØRGENSEN, P., and CLAUSEN, O. K.   German grammar.   Translated by G. Kolisko.   London, Heinemann, 1959–66.   3 v.   25s., 30s., 45s.

This is a descriptive grammar of German usage of the most academic kind, of little relevance for the ordinary reader. V. 1 deals with word formation and accidence; v. 2, with number and case; v. 3, with verbal forms, congruence, word order and the sentence.

MCLELLAN, F. R. H.   A school grammar of modern German.   Cambridge, University Press, 1950.   xii, 211 p.   6s. 6d.

All German-language examples are printed in Gothic.

ROSS, A. S. C.   The essentials of German.   London, Mason, 1963. 28 p.   5s.

In spite of a basically healthy approach, designed to clear away much of the dead wood that litters old-fashioned grammars of German, this booklet can only be recommended as a curiosity, being sufficiently lacking in common sense to print non-existent putative forms in bold type, to use no capital letters for nouns, and to print genitive before nominative forms. These *essentials* (see footnote on last page) are solely concerned with 'inflexional grammar', *i.e.*, with no aspect of syntax, including compound verb tenses.

WELLS, G. A., and ROWLEY, B. A.   The fundamentals of German grammar on one card.   London, Arnold, 1963.   3s. 6d.

Ingenious potted aide-mémoire, principally on declensions and conjugations.

GENERAL DICTIONARIES

BARKER, M. L., and HOMEYER, H.   The pocket Oxford German dictionary [German-English].   2nd ed.   Oxford, Clarendon Press, 1962.   xxii, 448 p.   12s. 6d.

CARR, C. T.   The pocket Oxford English-German dictionary. Oxford, Clarendon Press, 1951.   [4], 222 p.   7s. 6d.

These two dictionaries are also available in one volume,– *The pocket Oxford German dictionary* (1951, 18s.).   Gives help with pronunciation, an outline of grammar, plurals and verb forms. Clear print on India paper. Full coverage for its handy size ($5'' \times 3\frac{1}{4}''$). Recommended.

BELLOWS, J. E. Bellows' German dictionary, German-English, English-German. 3rd rev. ed. London, Longmans, Green, 1956. 696, 117 p. (pocket ed. 1959. 17s. 6d.).

The two parts of the dictionary are not associated in page units, as in *Bellows' French dictionary*, but appear in separate sequences. Gives assistance with pronunciation and grammar. Currency tables. Recommended.

BETTERIDGE, H. T. Cassell's German & English dictionary, based on the editions of Karl Breul; completely rev. and re-edited. London, Cassell, 1957. xx, 629, [1], 619 p. 36s.; with thumb index, 45s.

Reset in Roman type. Full coverage; synonyms are distinguished. Appendices of geographical and personal proper names, common abbreviations, irregular verbs, weights and measures, clothing sizes in both parts. Phonetics for English pronunciation. Clear type, well set out. Vocabulary has not yet caught up with the TV age. Recommended.

BITHELL, J. German-English and English-German dictionary. 4th ed. London, Pitman, 1949. 1,034 p. o.p.

Includes appendix on recent terms. Not as full as the Cassell's dictionary. Not recommended.

BOMSKY, L., and BUSSMANN, H. B. Wichmann's Dictionary of the German and English languages. Rev. ed. London, Routledge, 1952. xiv, 272, 273–513. 7s. 6d.

A pocket dictionary; chiefly single-word equivalents. Help is, however, given with pronunciation, abbreviations, verbs, plurals. List of proper names. Recommended.

CLARK, V. M. Collins' German gem dictionary. London & Glasgow, Collins, 1953. 752 p. o.p.

Pocket dictionary, both ways. Capitalised entry words. No grammar information except word lists. Pronunciation guide, both ways. Not recommended.

COLLINSON, W. E., and CONNELL, H. An English-German and German-English dictionary. London, Pordes, 1962. 576 p. 16s.

A valuable dictionary, with a difference; first published (1954) in Penguin edition, based on modern linguistic science. Full assistance given with grammar for fitting words into sentences. All verbs are listed under the first-person-singular form. Colloquial German included; pronunciation help. Recommended for beginners up to intermediate stage, and for user with general interests. Not pocket size.

Duden Bildwörterbuch der deutschen Sprache. Rev. ed. Mannheim, Bibliographisches Institut AG, 1958. 760 p. DM 12.60.

Monolingual. 368 large illustrations, with German terms opposite. Index of terms.

Englisch-Deutsch, Deutsch-Englisch. Zürich, Atrium-Verlag, 1950. 804 p. 8s. 6d.

For German-speaking rather than English-speaking user (e.g. gives phonetic pronunciation for English words and lists English irregular verbs).

JONES, T. Harrap's Standard German and English dictionary. London, Harrap, 1963–. Part 1: German-English, v. 1: A-E. 80s.

Compiled in line with the principles of Harrap's excellent *Standard English and French dictionary*. It aims to be a large, reliable German and English dictionary. Part 1 is to be in 4 v., issued at 2-yearly intervals; part 2 is also to be in 4 v. Rich in colloquialisms and technical terms (categorised), and outstanding for fullness of context-quotations (e.g., 'Boden': c. 120 lines). International phonetic alphabet used. Good stout, white paper and clear typography (e.g. bold for sub-entries, despite a three-column page).

JOHNSON, V. An advanced modern German vocabulary. London, Harrap, 1965. 62 p. 5s.

In 10 major topics, with some sub-divisions, a useful browse and help in essay-writing and debating.

KLATT, E. Langenscheidt's Pocket German dictionary: English-German. 29th ed. Berlin, Langenscheidt (London, Methuen), 1962. 608 p. 10s. 6d.

KLATT, E., and KLATT, G. Langenscheidt's Pocket German dictionary: German-English. 13th ed. Berlin, Langenscheidt (London, Methuen), 1959. p. 609–1,235. 10s. 6d.

These two dictionaries are also available in one volume, – *Langenscheidt's shorter dictionary* (20s.). Assistance is given on verbs and noun declensions in the German-English part. Both parts are very full, considering their small format. Symbols are used to distinguish synonyms. British and American-English covered. For German user. Not quite up to recent terms. Recommended.

Marlborough's German self-taught. 5th ed. Glasgow, Brown, Son & Ferguson, 1957. xii, 192 p. 8s. 6d.

A classified dictionary and phrase-book. Pt. 1: 134 pages of word lists (mostly nouns), English-German, with "imitated pronunciation" (e.g. dahss Klee'mah). Separate lists of verbs, adjectives, etc. "Flying saucer" is given on p. 1. Pt. 2: conversational phrases, strictly for travellers. Subject index.

MESSINGER, H., Langenscheidt's Handwörterbuch Deutsch-Englisch. Berlin, Langenscheidt (London, Methuen, as Langenscheidt's Concise German-English dictionary), 1959, 672 p. 17s. 6d.

German-English only. Aids to German pronunciation: lists of abbreviations, weights and measures, numerals. No assistance with German grammar, plurals or verbs. Speciality: up-to-dateness with modern technical, business, etc., terms (e.g. includes 'Managerkrankheit' (stress disease)).

Bound with the English-German part to form Langenscheidt's *Concise German dictionary* (4th ed., London, Methuen, 1964. 744, 672 p. 36s. 6d.). The German-English part has *c.* 15,000 entry words, the English-German, *c.* 18,000. This 4th ed. contains minor additions.

MOTEKAT, H., and BOURKE, J. Brockhaus illustrated dictionary, German-English, English-German. London, Pitman, 1961. xvii, 766, xii, 728 p. illus. 50s.

Based on the monolingual *Sprach-Brockhaus*. Phonetic pronunciation for German and English words: assistance (in German-English part) with plurals and verb forms. Very rich in synonyms and idiomatic expressions. Special feature: minutely keyed illustrations and multiple cross-reference, assisting with technical terms. Very good value; a book to browse in as well as use for reference. Recommended.

PARKER, F. G. S. Essential German vocabulary. London, Harrap, 1966. 237 p. 14s. 6d.

Lists of words and expressions by topics, but graded according to difficulty into sub-divisions; sections of verbs and abstracts; in second part, contents in one alphabetical list (English-German, as in rest of book). Standard 'A' level plus.

SASSE, H.-C., and others. Cassell's New compact German-English, English-German dictionary. London, Cassell, 1966. 12s. 6d. 541 p. School edition (identical), 1967. 9s.

Restricted in extent, but includes archaic terms essential for reading the classics. Phonetic transcriptions for all entries and basic grammatical and syntactic information included.

Der Sprach-Brockhaus. 7. durchgesehene Aufl. Wiesbaden, Brockhaus, 1958. 800 p. illus. DM 15 (London, Bailey Bros. & Swinfen. 28s.)

First published 1935. An illustrated abridgement of *Der kleine Brockhaus* (1950. 2 v.) and an excellent monolingual dictionary. A feature is the lavish use of accurate line-drawings – 5,400 in all, with keyed parts – at head and foot of pages. About 80,000 entry-words.

SPRINGER, O. Langenscheidt's encyclopaedic dictionary of the English and German languages, by E. Muret and D. Sanders. Berlin, Langenscheidt (London, Methuen), 1962–.

Pt. 1, *English-German*. 2 v. (xxxvii, 1,844 p.) ea. 110s. The largest English-German reference dictionary, originally published in 1908. Pt. 1 has over 180,000 main entries and is rich in appendices. Clear typography, despite three columns; numbered sub-entries.

WAHRIG, G. Deutsch-englisches Wörterbuch. Leipzig, Verlag Enzkylopädie, 1958. xix, 786 p. DM 10.80.

An East German publication, with about 40,000 entries. A handy size (5·6″ × 4·1″) and particularly handy for colloquialisms and idioms, as well as technical terms. Appendices include a list of abbreviations.

The companion *Englisch-deutsches Wörterbuch* was published in 1956. (769 p. DM 10.80).

WEIS, ERWIN, and WEIS, ERICH. The Schöffler-Weis compact German and English dictionary. London, Harrap, 1962. xvi, 1,174 ix, 626 p. o.p.

More useful for Germans. Gives phonetic pronunciation of English words; British and U.S. abbreviations. No help with noun declensions; synonyms explained in German. German strong verbs and numerals listed. Large, ugly print. Not recommended.

WILDHAGEN, K., and HÉRAUCOURT, W. English-German and German-English dictionary. 12th ed., rev. and enl. Wiesbaden, Brandstetter; London, Allen & Unwin, 1963–65. 2 v. (xxi, 1,061 p.; xxvi, 1,347 p.) 105s.; 100s.

"At the opposite pole to the small and dangerous type of dictionary that presents after each word a string of *more or less* equivalents without guidance as to their distinctive nuances of meaning" (*Babel*, v. 9, no. 4, 1963, p. 203–4). In this new ed., the German-English part is virtually unaltered since the 1953 ed.; it is the English-German part that has been enlarged by about 25%. Less easy to refer to, although only 2 columns to the page, than Trevor Jones or Springer. For the serious student and the conscientious translator who is not in too much of a hurry, concludes *Babel*.

Smaller, pocket-sized dictionaries include: *The E.U.P. concise German-English, English-German dictionary* (London, English Universities Press, 1945. 307 p. (Teach yourself series). 7s. 6d.), with a concise summary of German grammar; *Hugo's German-English, English-German dictionary* (London, Hugo's Language Institute, 1933. 5s.), with simulated pronunciation; Schöninghs Deutsch-englisches Wörterbuch, by E. Schlupp (Paderborn, Schöningh, 1954. 504 p. 9s.); and the *Tauchnitz dictionary, English-German, German-English*, compiled by W. Ebisch (2nd ed. Hamburg, Tauchnitz, 1949. 328 p. 9s.), with German in Gothic type.

Technical Dictionaries

DE VRIES, L. German-English technical and engineering dictionary.
New York, Toronto & London, McGraw Hill, 1950. xiv, 928 p.
$20. Supplement, 1959. xxvii, 386 p. o.p.

The two volumes constitute what is probably the fullest general German
and English technical dictionary. The main volume has more than 125,000
entries; the *Supplement* adds about 50,000 entries. Many compounds. The
corresponding English-German volume was published in 1954.

— German-English science dictionary. 3rd ed., including supplement
of new terms. New York, Toronto & London, McGraw-Hill,
1959. xlii, 592 p. o.p.

Intended as complementary to the foregoing. About 50,000 entries,
including terms in agriculture and medicine as well as the pure sciences.

ERNST, R. Wörterbuch der industriellen Technik ... 5–9. Aufl.
Wiesbaden, Brandstetter, 1959–60. 2 v. DM 57.80.

V. 1, German-English, contains "well over 75,000 key words" (*Preface*)
and includes many terms in nuclear physics and electronics.

LEIBIGER, O. W., and LEIBIGER, I. S. German-English and English-
German dictionary for scientists. Ann Arbor, Michigan, Edwards,
1950 (reprinted 1958). iv, 380, 360 p. $12.

Claims to contain 90,000 entries, but is certainly less complete than De
Vries and is prone to include non-technical words with their ordinary
meanings. Compounds are given separate entries.

PATTERSON, A. M. A German-English dictionary for chemists.
3rd ed. New York, Wiley, 1950 (and reprints). xviii, 541 p. 44s.

Though primarily for chemists and chemical engineers, it contains many
terms from related fields of science. About 59,000 entries. Praised for its
organisation, dependability and consistency. Clear layout, as in the De Vries
volumes.

WEBEL, A. A German-English dictionary of technical, scientific and
general terms. 3rd ed. London, Routledge & Kegan Paul, 1952
(reprinted 1963). xii, 939 p. 60s.

Much used in its day and even now by translators. About 60,000 entries,
with separate entries for compounds.

Commercial dictionaries

EICHBORN, R. von. Wirtschaftswörterbuch. Düsseldorf, Econ-
Verlag GmbH, 1961; London, Pitman, 1963. 2 v. ea. DM 56;
105s.

A reliable and extensive business dictionary, with some 25,000 main entry-words in each volume (v. 1, English-German; v. 2, German-English). Distinguishes between British and U.S. terminology. Idiomatic translation of British and U.S. terms that have no German equivalent.

GUNSTON, C. A., and CORNER, C. M. Deutsch-englisches Glossarium finanzieller and wirtschaftlicher Fachausdrücke. 4 erw. Aufl. Frankfurt am Main, Knapp, 1962. 1,060 p. DM 49.80.

About 15,000 main entries. Most terms are not merely translated; their precise application is stated in italics. A reliable and extensive commercial dictionary.

HERBST, R. Wörterbuch der Handels, Finanz und Rechtssprache. 2. Aufl. Lucerne, Thali, 1962–66. 3 v. ea. Sw. fr. 98.50.

A trilingual dictionary (v. 1: English-German-French. (1962); v. 2.: Deutsch-Englisch-Französisch (1966)), but included here for up-to-dateness, careful compilation and many idioms. About 50,000 entry-words in each volume.

RENNER, R., and others. German-English economic terminology. Munich, Hueber, 1965; London, Macmillan, 1966. 556 p. DM 27.80; 63s.

7,000 terms, arranged in 25 sections, with sub-divisions. Highly recommended in *The incorporated linguist* (v. 5, no. 2, April 1966, p. 56–57). Despite its title, concentrates on commercial terms.

7

DUTCH

by P. K. KING, M.A.

The choice of available grammars for English students is small and the standard is poor. This is not solely due to commercial factors, for the best of them, Shetter's, is selling well and the E.U.P. booklet which it supersedes has run to nine impressions and editions in 25 years. But there is no authoritative standard grammar of the language even for Dutch students, and current trends in linguistics not unnaturally deter even the boldest from applying a method which may be outdated by the time the ink has dried. And while it is true that at the elementary level of these grammars the real problems of analysis, description and prescription can be evaded, they all suffer to some extent from an uneasy compromise between the requirements of the tutored and untutored student.

GRAMMARS

BIRD, R. B., and SHETTER, W. Z. Een goed begin . . . : a contemporary Dutch reader. The Hague, Nijhoff, 1963. 2 v. (102 p.; 108 p.) 26s.

> The first part contains poetry and prose by twenty-six of the better-known Dutch writers of this century arranged in increasing order of difficulty. This is intended as a companion to Shetter's grammar, so that the grammatical summary, included with the notes and vocabulary to the Reader, is restricted to a tabular presentation of the basic paradigms. Despite some inaccuracy which is the price of such compression, it provides a clear, at-a-glance revision reference for those who can afford the high price.

HOLCH JUSTESEN, A. Hollandsk grammatik. Copenhagen, Jespersen & Pio, 1952. 158 p. fl. 16.

> This is undoubtedly the best grammar of Dutch for foreign students, but since it is written in Danish the justification for including it here is the excellent phonetic description (p. 13–50) by Eli Fischer-Jørgensen. This includes a scholarly phonetic and morphemic analysis (including loanwords) and sections on assimilation, stress, intonation and orthography.

Dutch in three months: Hugo's simplified system. London, Hugo's
Language Institute, [n.d.] 175 p. 7s. 6d.

The so-called simplification of the "imitated pronunciation" used throughout is both confusing and inaccurate. A semi-direct method of phrase
building is used from the start with intermissions of rather superficial
grammatical descriptions in three sections. An index does not entirely meet
the disadvantages of this piecemeal arrangement, though the method of
teaching by giving specimen parallel translations as well as exercises and
keys may be of some use in the most elementary stages.

KOOLHOVEN, H. Teach yourself Dutch. London, English Universities Press, 1964. 223 p. 7s. 6d.

Although this has been revised since its original, conservative version of
1941, it is still out of date and suffers from the intrinsic faults of muddled
arrangement. Unrelated categories are introduced almost at random so
that, e.g., the plural of nouns is partly dealt with in six different chapters
scattered through the first half of the book. The ostensible aim of construc-
ting interesting exercises in the early stages is at the cost of orderly learning
and revision, though the student with least linguistic ability is likely to be
least handicapped by this. More advanced grammatical and stylistic points
that are touched on would be a greater asset if they were more systematically
presented and developed. There is a key to the exercises, a separate list of
strong verbs and a Dutch-English vocabulary. Pronunciation is dealt with
quite fully, and a serious attempt is made to establish an accurate use of
phonetic transcription, though with some curious lapses.

RENIER, F. G. Learn Dutch! London, Routledge & Kegan Paul,
1964. viii, 182 p. 9s. 6d.

This is clearly intended for use in supervised classes, and what it gains in
phonetic drills it loses in grammatical detail and arrangement. Most chapters
contain dictation passages, preceded in the earlier stages by pronunciation
and spelling exercises. In the grammar sections, in which two or more
categories are often quite arbitrarily lumped together, the general lay-out is
not always clear and the treatment is scant. On the other hand, this is the
only text-book which attempts some Direct Method with text and exercises
related to illustrations (albeit of a crudely inartistic kind) so that the book
may be of some limited, supplementary use to a teacher or student under
instruction, but it cannot be recommended for the autodidact.

SHETTER, W. Z. Introduction to Dutch: a practical grammar.
2nd rev. ed. The Hague, Nijhoff, 1965. viii, 196 p. fl.12.

This is the most reliable grammar for general purposes, giving "a concise
presentation of the essentials of the Dutch language which could be used
both for independent home study and in groups or classes under formal
instruction". The chapter on pronunciation suffers most from this dual

purpose since it is inadequate for an untutored learner and largely redundant where proper instruction is available. The basic structure of the grammar is dealt with fairly thoroughly, including sections on the word *er*, diminutives and word formation and derivation. The chapters deal with more than one category at a time only when these are closely related, and apart from occasional revision sections consisting of reading passages, each chapter contains an accumulative vocabulary, idiomatic phrases and exercises based on the grammatical matter. They are arranged so as to be adaptable for class-work, and keys are given for the independent student. The limited scope necessitated some omissions of course, the most serious of which are sections on negation and the modal particles.

SNELLENBERG, J. van, and GIBBONS, G. Dutch self-taught. 4th ed. London, Marlborough, 1957.   126 p.   7s. 6d.

This is a rather unsatisfactory hybrid of classified word-list and grammatical summary. Into a short dictionary (62 p.), divided under the headings of adjectives; adverbs, conjunctions and prepositions; verbs; nouns and short phrases headed sport, commerce etc. is slotted a 'phonetic' description with a transcription not unlike Hugo's and about as valueless, and an outline grammar (31 p.) which is almost comically antiquated in its approach, though the faults are more in the English than in the Dutch.

SMIT, J., and MEIJER, R. P.   Dutch grammar and reader.   2nd ed. Melbourne, University Press, 1963.   207 p.   12s. 9d.

Here the grammar (58 p.) is kept quite separate from the exercises (27 p.) and reading texts (79 p.) and the advantages of this arrangement are immediately apparent. Grammatical points are dealt with clearly and systematically at two levels, the more advanced being indicated both in the grammar and the exercises in the centre section. These levels are meant to correspond to the requirements of secondary schools and the first year of university courses for which this book is intended. Unfortunately even in reprint the grammar contains so many inaccuracies, omissions and untidy formulations, that even where a teacher uses it, he will have to exercise caution. The phonetic description is unreliable and the double-standard arrangement is largely illusory since so much elementary material is omitted that in its entirety the grammar is quite inadequate for upper school, let alone university work. Nevertheless, the graded drills and translation and composition passages are thoughtfully chosen and would be useful in class-work, where the lack of keys will be an advantage.

GENERAL DICTIONARIES

BAARS, F. J. J., and SCHOOT, J. G. J. A. van der.   Prisma-woordenboek Engels-Nederlands.   12th rev. ed.   Utrecht, Het Spectrum, 1965. 336 p.   fl.1.50.

40,500 words. Small-type, fairly comprehensive and reliable paperback dictionaries printed on poor quality paper. Intended for the Dutch user. Conversion tables are given in the Dutch-English volume (see VISSER, G. J., below).

BROUWERS, L. M.   Het juiste woord.   4th rev. ed.   Brussels, Brepols, 1965.   1,445 p.

The only synonym-antonym thesaurus. Its scope is comparable to Roget's *Thesaurus*.

BRUGGENCATE, R. ten, and BROERS, A.   Engels woordenboek.   16th rev. ed., by R. W. Zandvoort and J. Gerritsen.   Groningen, Wolters, 1963.   2 v.   (960 p.; 1,106 p.)   ea. 25s.

The most comprehensive two-way dictionary with 67,000 English and 66,000 Dutch words. It is kept up to date by leading scholars so that artificial 'dictionary' equivalents and idioms are rare. Indispensable for idiom but, since it is intended for Dutch students, a serious lack is its omission of genders and phonetic descriptions of the Dutch words.

DALE, J. H. van.   Groot woordenboek der Nederlandse taal.   8th rev. ed., by C. Kruyskamp.   The Hague, Nijhoff, 1961.   2,632 p. fl. 78.

At nearly £8 this would fall outside the scope of this bibliography if the *Nieuw handwoordenboek der Nederlandse Taal*, a concise extract of the greater Van Dale, had been revised since 1956 when the 7th impression (1,097 p.) appeared from the same publishers at fl. 10.90. The greater dictionary is an entirely reliable and admirably produced standard work which is frequently revised. 180,000 Dutch words are given; stress and gender is shown but not pronunciation.

JANSONIUS, H.   Groot Nederlands-Engels woordenboek.   Leiden, Nederlandse Uitgeversmaatschappij, 1950.   2 v.   (912 p.; 920 p.); Supplement., 1959.   428 p.   fl. 35, fl. 40, fl. 35.

One-way dictionary of 115,000 words in the old spelling, with no genders or pronunciation. Extensive use of contexts demonstrates the nuances in the meaning of words, but since the work is intended for the advanced Dutch student of English, it will be most useful to the English student who already has a sound knowledge of Dutch.

KING, P., and KING, M.   The E.U.P. concise Dutch and English dictionary.   London, English Universities Press, 1958.   397 p. 10s. 6d.

This gives 17,000 Dutch and 14,000 English words with a bias towards the spoken rather than literary language. Genders and stresses are shown but not pronunciation. An introduction containing a summary of the phonetics and orthography and grammar (including classified lists of verbs) makes this a practical elementary reference.

RENIER, F. G. Dutch-English and English-Dutch dictionary. London, Routledge & Kegan Paul, 1964. xviii, 571 p. 10s. 6d.

This is a straightforward, reliable dictionary for word sense and some idiom, with a clear lay-out in a convenient format containing 16,000 Dutch and 12,000 English words. The genders and pronunciation of Dutch words are shown.

VISSER, G. J. Prisma-woordenboek Nederlands-Engels. Utrecht, Het Spectrum. 9th rev. ed. Utrecht, Het Spectrum, 1965. 320 p. fl. 1.50.

38,500 entry-words. See BAARS, F. J. J. above, for English-Dutch counterpart.

WELY, F. P. H. Prick van. Cassell's English-Dutch, Dutch-English dictionary. 6th ed. London, Cassell, 1965. 1,354 p. 42s.

This work is intended for both English and Dutch users. The inclusion of phonetic and lexical notations on both sides necessarily reduces the amount of translation given for English and Dutch words. It is conservative, accurate and somewhat dull, with 40,000 Dutch and 49,000 English words.

— Cassell's Compact Dutch dictionary. 5th ed. London, Cassell, 1965. 676 p. 18s.

An abridged version of the foregoing, containing 16,700 Dutch and 18,000 English words.

Woordenlijst van de Nederlandse taal. The Hague, Nijhoff, 1954. lxx, 635 p. fl. 6.

An extensive list showing the spelling and genders (but not the meaning) of 75,000 words, as authorised by the Dutch and Belgian government agreement of 1954. The introduction summarises the orthographic changes affected by this most recent spelling reform.

Technical Dictionaries

BAKKER, J. 3,200 vaktermen en belangrijke gegevens voor het grafisch bedrijf. Nederlands-Engels. Hoorn, Edecea, 1952. 96 p. fl. 2.75.

BONS, A. Engels handelswoordenboek (Nederlands-Engels), tevens algemeen woordenboek. 2nd ed. Deventer, Kluwer, 1957. 1,172 p. fl. 45.

Dutch-English commercial dictionary, with English equivalents of more than 32,000 Dutch business, trade and legal terms.

BOS, K., and PEN, F. A. 1. Technisch Engels. Haarlem, Stam, 1958 (10th–11th imp.). 200 p. fl. 5.25.

— and NONNEKES, C. J. 2a. Bouwkunde, weg-en waterbouwkunde. Haarlem, Stam, 1958 (9th imp.). 143 p. fl. 5.50.

— and GRAUS, J. M. A. 2b. Werktuigbouwkunde, elektrotechniek, scheepsbouwkunde en chemie. Haarlem, Stam, 1960 (10th imp.). 149 p. fl. 5.50.

— and STREUMER, J. J. 3a. Bouwkunde, weg- en waterbouwkunde, correspondentie. Haarlem, Stam, 1958 (5th imp.). 166 p. fl. 6.50.

— and GRAUS, J. M. A. 3b. Werktuigbouwkunde, elektrotechniek, scheepsbouwkunde en chemie, correspondentie. Haarlem, Stam, 1958 (6th imp.). 224 p. fl. 8.95.

BOSCH, A. ten. Ten Bosch' Engels-Nederlands technisch woordenboek. 4th rev. ed., revised by E. L. Oberg in collaboration with G. Schuurmans Stekhoven and D. B. J. Voortman. Deventer, Kluwer, 1964. 436 p. fl. 22.50.

About 12,000 English technical terms, with Dutch equivalents. The Dutch-English part is included in the quadralingual *Nederlands-Engels-Frans-Duits* dictionary 6th ed. 1963. [vii], 692 p. fl. 27.50.

FITZ-VERPLOEGH, A. Engelse vaktermen en uitdrukkingen voor scheepswerktuigkundigen, monteurs, machinisten, metaalbewerkers en andere practici. 2nd ed. Deventer, Kluwer, 1955. ix, 100 p. fl. 4.50.

Dutch-English and English-Dutch technical terms in engineering.

GRAUS, J. M. A. Technisch Engels woordenboek. Deel 1. Engels-Nederlands. Haarlem, Stam, 1956 (4th imp.). 279 p. fl. 7.75.

— — Deel 2. Nederlands-Engels. Haarlem, Stam, 1955 (2nd imp.). 224 p. fl. 6.50.

Each volume contains equivalents of about 24,000 technical terms.

SCHOENMAKER, P. W. Nautisch-technisch woordenboek. I. Engels-Nederlands. Amsterdam, Duwaer, 1963. 326 p. fl. 12.50.

About 6,000 English nautical terms, with Dutch equivalents, for ships' officers.

COURSES ON RECORDS AND TAPES

Linguaphone Dutch. 16 records or two tapes, with Vocabularies (89 p.), Texts of the lessons (159 p.) and Grammar (60 p.) London Linguaphone Institute, 1957. £18 10s.

A well-conceived course, moving somewhat too fast in the early stages. There is a good variety of excellent voices and the text is clearly if sparsely illustrated. The grammar contains a wide range of information and is generally reliable.

LAGERWEY, W. Modern Dutch. A first-year college-level audio-lingual course for the Dutch language. Michigan, Calvin College (1331 Franklin Street S.E., Grand Rapids), 1965. 458 p. $6, and five dual-track tapes $30.

This cannot, unfortunately, be recommended. Part of the dialogue is set in America; one of the speakers claims to be foreign to Dutch (and indeed sounds it at times!), and even where the pronunciation is impeccable the intonation is faulty. As much recording time is devoted to English as to Dutch, and a most important part of the text, the substitution drills, is not recorded at all. Since the pronunciation drills are based on American-Dutch comparisons, their usefulness is limited for the British student who will find these comparisons misleading.

8

SCANDINAVIAN LANGUAGES

by A. G. Curwen, f.l.a.

The Scandinavian languages are not taught in British schools, with a very few exceptions. People who decide to learn one or more of them do so therefore as the result of a deliberate choice and for reasons which are entirely personal, and which may dictate which of the languages is studied (or studied first). They can be read as a main or subsidiary subject at one of ten universities, studied at night school, or studied privately, with or without the aid of recordings. Whatever the method, the position is that very much more material is available to help the student than is immediately apparent from browsing in bookshops or searching British book trade lists or bibliographies.

Other things being equal, it might be considered that Swedish is the most useful of the languages to learn, inasmuch as it has the greatest number of native speakers. Furthermore, it is no very great step from Swedish to Norwegian. Norwegian has been in a state of flux for the past hundred years or so: the resulting confusion and rivalry between the different forms of the language pose some difficulties for the student, but also add to the interest of learning it. All the textbooks seen deal with the *bokmål* (or *riksmål*) form of Norwegian, which is used by the majority of educated urban speakers and in most of the printed material the student is likely to see. Those who are attracted to the *nynorsk* (or *landsmål*) form will either have to learn it direct by staying in a part of Norway where it is spoken and taught, or will have to learn *bokmål* and then study *nynorsk* from Norwegian textbooks. In some ways Norwegian is the easiest language to begin with if one intends to study the others subsequently: the pronunciation leads fairly naturally to Swedish, and *bokmål* to written Danish. Danish, while fairly static in its written form, is a problem on its own when one comes to the spoken language. Help from recordings or native speakers is more than ever necessary. Modern Icelandic is dealt with in this chapter, but not Old Icelandic. However, although the pro-

nunciation has changed over the centuries, the grammar and orthography have remained remarkably static, enabling the modern reader
to enjoy the sagas in a way which is denied to the modern English
reader faced with Middle English of the twelfth and thirteenth centuries. Finally, the sole extended work on Faroese (now in print again)
h s been included to complete this family of languages.

NOTE. An abstract of a paper on the Scandinavian languages by D. M.
Mennie appeared in the Aslib *Technical translation bulletin*, v. 8, no 3,
December 1962, p. 8–13, with the following headings: 1. The Scan-
dinavian languages and which shall I learn? II. Some characteristic
features of Swedish. III. Aids to learning Danish, Norwegian and
Swedish: a short bibliography.

Dictionaries. Nearly all Scandinavian-English and English-Scandinavian dictionaries originate in Scandinavia and are clearly designed for
Scandinavian readers, even though some are issued with British and
American imprints also. Thus while nearly all the English-Scandinavian
volumes give the pronunciation of English words, and irregular
plurals of nouns and parts of verbs, hardly any of the Scandinavian-
English volumes will do the same for the Scandinavian languages: the
Scandinavian user knows the plurals, genders and pronunciation of his
own vocabulary. This is a very serious disadvantage for the English-
speaking user.

Only the little Niloé's English-Swedish and Swedish-English
dictionary gives the pronunciations for both languages; only the great
Danish-English dictionary by Vinterberg and Bodelsen, the smaller one
by Magnussen, Madsen and Vinterberg, the unfinished Swedish-
English dictionary by Harlock, with the smaller school edition in one
volume, and the excellent new Norwegian-English dictionary by
Haugen give the genders and plurals of Scandinavian nouns and the
parts of verbs, and refer back from irregular forms in their alphabetical
place to the main article (e.g. from *böcker* to *bok*, from *er*, *var* to *være*);
and even these dictionaries do not indicate pronunciations (except
Haugen's).

There is room for much improvement in this field: Scandinavian
publishers should remember that Scandinavian-English dictionaries
are used by English-speaking persons as well as by their own people.

Those who have learnt one of the Scandinavian languages may well
be led on to study one or more of the others. This is a rich and often

amusing field. Despite their common origin, the differences between the languages are by no means limited to spelling and pronunciation. For example, the student who knows Danish or Swedish and is studying the other (or who thinks he knows both) should not overlook

MUNCH-PETERSEN, V. P., and HARTMANN, E.   Farlige ord og lumske ligheder i svensk og dansk. 3. forøgede udg. Copenhagen, Gyldendal, 1962.   260 p.   D. kr. 18.25.

which is a surprising and entertaining dictionary of linguistic 'false friends', etc., arranged in parallel columns, Swedish-Danish and Danish-Swedish. Nevertheless it is a perfectly serious and scholarly work designed to promote the better understanding of the two languages.

Several bilingual inter-Scandinavian dictionaries of varying degrees of fullness are available, and there is at least one trilingual Danish-Norwegian-Swedish volume, but they fall outside the scope of this guide, as do textbooks in Scandinavian languages for learning other Scandinavian languages.

There is one fairly comprehensive work on the Scandinavian languages as a group currently available in English:

WALSHE, M. O'C.   Introduction to the Scandinavian languages. London, André Deutsch, 1965.   187 p.   (The language library). 32s. 6d.

This is divided into two parts. The first deals with the distribution, history and current position of the languages. The second deals with the pronunciation of Danish, Norwegian and Swedish, and then continues with a comparative grammar of Danish and Swedish on facing pages, a chapter on the grammar of the two forms of Norwegian, a select classified vocabulary of Danish words with English translations and the corresponding Swedish and Norwegian words in parallel columns, and finally a brief bibliography. It is definitely not a textbook for learning any or all of the languages, but is excellent value for those who are interested in languages generally, those who know some German, and not least those who know one of the Scandinavian languages already.

A volume on the Scandinavian languages by the late Alf Sommerfelt was for many years advertised as projected for Faber's 'Great languages' series. Einar Haugen has now taken over this task, but the publishers write (January 1966) that the book will not be published for, possibly, several years.

Prices. Throughout this chapter the latest known prices in Scandinavian currencies have been quoted for books published there, as far as possible. Where there is a British *publisher*, as opposed to an importing bookseller, the price is given in sterling. Prices are generally mid-1966, though some are earlier. Prices quoted in national bibliographies, publishers' and booksellers' lists may well differ, depending on whether Scandinavian purchase tax has been included or not. Despite these variations, and any increases which may have occurred, it is hoped that sufficient information has been given to enable libraries and individuals to estimate their expenditure, and to judge whether their booksellers are making reasonable charges for imported titles. It is often worth quoting the Scandinavian price (if known) when placing the order. The advantages of using one or more Scandinavian booksellers should not be overlooked, particularly if their purchase tax is not charged on books exported. This may balance the cost of postage.

'Self-taught' Series. In the titles volume of *British books in print* 'Danish self-taught', 'Norwegian self-taught' and 'Swedish self-taught' are all attributed to Brown, Son & Ferguson, Ltd. These publishers deny having taken over this series, and E. Marlborough & Co. Ltd. state that these titles are still available from them at 5s. each, although many other titles in the series are now out of print.

DANISH

The current Danish norm dates from the spelling reform of 1948. This was very slight. Å (å) is now used in place of AA (aa), and comes last in the alphabet; it is no longer necessary to begin all nouns with a capital, German fashion; the auxiliary verbs *kunde, skulde, vilde* are now *kunne, skulle, ville*; and there are a number of minor changes which are unlikely to affect the student. Books published prior to 1948 can still be used without difficulty. Some conservative newspapers stick to the old orthography, and some dictionaries and encyclopaedias on which work was begun prior to 1948 have been published since with the old orthography; one encyclopaedia even changed horses in midstream. It should be noted that the order of the Danish alphabet, ending x y z æ ø å, now agrees with Norwegian, while both differ from Swedish, ending x y z å ä ö.

There is a move to simplify Danish numbers and bring them into line with Norwegian and Swedish practice. To a limited extent this has been carried out for cheques, etc., e.g. *femtito kroner* = 52 kroner, but otherwise the student will have to master the old longwinded forms which are still standard in the written and the spoken language, e.g. *tooghalvtreds* = 52 (abbreviated, at that), and *tooghalvtredsindstyvende* = 52nd, or, "two and halfway [between four tens and] thrice twenty-th".

GRAMMARS AND READERS

ANDERSEN, G. M. Say it in Danish. New York, Dover; London, Constable, 1958. 165 p. 6s.

> A companion volume to Abrahamsen's *Say it in Norwegian* (see p. 145).

BREDSDORFF, E. Danish: an elementary grammar and reader. Cambridge, University Press, 1956 (4th rev. imp., 1965). xi, 301 p. 35s. (Students' paperback ed. 18s. 6d.).

> Author is Reader in Scandinavian Studies at Cambridge. Contents of book tried out on students at London and Cambridge. For beginners and up to first-degree standard (many university students not having studied any Danish previously).
>
> Pt. 1: Introduction to Danish (Danish alphabet; the written language; the spoken language, p. 1–17). Pt. 2: Danish phonetics (the sound system; spelling and sound values; special pronunciations; stress; weak forms of words, p. 18–45). Pt. 3: Grammar (nouns, adjectives, etc., through to word order and word formation, p. 46–182). Pt. 4: Useful words and general information (idioms, weights and measures, money, abbreviations, etc., p. 183–200). Pt. 5: Danish texts (vocabulary notes at foot of each page, p. 201–88). Pt. 6: 20 texts for Danish composition (p. 289–301). No vocabularies.
>
> Probably the best available book for those who want a fairly formal approach.

DEARDEN, J., and STIG-NIELSEN, K. Spoken Danish. New York, Holt, [1946]. 2 v. [Holt, Rinehart & Winston; Book I: 40s.; Book II: 52s.].

> Linguistic analysis and presentation by Dearden; Danish material by Stig-Nielsen. Course created primarily to teach U.S. military personnel the *spoken* language. So arranged that, in the absence of a qualified teacher, a

group of students can choose one of their number to be 'leader' and organiser of the lessons, while a native speaker reads (and repeats) the text as required, by signal if necessary: the speaker need not know English. Subsequently disc recordings were produced for Book 1 (see under Gramophone Records and Tapes).

Divided into 5 parts, each sub-divided into 6 units. Every sixth unit is revision; the others each deal with a topic (e.g. Meeting people, Weather). Each unit is divided into a set of basic sentences, and notes, exercises, etc., on the sentences. The sentences are arranged in 3 parallel columns: (i) English equivalents (ii) Aids to listening, i.e. the Danish in International Phonetic Alphabet transcription, which the students concentrate on, and (iii) conventional Danish spelling. Identical Danish-English and English-Danish word lists at the end of each volume. The Danish-English list is arranged under the I.P.A. forms with the conventional spelling in brackets. Gives genders etc., translation, and reference to unit where word first appeared. English-Danish list gives Danish translation in I.P.A. form only.

An ingenious attempt to solve a wartime problem. Now very dated in content and method, and very cramped and unimaginative in its physical appearance. Table of contents gives a brief idea of the major grammatical points introduced in the units, but there is no detailed index. Not up to modern standards, and very expensive. It is to be hoped that this course will be revised as successfully as Haugen's *Spoken Norwegian* (q.v.), which was a similar wartime compilation.

DIDERICHSEN, P. Essentials of Danish grammar. Copenhagen, Akademisk Forlag, 1964.   78 p.   D.kr. 16.–

Written at the request of Danish organisations concerned with teaching Danish to foreigners. Based on the same principles as the author's *Elementær dansk grammatik* (3rd ed., Copenhagen, Gyldendal, 1962, D.kr. 25.–), which is by no means an elementary book, entirely in Danish.

Outline of history of language, (p. 11–14). Grammar: Part I: Sounds and letters: spelling and pronunciation (p. 15–33). Part II: Words and forms: inflection and use (p. 34–66). Part III: The sentence: sentence structure (p. 67–75). Excerpt from a short story by H. C. Branner (p. 76–78).

A very useful brief reference grammar to supplement readers and class and individual tuition. Gives many examples of Danish usage which are explained by parallel English examples, avoiding grammatical technical terms as far as possible. The section on pronunciation uses the International Phonetic Alphabet with modifications.

The author has recorded a 45 r.p.m. E.P. gramophone record to accompany the book (D.kr. 9.–). The pronunciation represents that of educated Danes born in the early twentieth century. Side 1 contains the 173 words from the systematic survey of pronunciation in Part I of the grammar; Side 2 is the text by Branner.

DUGDALE, J. S.   Danish: a six weeks' primer in essential grammar and vocabulary. [New ed.]. London, Foyle, 1962. 87 p. (Foyle's language tutors). 4s.

> This was recorded as a new edition in the *British national bibliography*. (1st ed. 1952). One suspects that, in fact, it is a re-issue, with a more cheerful paper-cover. Whether or not one thinks that primers of this sort have any value, this one should not be put into the stock of any library, nor should it be recommended to anyone, until it has been completely revised. There are so many errors that it is dangerously misleading to a beginner. If one knows enough Danish to spot all the errors, one does not need the primer. In a letter (October 1962) the publishers state that they "will certainly not reprint until the book has been completely checked".

FENNEBERG, P.   Speak Danish: a practical guide to colloquial Danish. 7th ed. Copenhagen, Gad; London, Oxford University Press, 1959. viii, 138 p. 12s.

> First published 1938; 2nd ed. 1945. Later editions use the revised orthography of 1948. A popular work for the teach-yourself student. Pronunciation explained at some length, using a simple phonetic transcription, easily understood (knowledge of the International Phonetic Alphabet is not required). In the course of this explanation (p. 1–28) the author also introduces a sizeable vocabulary and the student finds he has progressed from the Danish for "An uncle and an aunt" to "I am sending a red rose to Miss Rasmussen"! The rest of the book works through various grammatical topics in conventional order, at the same time giving much useful information about Danish life and customs, and a good idiomatic vocabulary. By no means an academic work in appearance, it is sound, entertaining and instructive. The Danish-English vocabulary (p. 121–38) has about 1,050 entry-words.

HARVEY, W. F.   Danish self-taught, with phonetic pronunciation. (Thimm's system). 3rd ed. Marlborough, [1914?]. 120 p. 5s.

> Apparently no revision since 1914. If so, it is fearfully dated as well as suffering from the other disadvantages of the series. Not recommended.

HUGO'S LANGUAGE INSTITUTE.   Danish simplified: an easy and rapid self-instructor. London, the Institute, [n.d.]. o.p.

> Probably better value than the Marlborough self-tutor by W. F. Harvey, but not necessary for libraries while there are several infinitely superior works available. (For typical layout see the note on the Norwegian volume in this series, p. 151)

KOEFOED, H. A.   Teach yourself Danish. London, English Universities Press, 1958. xiv, 232 p. 7s. 6d.

> Author formerly Queen Alexandra Lecturer in Danish at University College, London. Attempts compromise between the modern, informal and the more conventional grammatical methods. 32 text groups are not lessons – no "Danish in 32 hours" course; each student must do several or few accord

ing to ability and progress. Pronunciation (simplified I.P.A., p. 1–11); texts and exercises (p. 13–152); grammar (p. 153–210); key to exercises (p. 211–24); index of Danish words (no translation given; refers to occurrence in text, p. 225–32). Each text-group consists of one or more passages in Danish, with vocabularies, questions in Danish, *ordsprog* (i.e. proverbs, idioms and sayings) and grammatical notes. Later on there are also exercises for translation into Danish.

By far the most informal of the E.U.P. Scandinavian 'Teach yourself' books. The student learns grammar as he goes on – instead of 'doing' nouns, adjectives, articles, etc., a chapter for each, with exercises and vocabulary subsidiary to and illustrating the grammatical topic.

Details of the records of this course are given under Linguaphone in the section below.

Koefoed is also joint author of:

NORLEV, E., and KOEFOED, H. A.   The way to Danish: a textbook in the Danish language.   2nd ed.   Copenhagen, Munksgaard, [1964]. 306 p.   D.kr. 38.50.

First ed. 1959. 2nd ed. has some corrections and revisions, but the basic Danish text is unaltered. Introduction on grammatical terminology, pronunciation, spelling, etc. (p. 11–27). The bulk of the book (p. 28–261) consists of 30 chapters, each divided into (A) Text, (B) Explanations of difficult terms in the text, (C) Word list with phonetic transcription, (D) Words and usage, (E) Grammar, and (F) Exercises. The texts introduce about 1,500 of the most commonly used words, and are woven into an amusing continuous story about two young men on holiday in Denmark. The word index (p. 262–302) gives all the Danish words used, with spelling, pronunciation, inflexion and meaning. When a word has been specially discussed, reference is made to the relevant chapter and section. Grammatical index; index of special terms; index of practical information, e.g. weights and measures, telephone, expressions of time, etc. (p. 303–6).

An excellent unconventional textbook, with clear explanations, lively, interesting, well printed. No illustrations, and no recording of the text available. Written in the first place for use in American colleges, it can equally well be used in other English-speaking countries. It can also be used by students working alone, but they will need help with pronunciation.

SALLING, A. Lær at tale dansk. 2. udg. Copenhagen, Grafisk Forlag, 1966.   241 p. illus.   D.kr. 24.75.

Textbook for learning Danish by the direct method, mainly in class, but also for self-tuition. Vocabulary of some 1,100 words (apart from grammatical terms and proper names), mostly selected from the most-used Danish words. There is no help with pronunciation, as it is assumed that the student will either have a teacher or the use of audio aids. However, no tape or gramophone record is issued to accompany the book.

Divided into 72 sections (*stykker*) (p. 7–182), each containing conversation pieces or a prose passage, exercises, and lists of new words. Grammar (fairly brief, and all in Danish), with examples (p. 183–201). Danish-English vocabulary (p. 202–241) gives translation of words and also the page on which they first occur. Genders of nouns given, but not the parts of irregular verbs, which are listed individually, e.g. *bad* (asked) p. 108, *bede* (ask) p. 81.

Clearly printed. Up-to-date, fairly informal. Good value for class use or for individual tuition, but help with pronunciation essential.

STEMANN, I., and others.   Danish: a practical reader, by Ingeborg Stemann in collaboration with Angus Macdonald and Niels Haislund. 4th ed.   Copenhagen, Hagerup, 1965.   viii, 287 p.   D.kr. 25.–

1st ed. 1938; 2nd ed. 1953. 3rd and 4th editions are corrected reprints of 2nd ed. Translated and enlarged from original edition prepared for German-speaking students. Texts and examples of newspaper reports, letters, descriptive writing, etc. A grammar as well as a reader, intended both for those who have had university education and those who have not. Pt. 1: Rules for pronunciation (very full for a work of this sort, with accurate phonetic transcription using International Phonetic Alphabet, p. 1–29, and Hans Andersen's story *Hvad hele familien sagde*, with phonetic transcript in parallel columns, p. 30–34). Pt. 2: Lessons, etc., which include further pronunciation notes, phrases, grammar, vocabulary and exercises (p. 35–130). Pt. 3: List of phrases, with translations and phonetic transcriptions (p. 131–158). Pt. 4: Danish texts, with no translation or pronunciation (p. 159–207). Pt. 5: Grammar (p. 208–287). This last is in numbered paragraphs to which the lessons refer.

The second edition was reset using the 1948 orthography, and was somewhat revised at the same time. Some text passages were improved; some words were added to the vocabularies, which were re-arranged into alphabetical order; factual information was brought up to date; and some newspaper extracts were replaced by more modern ones.

A key to this work is: *Danish-English vocabulary*; prepared by Angus Macdonald and with phonetic transcription by Gunnar Skov (Copenhagen, Hagerup, 1938. 163 p. D.kr. 3.75). This is still in print. It should be noted, however, that it was prepared to accompany the *first* edition, and has not been revised. Contents: Value of phonetic symbols (p. 1–10). Danish-English vocabulary (p. 11–148), giving pronunciation, genders, plurals, principal parts, etc., as well as translation. Key to the lessons (p. 149–163), i.e. translations of the exercises for translation into Danish.

A second stage (*andet trin*) continuation reader is available:

STEMANN, I., and NISSEN, M.   Moderne dansk for udlændinge. Andet trin.   Copenhagen, Gyldendal, 1962.   196 p.   D.kr. 18.–

Entirely in Danish. Conversation pieces, menus, telephone conversations, letters, etc. (p. 7–39). Prose and verse pieces by modern authors (p. 40–163). Everyday phrases and conversational forms (p. 164–9). Interjections (p.

170–3). Expressions of time (p. 174–5). Outline of grammar (p. 176–194). Not indexed.

There is also a third stage reader by Stemann: *Dansk for udlændinge*. 2. omarbejdede udg. (Copenhagen, Gyldendal, 1945. 356 p. o.p. Not to be reprinted).

GRAMOPHONE RECORDS AND TAPES

DEARDEN and STIG-NIELSEN (Holt, Rinehart and Winston). Six 33⅓ r.p.m. 12″ records for Book 1 of *Spoken Danish*, £28 10s. Key to recorded units 1–12, 8s.

DIDERICHSEN (Akademisk Forlag). One 45 r.p.m. E.P. record to accompany *Essentials of Danish Grammar*, D.kr.9.–

KOEFOED (Linguaphone). Five 45 r.p.m. records to accompany *Teach yourself Danish*, £10. (£10 7s. 6d. with the book).

One side is devoted to the sounds of Danish. The other 9 record the reading exercises and conversations from the book. The early pieces are read slowly and the last ones at normal conversation speed, with the tempo steadily increased in the course of the middle ones. The speakers are an actor and an actress trained at the Royal Theatre, Copenhagen.

The Danish Institute (3 Doune Terrace, Edinburgh, 3) is preparing a course on tape, but it will probably be some time before it is available.

RADIO COURSES

Danmarks Radio does not broadcast a "Danish by radio" course for English-speaking listeners, and has no plans for doing so at the moment (September 1966).

DICTIONARIES

Standard Orthography

DANSK SPROGNÆVN. Retskrivningsordbog. [4. udg.] Copenhagen, Gyldendal, 1955. xxxi, 299 p. D.kr. 15.–

The bulk of the book is the work of Jørgen Glahder (who also prepared the earlier editions), and is a listing, without definitions, of the vocabulary of current Danish according to the 1948 rules. It gives parts of speech, genders and plurals of nouns, past tenses of all verbs and principal parts of strong and irregular verbs, irregular comparisons of adjectives, and any accepted alternative forms and spellings. Only a selection of compound words is given, unless there is a possibility of confusion; otherwise the constituent parts must be sought individually. Omissions: (1) special professional, technical, etc., terminology used only by those concerned (this makes it the more regrettable that Warrern omits grammatical information in his technical dictionaries); (2) archaic words, except those of a literary nature which may be used in historical and critical works; (3) proper names (but derived adjectives, etc., are included); (4) dialect words which have not been assimilated into the standard language; (5) slang.

The preliminary matter includes *Retskrivningsvejledning* by Erik Oxenvad, which deals with the Danish alphabet, use of capital initial letters, division of words at the ends of lines, words written together or separately, rules for inflexions, and punctuation.

Translating Dictionaries (in descending order of size)

VINTERBERG, H., and BODELSEN, C. A. Dansk-engelsk ordbog. 2. reviderede og udvidede udg. ved C. A. Bodelsen. Medredaktører: Jens Axelsen, B. Kjærulff Nielsen og Edith Frey. Copenhagen, Gyldendal, 1966. 2 v. D.kr. 320.–.

1st ed. 1954–56. One of the finest modern bilingual dictionaries. The sole significant defect for the English-speaking reader is the omission of pronunciation for the Danish entry words. Very full vocabulary, including many specialised trade, professional and technical terms. Indicates gender and plurals of nouns, past tenses of weak verbs and principal parts of strong and irregular verbs, etc. English translations given with many examples of usage; different meanings clearly defined and separated. Under each heading combinations of the entry word with prepositions, verbs, etc., are set out systematically. Small, but beautifully clear printing, coupled with carefully thought-out typography, combine to facilitate use. At about 15 gns. this is beyond the reach of most students, but should be in every major reference library; there is no other comparable Danish-English dictionary. This 2nd ed. has been re-arranged and reset, using the 1948 orthography (the first ed. used the earlier forms, as work on it was well advanced prior to 1948).

The corresponding English-Danish dictionary is of an equally high standard in all respects:

KJÆRULFF NIELSEN, B. Engelsk-dansk ordbog. Medredaktør: Jens Axelsen. Konsulent: C. A. Bodelsen. Copenhagen, Gyldendal, 1964. xi, 1,294 p. D.kr. 198.–

Translates some 130,000 English words, and gives the Danish equivalents of about 100,000 expressions and figures of speech. Nevertheless, by exemplary typography and printing, all this material is contained in one reasonably-sized volume with no loss of clarity. In this volume, typically, the pronunciation of all the English entry words is given.

There is no other comparable pair of dictionaries for any of the other Scandinavian languages.

MAGNUSSEN, J., and others. Dansk-engelsk ordbog, af Hermann Vinterberg. Grundlagt af Johs. Magnussen, Otto Madsen og Hermann Vinterberg. 6. rev. og forøgede udg. Copenhagen, Gyldendal, 1959. 447 p. (Gyldendals røde ordbøger). D.kr. 21.50. (7. rev. og forøgede udg. 1967. viii. 464 p.)

The best medium-sized Danish-English dictionary. Gives genders and plurals of Danish nouns, parts of verbs, and references from irregular plurals (e.g., from *bøger* to *bog*, *mænd* to *mand*, etc.), all very useful for non-Danish users and features rarely found in Scandinavian dictionaries. No pronunciations of Danish words. 6th ed. uses new orthography of 1948 and is 40 pages larger than 5th ed. (1944). 5th and all earlier editions to a greater or less extent out of date. Excellent printing.

Magnussen, Madsen and Vinterberg also produced the corresponding English-Danish dictionary, although their names no longer appear on the titlepage of the latest edition:

VINTERBERG, H., and AXELSEN, J. Engelsk-dansk ordbog. 8. ændrede udg. Copenhagen, Gyldendal, 1964. [8], 496 p. (Gyldendals røde ordbøger). D.kr. 23.–

A good dictionary, intended mainly for Danes. Hence inclusion of English pronunciation, and lack of explanatory matter when there is a choice of Danish words translating a given English one (except when completely different subject fields are involved; these are specified). 6th ed. (1954) introduced 1948 orthography and was some 75 pages larger than 5th ed. (1937). The 8th ed. is again revised and enlarged, and improved typographically. If a word is used as noun, adjective, verb, etc., (e.g. 'light'), it has separately numbered articles for each.

The two volumes are available bound together (D.kr. 44.50).

Allen & Unwin have had these dictionaries on their list for about 20 years. These were special printings of the 5th edition made in 1947, and so dated, although Gyldendal published them in 1944 (D-E) and 1937 (E-D) respectively. The situation was further complicated by the fact that the edition dates for 4th and 5th Gyldendal Danish-English volumes were printed on the verso of the titlepages of the Allen & Unwin English-Danish volumes! Allen & Unwin state (February 1966) that the Danish-English volume is almost sold out, and that the English-Danish was sold out some time ago; they are now importing from Gyldendal. Nevertheless purchasers should make sure they are getting the latest editions.

BOLBJERG, A. Dansk-engelsk ordbog. 4. udg. Copenhagen, Berlingske Forlag, 1963. 558 p. (Berlingske ordbøger). D.kr. 19.75.

Designed for Danish users, it does not indicate genders and plurals of nouns or parts of verbs. Apart from that, it is a sound medium-sized dictionary, well revised and excellently printed. There are over 50,000 entry-words and compounds.

The companion volume is:

HAISLUND, N., and SALLING, A.   Engelsk-dansk ordbog.   3. stærkt forøgede udg.   Copenhagen, Berlingske Forlag, 1964.   564 p. bibliog. (Berlingske ordbøger).   D.kr. 19.75.

Previous edition 1950. Much revised and enlarged. Gives irregular plurals of English nouns and parts of verbs, and pronunciation, using Otto Jespersen's system. The phonetic transcription has been revised and brought into line with Daniel Jones' *English pronouncing dictionary*, 1963 edition.

English proper names and their pronunciation, and Abbreviations, formerly Appendices 1 and 2, are now incorporated in the body of the text. Appendix 3: English irregular verbs, is retained, and the rather dated Appendix 4: How does one write a letter in English? has been dropped.

SCHIBSBYE, K., and KOSSMANN, J., ed.   Dansk-engelsk ordbog.   Copenhagen, Politiken, 1957.   565 p.   (Politikens blå ordbøger).   D.kr. 16.25.

— — Engelsk-dansk ordbog.   Copenhagen, Politiken, 1957.   556 p. (Politikens blå ordbøger).   D.kr. 16.25.

A pair of dictionaries in the long series of excellent popular reference books published by the Copenhagen daily *Politiken*. They are intended primarily for Danes, but the editors hope others will find them useful. Clearly printed. The Danish-English volume does not give pronunciations, genders, inflexions, etc. for Danish words, but the pronunciation of English words *is* given in the companion volume. About 50,000 entry words.

(Gyldendal publish, in addition to the major works and the medium-sized 'red' series mentioned above, a 'blue' series of dictionaries (Gyldendals blå ordbøger). The publishers state that these are intended for first-year English studies in Danish schools. The Danish-English volume is by Evald Munck (312 p.), and the English-Danish by E. Høegh Nielsen (260 p.). Both appeared in 1963, and cost D.kr. 14.75 and 12.75 respectively. Not seen.)

Høsts engelsk-danske og dansk-engelske lommeordbog.   3. nye [udvidede] og stærkt reviderede udg. ved David Hohnen.   Copenhagen, Høst, 1966.   512 p.   D.kr. 7.75.

First published 1930; new, revised and enlarged edition by C. V. Løye, 1945. Includes some phrases, elements of English grammar (in Danish), elements of Danish grammar (in English; 4 pages); also useful note on the new orthography of 1948, in later printings. (Latest ed. not seen).

Pocket dictionary for the traveller; not for the serious student or the library.

Synonyms

NÆSTED, H. Engelsk-dansk Synonym-ordbog: engelske Synonymer
forklaret paa Dansk. Udarbejdet paa Grundlag af J. A. Afzelius
Svensk-engelsk synonymbok. Copenhagen, Grafisk Forlag, 1946 (4th
corrected reprint 1964). 531 p. D.kr. 32.50.

> Arranged under some 850 Danish headings, each of which may be a single
> Danish word with several possible translations, or a group of Danish partial
> or near synonyms. Under each heading the various English translations are
> given, with many examples of usage.
> Intended for Danes, it is also valuable for English-speaking students who
> are past the beginners' stages. Its use is facilitated by indexes of English and
> Danish words, with approximately 4,000 and 1,200 entries respectively.

Technical Dictionaries

WARRERN, A. Dansk-engelsk teknisk ordbog. 3. udg. Copenhagen, J. Fr. Clausen, 1964. 288 p. D.kr. 52.–

> 1st ed. 1949, 2nd ed. 1957. 35,000+ entry words. Gives translations, but
> neither pronunciations nor grammatical information about the words. No
> tables; not illustrated. Completely reset since its first appearance; revised
> layout made possible substantial increase in content without enlarging the
> physical size of the book.
> The companion volume is:

— Engelsk-dansk teknisk ordbog. 4. udg. Copenhagen, J. Fr.
Clausen, 1965. 291 p. D.kr. 52.–

FAROESE

LOCKWOOD, W. B. Introduction to modern Faroese. Copenhagen,
Munksgaard, 1955. xii, 244 p. (Færoensia: textus et investi-
gationes . . . v. 4). D.kr. 43.–. (reprinted 1964).

> A sound piece of work published for a learned society specialising in
> Faroese studies. Probably nothing else comparable and up-to-date available
> in English. Pronunciation (p. 5–27); Grammar (p. 28–157); Reader (p. 158–
> 200); Glossary (p. 201–44).

MODERN ICELANDIC

The position for students of Icelandic is not satisfactory. Of the
available grammars, that by Einarsson is very good, but also very

detailed, so that while it is indispensable for reference, it is not ideal for the beginner, who will have difficulty in picking out the essentials; Jónsson's primer is a better length for the beginner, but is now dated in its readings, and is said to have a somewhat peculiar vocabulary; and Glendening's book virtually ignores the spoken language, and is marred by some misprints. As far as dictionaries are concerned, there is great need for a good modern Icelandic-English work.

NOTE. Icelandic authors are entered below under their last names, English style, for convenience. In other catalogues, lists and bibliographies (especially those originating in Iceland) they may well appear under their first names (e.g. SNÆBJÖRN Jónsson, STEFÁN Einarsson), the last name being regarded as a patronymic rather than a surname.

GRAMMARS AND READERS

EINARSSON, S. Icelandic: grammar, texts, glossary. 2nd ed. Baltimore, Md., Johns Hopkins Press; London, Oxford University Press, 1949. xxxvii, 502 p. illus., maps, bibliog. 45s.

Originally designed for American officers going to Iceland in the 1940s. Because the grammatical treatment in Snæbjörn Jónsson's *Primer* is brief, in this work it was dealt with in considerable detail. The pronunciation is that of the Eastern region, but the Reykjavik (Southern) pronunciation is indicated where significantly different. Grammar: Pronunciation, using modified International Phonetic Alphabet (p. 1–31); Inflexions (p. 32–104); and Syntax (p. 105–80). Texts: I, Nos. 1–30, *Æfingar med málfrædi*, i.e., translation exercises, etc., on the preceding grammar, with vocabularies for each (p. 181–246); II, Nos. 31–72, *Daglegt líf og daglegt tal*, i.e., newspaper extracts, letters, conversations, folk tales (p. 247–93). Glossary (p. 297–502). The glossary, Icelandic-English only, gives details of noun declensions, parts of verbs, cross-references from inflected forms with different vowel stems, pronunciation and translation. There are also references to the syntax, but it is not a full index to the grammar.

First edition 1945 – still usable; 2nd ed. has very slight changes.

By far the fullest and best grammar of the modern language for English-speaking students; first-class by any standards. A note in the book states that a copy should go with every Linguaphone Icelandic set sold.

GLENDENING, P. J. T. Teach yourself Icelandic. London, English Universities Press, 1961. xvii, 190 p. 10s. 6d.

For beginners wishing to acquire a reading knowledge of the language. Because few people can hear Icelandic spoken, the section on pronunciation has been kept to a minimum. Each lesson deals with a particular grammatical point; there is no attempt to minimise difficulties of the many inflected forms. Looks like conventional Latin grammar, but very clearly printed. Each lesson has vocabulary and 2 exercises for Icelandic-English and English-Icelandic translation. Book comes to life in examples of usage quoted and in exercises. "The pen of my aunt" is not to be found; "He was blind drunk" is! Pronunciation (p. xi–xvii); Lessons (p. 1–108); idioms and proverbs (p. 109–17); appendix of declensions and conjugations (p. 118–27); key to exercises (p. 128–37); English-Icelandic vocabulary (p. 138–55); Icelandic-English vocabulary of c. 1,750 entry words, indicating conjugations and declensions (p. 155–90).

JÓNSSON, S.   A primer of modern Icelandic.   Oxford, Clarendon Press, 1927.   ix, 283 p.   25s.

Prior to the publication of Stefán Einarsson's and Glendening's books, the only grammar of any note for English-speaking students. It is still in print and is perfectly sound, though rather formal and inevitably a bit dated in some of its readings, etc. Pronunciation (p. 1–11); Grammar (p. 12–67); exercises and dialogues (p. 68–122); Icelandic readings (p. 123–91); vocabularies (p. 192–204, 205–83). Can still be justifiably added to stock, and should be placed in reserve rather than withdrawn, despite the existence of the later works.

SHEPSTONE, J. G.   How to say it in Icelandic: an English-Icelandic phrase-book enabling the English-speaking visitor to get along in Iceland without any previous knowledge of the country's national language. Reykjavík, Leiftur, 1955. 38 p. (London, Bailey Bros. & Swinfen.   7s. 6d.).

Purely a phrase-book. No grammar. Very simple pronunciation.

GRAMOPHONE RECORDS

LINGUAPHONE. Sixteen 78 r.p.m. records, £18 18s. Course prepared by Stefán Einarsson. The set of books for the course includes Einarsson's *Icelandic: grammar, texts, glossary.* Recorded about 1947 by 5 Icelandic actors, teachers and authors.

RADIO COURSES

The Icelandic state radio does not broadcast an "Icelandic by radio" course for English-speaking listeners. (Information from the Embassy in London.)

DICTIONARIES

BOGASON, S. Ö. English-Icelandic dictionary. Rekjavík, Isafoldar-prentsmiðja, 1966. [8], 862 p.

First published 1952. 1966 ed. reset as far as p. 352 (i.e., Part I, A-I), but the remainder is reprinted unchanged. There is an increase of 16 pages in the first part compared with the 1952 ed.

Gives pronunciation of English entry words (International Phonetic Alphabet). Does not make cross references from parts of English strong verbs, etc., but has a table of English irregular verbs at the end.

Expensive, but by far the best English-Icelandic dictionary. Recommended by Glendening, who states that Cleasby and Vigfússon's *Icelandic-English dictionary* should be used in lieu of any comparable Icelandic-English dictionary.

CLEASBY, R., and VIGFÚSSON, G. An Icelandic-English dictionary, initiated by Richard Cleasby, subsequently revised, enlarged and completed by Gudbrand Vigfusson. 2nd ed. with a supplement by Sir William A. Craigie, containing many additional words and references. Oxford, Clarendon Press, 1957. xlv, 833 p. £5 15s.

1st ed. 1874. "Though the Dictionary is mainly intended for the old authors, both in prose and poetry, it endeavours to embrace an account of the whole language, old and new" – from the introduction. A major work of scholarship, it is very full and detailed, giving pronunciations, parts of speech, inflexions, etc., and translations with innumerable examples of usage and quotations from Icelandic literature, with their sources. Contains in addition Outlines of grammar (p. xv–xxxvi) – a considerable amount of information in 20 pages of small type, useful for reference but hardly to be recommended as a student's text; Alphabetical list of verbs, giving their principal parts (p. xxxvii–xlvi); Alphabetical list of irregular forms, (i) verbal, (ii) nominal, referring back to infinitive and nom. sing. forms respectively (p. xlii–xliv); Errata (p. 770); Addenda (p. 771–9); and Supplement I (p. 781–833).

Bearing in mind that this is not in the first instance a dictionary of modern Icelandic, and that Cleasby began work on it in 1840, it is nevertheless still of great value. Moreover, for a quarto volume containing a vast amount of information, it is modestly priced.

TAYLOR, A. R. Icelandic-English pocket dictionary. Reykjavik, Orðabókaútgafa, 1956. 172 p. I.kr. 53.–

A minute (16mo) dictionary, containing some 4,500 words. Has note on approximate pronunciation. Gives parts of speech, genders of nouns, a few plural forms, and translation. Brief table of some strong verbs and short note on noun declensions. Copy seen priced 12s. 6d.

There is a companion English-Icelandic volume by the same author, with some 5,500 words (208 p. I.kr. 53.–; copy seen priced 16s.). Pocket dictionaries for the traveller, not for the library or serious student. Expensive for their size.

ZOËGA, G. T.   Ensk-islenzk orðabok.   3rd ed.   Reykjavík, Bókaver-slun Sigurðar Kristjánssonar, 1951.   xi, 712 p.   (London, Bailey Bros. & Swinfen.   48s.).

   1951 is reprint date. Preface dated 1932. Basically older still. Introduction in Icelandic only. Gives English pronunciation.

   Zoëga also prepared the corresponding Icelandic–English dictionary, *Islenzk-ensk orðabók* (3rd ed., same publisher, 1942, 632 p. Postscript is dated 1922). Gives genders, declensions and conjugations of Icelandic words. Out of print for some time, and a new edition (or reprint?) is supposed to be in preparation. Both volumes are now very dated in content and appearance.

NORWEGIAN

Prior to 1907 Norwegian *riksmål* was virtually the same as Danish, as far as orthography was concerned. There have been three fairly drastic spelling reforms, in 1907, 1917 and 1938, to bring the spelling into line with Norwegian pronunciation, and, latterly, to bring the two kinds of Norwegian into line with one another. Students should not use textbooks published before 1938; when they have mastered the current forms they can take note of the earlier ones. Various stages of the language's development are to be seen in books, and in the names of firms, shops, etc. A rough guide to the dates of books on and in Norwegian can be made by checking the numbers 7, 20, 30 and 40, and also the method used for 21, 22, 23, etc. The old numerals were close to the Danish: 7 – *syv*, 20 – *tyve*, 30 – *tredve* (Danish *tredive*), 40 – *førr* (Danish *fyrre*, pronounced rather similarly). The newer 7 and 20 are *sju* and *tjue*, and 30 and 40 follow Swedish (and English) practice, *tretti* and *førti*. Other numbers were compounded in the Danish (and old-fashioned English) manner: *en og tyve*, *to og tyve*, one and twenty, two and twenty, etc. The modern practice is the reverse, *tjue en*, *tjue to*, etc. However, it would be wrong to make too much of this. Leaving aside official and educational works, the form and style of Norwegian may well reflect the generation (and preferences) of the author, and the type of Norwegian he was taught at school, rather than the official norm at the time of publication.

A masterly, non-partisan and very readable account of modern Norwegian language politics has recently been published:

HAUGEN, E. Language conflict and language planning: the case of modern Norwegian. Cambridge, Mass., Harvard University Press, 1966. xvi, 373 p. illus., bibliog. 80s.

While its detail would probably confuse the beginner, it should on no account be overlooked by the more advanced student.

GRAMMARS AND READERS

ABRAHAMSEN, S. Say it in Norwegian. New York, Dover; London, Constable, 1957. 142 p. 6s.

Author is Norwegian-born American. A phrase book, with no grammar. May have useful supplementary phrases for persons learning language with a grammar. Pronunciations are rather crude and assume an American readership. Orthography of 1938. 7=*Sju* (or *syv*); 20=*Tjue* (or *tyve*); 21=*Tjue en;* 30=*Tretti*. Not recommended for libraries.

BERULFSEN, B. Norwegian grammar. Oslo, Aschehoug, 1963. [6], 81 p. N.kr. 13.50.

First produced in mimeographed form in 1957. Following the further adjustment to (and stabilization of?) Norwegian orthography in 1959, the work was brought into line and prepared for printing.

Brief reference grammar in English (plus the Norwegian names of grammatical terms). Systematic review of *bokmål* in its most traditional form, dealing with the chief aspects of morphology and syntax. Introduction on phonetics, intonation and accent. High frequency words and phrases used for illustrations. No exercises; no index; no vocabularies.

A handy supplementary work for reference, produced to assist the teaching of courses in Norwegian at Oslo.

HAUGEN, E. Beginning Norwegian: a grammar and reader. 3rd ed., completely rev. London, Harrap, 1957. xii, 226 p. 15s.

First published 1938 (nevertheless, with 1917 orthography). Author is Professor of Scandinavian, Harvard University. A very good traditional grammar, written in the first instance for American students. 3rd ed. has 1938 orthography, and the chapters on pronunciation and spelling have been completely re-written. For students with no previous knowledge of Norwegian, either for class use or private study. Vocabulary restricted to some 800 of the 1,000 most used Norwegian words.

Introduction, giving outline of Norwegian linguistic history (p. 1–8); Pronunciation in fair detail (p. 8–18); Phrasing (p. 18–23); Spelling and pronunciation (p. 23–30); grammar exercises and readings (p. 33–208); Norwegian-English (p. 209–21) and English-Norwegian (p. 222–4) vocabularies; index (p. 225–6). Each 'lesson' is in 5 sections: 1. a passage in Norwegian for reading and translation; 2. Questions in Norwegian on the passage, to be answered in Norwegian; 3. Words and expressions to be learnt; 4. 'Observe the following examples' (i.e. specimens demonstrating grammatical points relevant to the passage, questions on the examples, then grammatical rules stated formally); 5. Drills on the foregoing. Norwegian-English vocabulary gives genders of nouns, including those now regarded as feminine, irregular plurals, and parts of verbs. Pronunciation is given when spelling is not wholly phonetic, and reference is made to the lesson in which each word or phrase is first used. English-Norwegian vocabulary only lists words used in English-Norwegian exercises that are not listed in the corresponding lesson vocabularies.

The entry in Harrap's catalogue has a note stating that a tape recording of the text is available from Magnetic Tracks Ltd. Unfortunately this firm has left its last known address in Vauxhall Bridge Road, London; Harrap's do not know where it has gone (August 1966).

HAUGEN, E.   Reading Norwegian.   New York, F. S. Crofts [*afterwards* Appleton-Century-Crofts], 1940.   vii, 200 p.   illus. $3.25.

Intended to expand the vocabulary and idiom acquired by those who have mastered *Beginning Norwegian*, and to give an idea of Norwegian life, beliefs, outlook, etc. The passages are selected because they are easy and interesting rather than great literature. Texts add some 700 words to the 800 in *Beginning Norwegian*. Some re-writing found necessary; rare and unusual expressions have been pruned. If they are essential to the story and the atmosphere, they are explained in footnotes, and are omitted from the vocabulary. 1938 spelling reforms used as basis; compiler tried to establish a norm not too far removed from the traditional.

I: *Eventyr og slikt* – folk tales by Asbjørnsen and Moe (p. 2–28); II: *Peik* – story about an orphaned South Coast boy in Oslo, by Barbra Ring (p. 30–93); III: *Folk forteller* – short stories and sketches (p. 96–119); IV: *Fra land og strand* – the variety of Norwegian life and landscape (p. 122–156); V: *Til Amerika* – the emigrants (p. 158–170). Vocabulary (p. 171–200), prefaced by note on 1938 spelling reforms as used in the book. Gives genders, plurals, parts of verbs, etc., and pronunciation, using modified International Phonetic Alphabet.

HAUGEN, E., and CHAPMAN, K. G.   Spoken Norwegian.   Revised. New York, [London], Holt, Rinehart & Winston, [1964].   xviii, 416, xli p.   illus.   60s.

First prepared in 1944 as part of a language project for U.S. forces abroad where they would find themselves without teachers but with a limitless supply of native speakers. Published for civilian use in 1947, it reflected the masculine, military situation in which it was conceived.

Now totally revised for peacetime situation in which most of the tuition is given by teachers in classrooms, and native speakers are not present or only present in the form of recordings. Consists of 25 lessons, each divided into two approximately equal halves. Each half begins with a dramatised conversation, with English translation and a guide to the pronunciation of the passage. New material is introduced in each passage, and is further developed in *repetisjon* – elements to be combined to form different sentences, *spørsmål* – questions in Norwegian, *samtaleøvelse* – suggestions in English for conversation in Norwegian, grammar – notes and comments etc. in English, *La oss lytte* – "Let us listen" i.e. further conversations, and finally references to passages in the companion reader (see below). Most of *La oss lytte*, and various other sections have been recorded; the recorded sections are specially marked. Every 4 or 5 lessons there is a vocabulary list, simply consisting of Norwegian words grouped according to their part of speech and referring to the lesson and section in which they occur. There is a Norwegian-English vocabulary at the end (p. iii–xxxv), giving pronunciation, parts of speech, genders and plurals, etc., English translation and a reference to the lesson and section in which the word first appears. Index of topics (a) grammar, and (b) pronunciation, at the end.

Very clearly printed and well set out; well illustrated. Up to date, fresh and lively, it deals with everyday situations. Authoritative and informative. By far the best book for class use, or for the individual with help from a Norwegian or the recordings. Also the most expensive of these textbooks.

The companion reader is:

CHAPMAN, K. G.   Basic Norwegian reader.   New York, London, Holt, Rinehart & Winston, [1966].   iv, 90, [17] p. illus.   30s.

The readings specified in lessons 11–25 of *Spoken Norwegian, Revised:* passages from 19th and 20th century authors. Some divided into two or three parts. Subject matter and vocabulary closely co-ordinated with relevant lesson. Mostly of high literary quality, but vocabulary content is the prime consideration. Also contains weather forecasts, two *nynorsk* poems and excerpts from Undset, Hamsun and Kielland in the orthography of their times. Marginal notes and footnotes on vocabulary: the former appear again or in *Spoken Norwegian, Revised*, and are included in the Norwegian-English vocabulary at the end of the book; the latter are peculiar to the passage in question. Has questions on the extracts for oral or written answer in Norwegian. Final vocabulary gives irregular pronunciations, grammatical details, translations, and reference to lesson and section in *S.N. c.* 1,300 entries (words and phrases). Fresh in content and appearance; well printed. Also expensive for its size.

HUGO'S LANGUAGE INSTITUTE.   Norwegian simplified: an easy and rapid self-instructor.   Standard ed.   London, the Institute, [1957].   160 p.   Also available in 2 paperback parts (6s. or 7s. 6d.).

Cover-title: *Hugo's Norwegian in three months.* For beginners. Standard Hugo layout: pronunciation (fair), then a series of lessons on various grammatical points, with exercises and phrases to illustrate usage and extend

vocabulary; imitated pronunciation and (intentionally) literal English translations. Half-way through the imitated pronunciations are omitted except
for new words, and later on the literal translations are omitted too. Finally
there are lists of irregular verbs, indispensable words, correspondence forms,
practical conversational phrases (12 double-column pages, with phrases in
no particular order) and 4 pages of commercial phrases and expressions.
(Even if it is useful to know the equivalent Norwegian commercialese, must
we perpetuate "I am in receipt of your letter of the 1st ult." and "Referring
to your favour of the 9th inst."?)

Better value than the Marlborough series in content and appearance, but
not a necessary purchase for libraries. Limited in scope; pronunciation needs
supplementing by listening to Norwegian, whatever the anonymous
compiler may claim.

Marlborough's Norwegian self-taught. . . .   7th ed., revised throughout by R. J. McClean.   London, Marlborough, [1939].   viii, 160 p.
5s.

The basic work is very old, but the name of the reviser, better known as
the author of the "Teach yourself" *Swedish*, should be some indication
that the current edition is much improved. However, not recommended for
libraries, which should stock Haugen, and Marm and Sommerfelt, in the
first instance.

Marm, I., and Sommerfelt, A.   Teach yourself Norwegian: a book
of self-instruction in the Norwegian riksmål.   London, English
Universities Press, 1943.   xii, 13–268 p.   7s. 6d.

Marm was Lecturer in Norwegian at the University of London and has
written the grammar; Sommerfelt, Professor of Linguistics at Oslo, has
written the introduction and the chapters on pronunciation. For beginners.
Authoritative and reliable; comprehensive and thorough up to stage reached
(i.e. subordinate clauses and word order). Sounds in Norwegian (in considerable, rather forbidding, detail), with modified International Phonetic
Alphabet (p. 13–58). Grammar, with exercises for translation both ways
(p. 58–184); translations of exercises (p. 185–213); appendix: irregular verbs;
vocabulary, each way; 7-item bibliography of dictionaries, grammars, etc.
(p. 214–68). The orthography of 1938 is used, and the introduction outlines
Norwegian linguistic history and the three spelling reforms. The existence
of feminine forms is recognised, but for the beginner's sake *en* is used instead
of the feminine indefinite article *ei* throughout, and the feminine definite
article *-a* is only used occasionally. 7=*sju, syv*; 20=*tjue, tyve*; 30=*tredve*;
40=*førti* or *førr*; 51=*en og femti*.

Typography rather dull. Conventional procedure of working through each
grammatical topic in order, with illustrative exercises. Norwegian-English
vocabulary of *c.* 1,100 words. Not as attractive, nor as modern in its approach
as Haugen's books, but sound and inexpensive.

POPPERWELL, R. G.   The pronunciation of Norwegian.   Cambridge, University Press, 1963.   xii, 229 p. diagrs., bibliog.   42*s*.

An advanced work following the methods of Professor Daniel Jones. Accompanied by a 7″ 45 r.p.m. record spoken by T. Støverud. Definitely not for beginners.

GRAMOPHONE RECORDS AND TAPES

CONVERSA-PHONE 'C' course.   One 10″ 33⅓ r.p.m. record.

HAUGEN (Magnetic Tracks Ltd).   Tape recording for *Beginning Norwegian*.   No details available (see p. 146).

HAUGEN and CHAPMAN (Holt, Rinehart & Winston).   Recorded sections of *Spoken Norwegian*.

Manual and key, 10*s*., plus *either* ten 12″ 33⅓ r.p.m. records, £24, *or* fourteen 7″ 1,200 foot double track reels, 7½ i.p.s., £28.

N.B. The tapes are available on a "loan for duplication" basis in the U.S.A.; this does *not* apply in the U.K.

LINGUAPHONE.   Standard Linguaphone set of textbooks and *either* sixteen 7″ 45 r.p.m. records, *or* two 5″ double-track reels, 3¾ i.p.s. £18 18*s*. in either form.

Prepared by an impressive list of authorities, including Berulfsen, Sommerfelt and Støverud, who figure in this chapter.

POPPERWELL (Cambridge, University Press).   The record accompanying *The pronunciation of Norwegian* is included in the price of the book and is not charged separately. T. Støverud, who made the recording, is W. P. Ker Lecturer in Norwegian at University College, London.

NOTE. Bjarne Berulfsen and Philip Boardman have produced a tape-recorded course in elementary Norwegian which is used at the International Summer School of the University of Oslo. The textbook is stencilled, but may be printed later and made generally available.

RADIO COURSES

Norsk Rikskringkasting does not now broadcast a "Norwegian by radio" course. This has been done in the past; future plans are unknown. (Information from another source: N. R. did not reply to enquiry.)

DICTIONARIES

Standard Orthography

There is no official Norwegian work corresponding to *Svenska Akademiens ordlista* or *Retskrivningsordbog udgivet af Dansk Sprognævn* (see pp. 170 and 140). While this may not surprise anyone who has studied Norwegian linguistic affairs, it is still regrettable from the student's point of view. Fortunately Haugen's Norwegian-English dictionary (see below) gives a great deal of information concerning inflexions, etc. Nevertheless there are times when one wants a more handy guide to the complications of *bokmål* and *nynorsk*, and the permitted alternative forms, etc., within each, with their various inflexions.

The fullest dictionary of this type is *Tanums store rettskrivningsordbok: bokmål* by J. Sverdrup and M. Sandvei (revised ed. Oslo, Tanum, 1961. xx, 460 p. N.kr. 33.75) which has some introductory pages on spelling, obligatory and optional forms, capitalisation, punctuation, etc. The dictionary proper has a few definitions, but in the main indicates spellings with all permitted forms, compounds, inflexions, stress. There are also many names of places, organisations, etc., with derived adjectival forms, etc.

Apart from this there are some dictionaries for converting one form of Norwegian into the other (e.g. L. Heggstad's *Fornorskings ordbok: bokmål-nynorsk*), and a prodigious output of smaller lists, mostly for use in schools. Aschehoug publishes a set of six small cheap lists which set out the different varieties of current Norwegian systematically:

Bokmål 1, by B. Berulfsen and E. Lundeby.
Nynorsk 1, by I. Eskeland and I. Torvik.
Bokmål 2, by B. Berulfsen.
Nynorsk 2, by I. Eskeland.
Bokmål 3, by H. Dalene.
Nynorsk 3, by H. Dalene.

The first of these is a 'complete' list, giving all forms and inflexions used in *bokmål. Bokmål* 2 is a 'traditional' list, giving the forms normally used by *bokmål* speakers, and excluding more modern innovations which have not been generally accepted; *Bokmål* 3 goes to the other extreme and lists the most recent forms designed to bring *bokmål* and *nynorsk* closer together. The lists use the orthography of 1938, with the 1959 amendments where appropriate. The three *nynorsk* lists follow the same pattern. The books are all about 100–120 pages long, and cost N.kr. 7.– each for *Bokmål* 1 and *Nynorsk* 1, 6.65 each for *Bm* 2 and *Nn* 2, and 7.15 each for *Bm* 3 and *Nn* 3.

It is worth noting that Dag Gundersen's *Norsk ordbok: bokmål og nynorsk* (Oslo, Universitetsforlaget, 1966. 247 p.) includes both forms (cf. Haugen's dictionary again): most Norwegian dictionaries have one *or* the other. Gundersen gives the words with their inflexions, and distinguishes those words or forms which are used only in *bokmål* or in *nynorsk*. It is not, however, a translating dictionary.

[I am indebted to dr. phil. Bjarne Berulfsen for much of the information given above. A.G.C.]

Translating Dictionaries (in descending order of size)

HAUGEN, E., ed.   Norwegian English dictionary: a pronouncing and translating dictionary of modern Norwegian (bokmål and nynorsk), with a historical and grammatical introduction.   Oslo, Universitetsforlaget; Madison, University of Wisconsin Press, [1965]. 500 p. bibliog.   N.kr. 97.50; 95s.

Also with Norwegian titlepage. Associate editors: Kenneth G. Chapman, Dag Gundersen, Jørgen Rischel.

Intended primarily as a tool to aid the learning of Norwegian by American students. The glosses have an American-English style as a consequence of this. With this sole reservation as far as the British user is concerned, this dictionary can be whole-heartedly recommended as one of the best available; moreover it is remarkably cheap. (It was produced with financial assistance from the American government.) Less elaborate than Vinterberg and Bodelsen's *Dansk-engelsk ordbog*, it is probably the best Scandinavian-English dictionary as far as the English-speaking user is concerned. There are 60,000+ entries in 452 triple-columned pages. Genders, declensions, etc., are indicated, and also pronunciation. *Bokmål* and *nynorsk* forms are listed in one alphabet, the main article being under the current *bokmål* form when there is no question of totally different words or meanings. Moreover, the work is richly provided with cross-references from the many variant spellings that have been used at one time or another.

To compress so much material into 500 pages a considerable amount of abbreviation has been used; the reader must study the first 45 pages carefully. Preface (p. 9–11). Introduction: 1. Instructions to users (p. 13–19); 2. Historical background of Norwegian – includes information on the two kinds of Norwegian and a paradigm of standard declensions, conjugations and comparisons (p. 20–34); 3. Guide to pronunciation (p. 34–42). 4. Reference bibliography (p. 43–45).

There is at present no comparable English-Norwegian dictionary. The next two are the fullest available:

GLEDITSCH, T., and others. English-Norwegian dictionary, by Th. Gleditsch, Margit Sahlgaard Borresen, Birger Krogh Johanssen. London, Allen & Unwin, 1950. vii, 855 p. 25s.

Reissue of the 2nd Norwegian edition, *Engelsk-norsk ordbok* (Oslo, Aschehoug, 1948). 1st edition, 1911. Revised with considerable difficulty during and just after the Second World War.

Gives English pronunciations (following Daniel Jones); pronunciations of derivatives only given if there is a shift of accent or quantity, etc. Adverbs formed regularly from adjectives are generally omitted, as are many substantives formed by the addition of -er or -ing to a verbal stem. There is no indication of Norwegian genders, plurals, etc. Some English abbreviations given in their alphabetical place (some wrong). There is a considerable number of examples of usage (sometimes dated).

Allen & Unwin report verbally that they still have stocks which will last a year or two; as far as Aschehoug are concerned the work is out of print and superseded by:

BJERKE, L., and SØRAAS, H. English-Norwegian dictionary. London, Harrap, 1964. xi, 562 p. 50s.

Reissue of *Engelsk-norsk ordbok* (Oslo, Aschehoug, 1963. N.kr. 59.50). While this work is undoubtedly more up-to-date than Gleditsch, it is also unfortunately only about two-thirds the size, the number of examples of usage particularly being considerably reduced. The dictionary may justifiably be purchased, but owners of Gleditsch should not discard their copies of the older work. Indicates neuter (*intetkjønn*) nouns by (n); others are assumed to be common gender (*fælleskjønn*). Gives pronunciation of English words. Dialect and old-fashioned words excluded; modern terms and slang included.

CHRISTOPHERSEN, R., and SCAVENIUS, H. Norsk-engelsk. Revidert utgave. 4. opplag. Oslo, Gyldendal Norsk Forlag, 1966. 341 p. (Gyldendals blå ordbøker). N.kr. 18.90.

Originally published in this edition (6th?) in 1954. Based on edition of 1949. Copyright dates, 1933 and 1947. Earlier editions by Scavenius alone. Standard medium-sized dictionary for Norwegians. No pronunciation, genders, plurals, etc. for Norwegian words. Attempts to be a dictionary of current usage, omitting old-fashioned and dated expressions from successive editions. Gives many examples of usage. Appendix of English irregular verbs. Excellent printing. Frequent 'editions' (*opplag*) are mainly reprints with small alterations. Not exhaustive, but very good value. The corresponding English-Norwegian dictionary is:

BERULFSEN, B. Engelsk-norsk. 14. opplag. Oslo, Gyldendal Norsk Forlag, 1965. 353 p. (Gyldendals blå ordbøker). N.kr. 18.90.

This is the edition of 1947 which introduced the orthography of 1938. Reprinted with numerous amendments since. 1st ed., 1933. Pronunciation of English words. Intended for Norwegians, it often gives several Norwegian words for each English entry-word, but gives no indication of the differences between the various Norwegian words. Printing again excellent.

The two volumes are also available bound together (45s.). This format, issued with an additional English title-page bearing Basil Blackwell's imprint, was first published as a photographic reprint of the 1933 Norwegian-English and 1938 English-Norwegian volumes for the benefit of Norwegians in this country during the war. Paper and printing were abominable, and copies were still being sold after the war (there were several reprints). Now the new Norwegian printings are bound together, but the printings (and sometimes editions) may not be the latest available as separate volumes. Let the buyer beware.

This pair of dictionaries deals with *bokmål*. A companion volume in the same series is:

HALLAND, N. Engelsk-nynorsk. Oslo, Gyldendal Norsk Forlag, 1955. 330 p. (Gyldendals ordbøker). N.kr. 18.90.

There is no corresponding *nynorsk-engelsk* dictionary.

JORGENSON, T., and GALDAL, P. Norwegian-English school dictionary. Rev. ed. [Northfield, Minn.], St. Olaf College Press, 1955. 448 p. $7.50.

1st ed. 1943. Revised edition has alterations in some 4,000 entries. *c.* 31,000 entries altogether. Simple definitions, comparatively few examples of usage but being designed for English-speaking students it gives all genders, plurals, etc., for the Norwegian entry words. Clearly printed. Far from exhaustive, but worth considering for the student and for lending library stock, though a bit expensive at about £3.

BJORGE, J. H. B. Engelsk-amerikansk-norsk ordbok. Oslo, Fabritius, 1959 [i.e. 1960]. 398 p. N.kr. 22.–

Not seen. *c.* 25,000 entry words plus compounds, derived forms, etc. List of 1,300 proper names with their pronunciation.

GUY, W. Norsk-engelsk ordbok for det praktiske liv. Oslo, Gyldendal Norsk Forlag, 1953. 292 p. N.kr. 30.25.

For Norwegians, especially for shops, firms and commercial colleges. Does not give genders, plurals, etc. Good within its stated limitations (not, however, a technical dictionary solely consisting of terms for goods, economics and business methods).

DIETRICHSON, J. W., and ØVERLAND, O. Engelsk-norsk, norsk-engelsk. Oslo, Gyldendal Norsk Forlag, 1965. 448 p. (Gyldendals lommeordbøker). N.kr. 10.–

Pocket dictionary. Also issued by Blackwell with English title-page (16s.; B65–7542).

MYKLESTAD, J. M., and SØRAAS, H. Engelsk-norsk og norsk-engelsk. Oslo, Damm, 1961. 345 p. (Damms lommeordbøker). N.kr. 8.50.

Pocket dictionary; useful for the tourist at a loss for the odd word. Not for the serious student, nor for libraries.

Idioms

FOLLESTAD, S. Engelske idiomer: ord og vendinger for muntlig og skriftlig bruk. Oslo, Fabritius, 1962. 512 p. N.kr. 48.–

An alphabetical listing of Norwegian idiomatic expressions with their English equivalents and sentences illustrating usage. Norwegian catchword index (p. 499–512). No English index.

Technical Dictionaries

ANSTEINSSON, J. English-Norwegian technical dictionary. The 3rd revised ed., by Alexander T. Andreassen. Trondheim, F. Brun, 1966. [8], 511 p. N.kr. 98.75.

Previous ed. 1950; 442 p.

Standard technical dictionary by the late librarian of the Norwegian Technological University in Trondheim. Clear layout and printing. For the English entry words it gives parts of speech, accentuation and also pronunciation when not straightforward. Introductory pages deal with the use of the dictionary (in parallel columns, English and Norwegian) – grammatical notes, etc. 6 tables at the end (p. 491–510): Abbreviations; Weights and measures; Greek alphabet, with mathematical and scientific meanings of the characters; Chemical elements, with symbols and constants; Paper sizes; and Norwegian irregular verbs.

The companion volume is:

— Norwegian-English technical dictionary. Trondheim, F. Brun, 1954. [7], 327 p. N.kr. 51.–

Produced under the auspices of the Norwegian Council for Technical Terminology. This volume *does* give the genders of Norwegian nouns, etc. Reprinted 1963. The publisher writes (March 1967) that there have been difficulties over the revision of these volumes. It is not known who will revise the Norwegian-English dictionary, or when.

SWEDISH

Spelling reform. Swedish last had a major spelling reform in 1906. The principal changes were that *hv*, *fv*, and *f*, when pronounced *v*, were replaced by *v* (e.g., *öfver* became *över*), and *-dt* was replaced by *-t* or *-tt*.

Written and spoken forms. Swedish is a language with several styles, of varying degrees of formality. The spoken language in particular differs considerably from the written norm. Modern textbooks tend to emphasise the colloquial forms, but many teach the written forms and draw attention to the colloquial ones by means of notes. A number of changes have been accepted in the written language, bringing it closer to everyday speech, e.g. the abandonment of plural verb forms, but this is a slow process. *Any textbook which teaches the plural forms of verbs, and states either directly or by implication that all the pronouns, auxiliary verbs and many other common words* (e.g. det, god, med, till, och, dag, bliva, giva) *are pronounced regularly according to their spellings, is definitely out of date and misleading to the student.*

Modern textbooks and recordings and their evaluation. The position has been transformed in recent years by the activities of the Institute for English-speaking Students of the University of Stockholm (IES). Several excellent textbooks have been produced, and they are being steadily revised and improved in the light of teaching experience at IES. The books are lively, modern in their approach, and attractively produced, and are (at the beginner's level) carefully integrated with one another. Moreover, tape and disc recordings have been made to accompany several of them. These books have been listed below as a group in systematic order.

The Institute has prepared duplicated lists of materials for the study of Swedish, covering a far wider range and in greater detail than can be attempted here. A new project which began in 1966 concerns the evaluation of all materials for teaching Swedish to foreigners. Each item will be reported on by two or three experts. A standard questionnaire has been produced enumerating a large number of headings under which information or opinions are required. It may be some time before the results of this work are generally available, but they will certainly be thorough and of the utmost value. The project is being undertaken by *Samverkande Bildningsförbunden: Pedagogiska nämden: Arbetsgruppen för bedömning av läromaterial i svenska för utlänningar*. Teachers wanting further information about this, and about the work of IES, should write to the Institute at Sveavägen 166 XV, Stockholm VA. The present Director is fil. mag. fru Elizabeth Brodda. (Her predecessor, fru Higelin, who features prominently in the following pages, is now a Council of Europe adviser on the teaching of foreign languages.) Information about courses in Britain is available from the Swedish Institute, 49 Egerton Crescent, London, S.W.3. The Institute also carries stocks of nearly all the worth-while Swedish books listed below.

History. A useful and inexpensive supplementary work is:

BERGMAN, G. A short history of the Swedish language; translated and adapted by Francis P. Magoun, Helge Kökeritz. Stockholm, Swedish Institute for Cultural Relations. 1947. 106 p. illus., bibliog. [London, The Institute, 4s. 6d.].

Augustana Press. Half a dozen quite useful titles in this field were produced by the Augustana Book Concern or Augustana Press of Rock Island, Ill. In January 1963 this was merged with Muhlenberg Press to form Fortress Press, publishers of Lutheran books. The Swedish textbooks are still in print and are available from Fortress Press, 2900 Queen Lane, Philadelphia, Pa., 19129.

Swedish National Bibliography. Users of the bibliography, *Svensk bokförteckning*, should note that in the classified index there is a special section for Swedish for foreigners: Fct – Svenska för utlänningar.

GRAMMARS AND READERS

A. IES series, in progressive order.

NOTE. The following publications are not, with the exception of *Facktexter*, published by the Institute.
See also Higelin: *Svenska på svenska*, and Hildeman: *Svenskt uttal*, in the section "Gramophone Records and Tapes".

(1) *Books for beginners.*

HILDEMAN, N. G., and others. Learn Swedish: Swedish reader for beginners; edited by Nils-Gustav Hildeman and Ann-Mari Beite, with exercises and comments by Siv Higelin. 2nd ed. Stockholm, Almqvist & Wiksell, 1961. 189 p. illus. S.kr. 13.50.

1st ed. 1959. 28 texts (prose and conversational pieces), beginning with one illustrating Swedish pronunciation, the remainder illustrating one or more grammatical topics (p. 9–58); 28 sets of exercises and grammatical comments on the texts (p. 61–124); Swedish-English word list, chapter by chapter (p. 125–165); complete alphabetical Swedish-English word list, giving genders and plurals of nouns and parts of verbs, etc., and referring to the place where each word first appears (p. 166–188); Index of exercises and comments, i.e., index to grammatical topics (p. 189). Covers the 1,000 most-used words. Lessons sensible, everyday and humorous. Excellently and attractively printed and laid out. The text is available recorded on discs or tapes.

This basic work in the series is being revised. The new edition, when it appears (in 1967?), will be entirely in Swedish, and the 28 texts will be somewhat revised. It will be complemented by a book of exercises and vocabularies, to be produced in some 8 languages, including English.

The companion grammar is:

BEITE, A. M., and others. Basic Swedish grammar, [by] Ann-Mari Beite, Gertrud Englund, Siv Higelin, Nils-Gustav Hildeman; [edited by Ann-Mari Beite]. 2nd ed. Stockholm, Almqvist & Wiksell, 1964. 168 p. S.kr. 14.50.

A systematic grammar to aid the teaching of Swedish. Concentrates on the modern language, and gives simple and clear explanations rather than exhaustive analyses. Begins with short account of Swedish pronunciation and spelling (this must be supplemented by teacher or records). Then deals with the various parts of speech one by one, and ends with four pages on word order (p. 152-155). Appendix: The translation into Swedish of some English words that need special attention (p. 156–164). Index (p. 165–8).

Very clearly set out. Includes a certain amount of internal cross-referencing.

These two books cover the essentials of modern Swedish. For further exercise at this level there is:

HILDEMAN, N. G., and others. Practise Swedish: exercises in the Swedish language, by Nils-Gustav Hildeman, Per-Axel Hildeman and Ingemar Olsson. 2nd ed. Stockholm, Almqvist & Wiksell, 1963. 103 p. S.kr. 8.–

1st ed. 1957. *Learn Swedish* was published in 1959 (2nd ed. 1963), and the 2nd ed. of this exercise book has been totally revised to bring its vocabulary and grammatical content into line with the basic reader. It can, however, be used with other textbooks. It is designed for class instruction but can also be used for individual study together with its key (see below). Some exercises are best answered in writing, others orally. The exercises are grouped under word classes for simplicity, but the order in which they should be tackled is indicated. References are made to the relevant chapters of *Learn Swedish*. Vocabularies: English-Swedish (p. 80–97), Swedish-English (p. 97–103). The latter is much briefer, but there are more exercises for translation into Swedish than from it. Both vocabularies give plurals and genders of nouns, parts of verbs, etc.

Intended primarily for those who study *Practise Swedish* on their own, there is:

HILDEMAN, N. G., and OLSSON, I.   Key to "Practise Swedish: exercises in the Swedish language".   Stockholm, Almqvist & Wiksell, 1963.   56 p.   S.kr. 7.50.

As *Practise Swedish* is closely adjusted to *Learn Swedish*, the authors have tried to choose the translation or answer that would come naturally to those who have used *Learn Swedish*. Alternatives are of course permissible, but are rarely suggested in this key.

(2) *Intermediate reader.*

HIGELIN, S.   Från Fakiren till Jolo: lätta svenska texter för utlänningar: en antologi av Siv Higelin.   2. uppl.   Stockholm, Folkuniversitetets Förlag, [1963].   79 p. illus.   S.kr.7.50.

For class use or self-tuition. The student should know the 1,000 most common Swedish words and something of the structure of the language. The texts are 23 short pieces, mostly contributed by journalists to their regular columns. ('Fakir' and 'Jolo' are the pseudonyms used by the oldest and the most recent of the authors represented). After the first two, the texts are arranged in order of increasing difficulty. Finally there are notes on the authors, books they have written, and journals to which they contributed (p. 77–79). Tape recordings are available.

There are complementary vocabularies in four languages, including:

HIGELIN, S.   Vocabulary to "Från Fakiren till Jolo: easy Swedish texts for foreigners", compiled by Siv Higelin in collaboration with Lilly Lorenzén.   Stockholm, Folkuniversitetets Förlag, [1964]. [32] p.   S.kr.3.50.

Lists words in order of appearance in the texts, divided up by the page numbers of *F. F. t. J.* Gives genders and plurals of nouns, parts of verbs, etc. Omits 1,000 most common Swedish words (and their compounds when the meaning is obvious), words which are exactly identical in English and Swedish, and a number of others which are easily recognised.

(3) More advanced readers.

HIGELIN, S. Om Sverige och svenskarna: texter för undervisning i svenska för utlänningar utgivna i samarbete med Svenska Institutet. Med svensk-engelsk ordlista. Stockholm, Almqvist & Wiksell, 1964. 241 p. illus. (Nordiskt kursbibliotek). S.kr. 22.50.

A selection for continuation students who have had the equivalent of about 3 terms' studies, made at the request of the Swedish Institute on behalf of its lecturers. A provisional stencilled ed. was tried out by them and also by IES. The aim is to give a picture of various aspects of Sweden and Swedish society, etc., and to give examples of various literary styles – poetry and prose, belles lettres and factual writing.

10 *århundraden* – 10 centuries (p. 9–96); *Resa i Sverige* – travel in Sweden (p. 97–130); *Svenska i tal och skrift* – spoken and written Swedish (p. 131–141); *Det moderna samhället växer fram* – the modern society develops (p. 142–177). Notes (p. 179–192): these are arranged piece by piece, and also include, where appropriate, references to supplementary audio-visual aids. Swedish-English word list (p. 193–241), giving genders and plurals of nouns, parts of verbs, etc. It omits many compounds, listing only the constituent words, and also many noun and adjectival forms which are directly derived from a root word without significant change in meaning.

STOCKHOLM. UNIVERSITY. *Institute for English-speaking Students.* Fack-texter för undervisning i svenska språket. Stockholm, The Institute, 1964. 15 leaves. no price. [London, Swedish Institute, 5s.].

Single-sided A4 size duplicated sheets. 15 pieces on politics, economics, welfare, agriculture, etc. Complemented by two separate word lists, one piece by piece and the other alphabetical, of 22 and 23 similar sheets respectively.

B. Other Grammars and Readers.

BJÖRKHAGEN, I. Modern Swedish grammar. 9th ed., rev. Stockholm, Svenska Bökförlaget, Norstedts, 1962. xii, 200 p. S.kr. 12.50.

First published 1922. (Some early editions also appeared with a Sidgwick & Jackson imprint; this no longer applies.) The author, the first Lecturer in Swedish at University College, London, "has keenly felt the want of a satisfactory grammar for the use of Englishmen. Most of the existing grammars of this kind are so full of mistakes as to render them almost useless" (from Preface to early editions). Established as the standard formal grammar for serious students: for beginners and up to first-degree standard. Prefaced by long section on pronunciation which attempts to explain Swedish tone system as well as values of individual vowels and consonants. Each part of speech treated fairly fully, with examples and phrases, and with notes on differences between formal, literary usage and colloquial Swedish.

Whereas earlier editions were somewhat formal and dull in appearance, the 9th ed. is a great improvement, revised and partly re-written. The phonetic transcription has been modified to make it easier, and some grammatical rules have been re-worded. Not least, the printing is exceptionally good and the appearance of the text is no longer a disadvantage. Nevertheless it is beginning to show its age in its examples, etc. It is not indexed, and has no vocabularies. The companion work is:

BJÖRKHAGEN, I. First Swedish book. 9th rev. ed. Stockholm, Svenska Bökförlaget, Norstedts, 1963. 176 p. S.kr. 12.75.

First published 1923. A reader and book of exercises, arranged in the form of lessons illustrating points raised in *Modern Swedish grammar*. In the latest ed. the first part is largely re-written. The introductory texts, composed to facilitate learning the grammar, should also help tourists wishing to master common phrases. The pronunciation system has been slightly modified. With a few exceptions the formal plural forms of verbs have been replaced by the singular, in line with modern Swedish usage. 56 sections. Early sections have simple words and phrases and pronunciation, with notes, exercises for translation into Swedish, pronunciation practice and vocabularies. Later on there are *Olle och Svante på landet* from Geijerstam's *Mina pojkar*, divided into 26 sections for translation from Swedish, and *The giant's treasures*, a fairy tale divided into 10 sections for translation into Swedish. This is very charming, but not the material of modern daily life in Sweden. Swedish-English vocabulary (p. 151–168) of words appearing in p. 86–150, giving genders and plurals of nouns, parts of verbs, etc. The earlier sections have their own vocabularies, but many words appear in both. The list at the end has about 1,500 words. English-Swedish vocabulary (p. 169–174) of words appearing in p. 109–150. Well printed.

BOSTRÖM, S. Från av till över: övningsbok i svenska sp åket för utlänningar. Stockholm, Folkuniversitetets Förlag, 1959. 61 p. illus. S.kr. 4.–

Entirely in Swedish. The first half of the book deals with the Swedish prepositions in alphabetical order from *av* to *över* (hence the title), with many examples of usage, and also illustrations for prepositions connected with motion and place. The second half of the book consists of a series of illustrations of everyday scenes, with a vocabulary beneath each. This is intended as material for exercises. No translations are given. Clear, lively, inexpensive. Intended for class use with a teacher, though the individual student could make use of the first half when he is past the beginner's stage.

HARVEY, W. F., and CEDERLÖF, C. Swedish self-taught by the natural method, with phonetic pronunciation (Thimm's system). 4th ed., rev. and enl. by J. W. S. Lindahl. London, Marlborough, [1932]. viii, 132 p. (Marlborough's self-taught series). 5s.

For beginners. Alphabet with phonetic pronunciation (p. 1–3); spelling (p. 4); classified vocabularies (p. 5–74); elementary grammar, including usual tables of declensions and conjugations (p. 75–83); conversational phrases and sentences (p. 84–131). The whole is extremely dull and much of it dated. (Swedish aviation has progressed since 1932, and few English travellers will have to tell the Swedish cavalry to cease fire.) Although it is stated (p. 4) "As this manual is intended for practical purposes, all purely literary forms have been ignored, and the stilted pedantic and antiquated [Swedish] phraseology carefully avoided", one finds nonetheless *Du må kallas*, translated *Thou mayest be called*, and the imperative passive forms *kallas, kalloms, kallens*, translated *be thou called, let us be called, be ye called*, which are stilted, pedantic, antiquated and of no practical use. Not recommended.

HUGO'S LANGUAGE INSTITUTE. Swedish simplified: an easy and rapid self-instructor. London, the Institute, [c. 1959]. 6s. or 7s. 6d. (In 1 v. or 2 paper-back parts).

Cover title: *Hugo's Swedish in three months*. For general appreciation, see entry under HUGO in the Norwegian section. The commercial phrases are not quite so obnoxious in this volume! Uses singular forms of verbs and draws attention to the old plural ones. The imitated pronunciation seems to be too carefully true to the spelling, rather than to natural speech.

JAMSET, B. I. Basic Swedish. London, Hirschfeld, 1947. 48 p. 3s.

Very basic Swedish alphabet and crude pronunciation (p. 6–9); basic grammar (p. 10–19); classified vocabularies (p. 22–42); useful conversational phrases (p. 43–48). Intended as first aid for travellers. Nothing on sentence formation, word order, etc. Not recommended.

LAYCOCK, G. K., and ALLWOOD, M. S. Idiomatic English sentences with Swedish equivalents. 5th ed. Stockholm, Almqvist & Wiksell, 1964. 282 p. (in print, but price unknown at the moment.)

Copyright date 1945. Arranged under English catchwords, A/Z. Does not give pronunciations, and has no index and no vocabularies. For English words with two or more meanings there are several examples illustrating each, with Swedish equivalents. Both languages are printed as spoken, e.g. "I'd" and "We won't" instead of "I had" (or "I would") and "We will not". The informal 2nd pers. sing. pronoun *Du* is used throughout except where it would be obviously unsuitable.

LEANDER, B., and LEANDER, Å. Say it in Swedish. New York, Dover; London, Constable, 1954. v, 122 p. 6s.

A companion volume to Abrahamsen's *Say it in Norwegian* (see p. 149).

See also *Pronounce it correctly in Swedish* in the section Gramophone
Records and Tapes.

McCLEAN, R. J.   Swedish: a grammar of the modern language.
London, English Universities Press, 1947.   xvi, 319 p.   (Teach
yourself books).   7s. 6d.

Author was lecturer in Swedish at University College, London. For the
beginner, but of more use to the serious student than to the tourist, being
somewhat formal and dull, and following the conventional practice of
dealing with one part of speech at a time, chapter by chapter. Pronunciation,
using modified International Phonetic Alphabet, and Swedish tone system
(p. 1–40); grammar, with exercises for translation both ways and short
vocabularies (p. 43–238); passages for translation from Swedish, partly
commercial, partly London University examination papers (p. 239–54);
strong verbs (p. 255–8); vocabulary, each way (p. 259–89); key to exercises
(p. 291–319). Exercises not very interesting; could do with more texts for
reading and translation in everyday speech. Reliable and authoritative;
would benefit from brighter texts and typography. Björkhagen's books
recommended for further study.

Professor McClean is also joint-author of a Swedish reader:

BRANDBERG, P., and McCLEAN, R. J.   A Swedish reader, with introduction and notes.   London, University of London, Athlone Press,
1953 (reprinted 1963).   174 p.   12s. 6d.

A selection of pieces by 15 authors from Geijer, Bremer and Strindberg
to the present; most are twentieth century. Has introductory notes on the
authors, and footnotes on vocabulary and idiom.

OSWALD, J. S.   The teach yourself Swedish phrase book.   London,
English Universities Press, 1958.   vii, 9–156 p.   (Teach yourself
books).   6s.

For the Briton in Sweden. 6 pages on pronunciation, using symbols of
International Phonetic Alphabet, but kept fairly simple. No attempt to
explain tone system. Classified vocabularies and phrases (p. 17–141). Heavy
type indicates main stress in words or phrases. I.P.A. equivalents given only
occasionally, when pronunciation is not obvious from spelling and the
introductory pages. Each section generally introduced by up to a page of
text giving much valuable information (e.g. about Swedish meals and
mealtimes, and the various types of shops and what they sell). "Some help
in forming new sentences" (p. 142–56) is a very brief grammatical section.

RICE, A. L.   Swedish: a practical grammar.   Rock Island, Ill.,
Augustana Press, 1958.   107 p.   [Fortress Press, $1.50].

Author, Professor of German and Swedish at Ursines College, Collegeville,
Pa., learnt Swedish himself as a American undergraduate, and views teaching

of the language differently from Swedish or Swedish-American authors. [This would certainly be true of the *older* writers of textbooks that Rice would have used as a student.] Object is to simplify intricacies of Swedish grammar as much as possible – many students faced by pages of rules on declensions and conjugations have got no further, or have got muddled. Author reckons to teach essential grammar within 2 months at college class meeting 3 times a week. After that he starts reading and building up vocabulary. 19 chapters. Chapter 1 on Swedish sounds (p. 12–17): absolute minimum, presupposes teacher; chapters 2–19 on various grammatical topics. Each chapter, bar one, contains explanatory matter, with examples, vocabulary and exercises for translation, both ways. Swedish-English glossary (p. 90–98) lists *c.* 500 Swedish words used in the book, with gender of nouns and only irregular forms of plurals and verbs; other inflexions are assumed to be normal. 500 words chosen at random, not from frequency lists. English-Swedish vocabulary (p. 99–104) lists words needed for English-into-Swedish exercises. Appendix (p. 105–7): "Schematic summaries", i.e. very brief tabular and other summaries of the main points of each lesson.

Worth considering for the beginner who prefers informal, unorthodox approach to grammar. Björkhagen is recommended by author as indispensable formal grammar for reference.

ROSÉN, G. Svenska för utlänningar. 11. uppl. Stockholm, Folkuniversitetets Förlag, 1965. 102 p. illus. S.kr. 5.50.

First published 1951. 4th (enlarged) ed. 1957. An illustrated reader, entirely in Swedish, for self study or for use with a teacher. Help with pronunciation is required, either from a teacher or from the recordings available (disc and tape).

It is complemented by a grammar, available in some 8 languages, including English: *A short Swedish grammar, word list and translation exercises for "Svenska för utlänningar."* (52 p. S.kr. 3.25).

There is also a book of exercises: *Öva svenska.* (3. uppl. 1964. 24 p. S.kr. 3.25) (Not seen). It has exercises in completing sentences, filling in blanks, etc. Reported unsuitable for the unaided student, as it lacks key, vocabulary, etc., and some of the examples are irregular.

The three books listed above, plus gramophone records and sundry other printed materials, are available as a set (see below under Gramophone Records and Tapes).

There is a similar set of more advanced materials. The textbooks for this are *Mera svenska för utlänningar* (1964. 62 p. illus. S.kr. 4.50) and *Öva mera svenska* (1964. 24 p. S.kr. 3.25).

SÖDERBÄCK, M. Elementary spoken Swedish. 6th printing, revised and enlarged. Rock Island, Ill., Augustana Book Concern, 1953. 68 p. [Fortress Press, 75*c.*].

First published 1947. Revised and enlarged edition of 3rd printing. A textbook for students without previous knowledge of Swedish. Everyday language. Students should study a good grammar concurrently. Presupposes instructor for pronunciation and practice in conversation. 30 simple dialogue type texts, with notes on Swedish words and phrases, questions in Swedish, and exercises for English-Swedish translation. Swedish-English vocabulary.

Söderbäck, M. Advanced spoken Swedish. Rock Island, Ill., Augustana Book Concern, 1947. 166 p. [Fortress Press, $2.25].

15 chapters, each consisting of a dialogue type text, notes on the text, and exercises on the notes. The notes are good, but the lack of an index makes it difficult to find particular grammatical points. No answers or key to the exercises, which are quite helpful in themselves. Swedish-English vocabulary.

Söderbäck, M. Swedish reader. Rock Island, Ill., Augustana Book Concern, 1952. 174 p. [Fortress Press, $2].

Modern short stories, suitable for second-year classes, with notes and Swedish-English vocabulary. (Not seen).

GRAMOPHONE RECORDS AND TAPES

Note. The Swedish Institute can supply lists of recordings of Swedish literature, dialect, ballads and folksongs.

Conversaphone.

One 7″ 33⅓ r.p.m. record. Not recommended by IES: poor Swedish translation of the original text, and unnatural pronunciation, too "letter-true".

Higelin. Från Fakiren till Jolo. (Bandcentralen, Box 1143, Solna 1, Sweden).

Text recorded without pauses on five 4″ double-track tapes, 3¾ i.p.s. S.kr. 150.– the set; 35.– each singly.

Higelin. Svenska på svenska. (Studiefrämjandet).

Three 7″ single-track tapes. S.kr. 95.– the set; 35.– each singly. Textbook S.kr. 8.50.

For use in the home, classroom, and language laboratory. Intended primarily for study with a teacher, the course can also be used by those studying by themselves if they have tape equipment. Sponsored by IES and Studiefrämjandet.

A selection of exercises to improve Swedish pronunciation, the ability to understand spoken Swedish, and to speak Swedish grammatically. Partly supplementary to conventional textbook courses, the course can also be regarded as a set of examples of exercises of different types which the teacher can extend as required.

Order from Föreningstjänsten, Box 190 72, Stockholm 19.

HIGELIN.   Swedish by radio;
Swedish: a first course.

See below under Radio Courses.

HILDEMAN, N. G., and others.   Learn Swedish (Almqvist & Wiksell).

Text recorded on six 45 r.p.m. records, or five 4″ double-track tapes 3¾ i.p.s. Discs: S.kr. 58.–; tapes: S.kr. 175.–

HILDEMAN, P. A.   Svenskt uttal: Swedish pronunciation. (Band-centralen).

One 5″ single-track tape, 3¾ i.p.s. Recorded with pauses. Mimeographed booklet with word and sentence patterns for pronunciation, and text of some conversations. S.kr. 40.– inclusive of one booklet; additional booklets 50 öre each.

LINGUAPHONE.   Set of textbooks and *either* sixteen 7″ 45 r.p.m. records, *or* two 5″ double-track tapes, 3¾ i.p.s.   £18 18s. in either form.

Standard Linguaphone plan. Course revised and reissued about 1962.

Tempo and pronunciation good, but the textbooks still give an out-of-date impression in spite of the more modern vocabulary, use of singular verb forms, etc. (IES comment).

PRONOUNCE IT CORRECTLY IN SWEDISH.   (New York, Dover Publications).

One 33⅓ r.p.m. record and leaflet giving full text. Material selected from *Say it in Swedish* by Birgit and Åke Leander (see p. 165-6); recorded by Åke Leander. $1.–. *Not handled by Constable.*

ROSÉN.   Svenska för utlänningar 1.   (Folkuniversitetets Förlag).

Two E.P. records; textbooks *Svenska för utlänningar, Öva svenska, A short Swedish grammar* [orders must specify English], various brochures etc. S.kr. 31.–

ROSÉN.   Mera svenska för utlänningar 2.

Three E.P. records; textbooks *Mera svenska för utlänningar, Öva mera svenska*, etc. S.kr. 31.–
Set of five records, alone, S.kr. 14.–, or two tapes, 3¾ i.p.s., S.kr. 32.–

RADIO COURSES

Sveriges Radio broadcasts "Swedish by radio" for English-speaking listeners. This is a 30-lesson course for beginners. The texts are based on the 1,000 most common words, and grammatical points have been kept to the essential minimum. For details of times and wavelengths, and a free copy of the textbook by Siv Higelin, write to Sveriges Radio, Box 955, Stockholm 1. The course is produced by Claude Stephenson.

An enlarged version of this course is to be published (in 1967?) by The Bedminster Press of Totowa, N.J., under the title *Swedish: a first course*. This will be illustrated. The enlargement consists of exercises for each of the 30 lessons. Gramophone records of the entire radio course will also be available. [Information from the author. The publishers have not replied to two requests for supplementary information.]

A continuation course by Siv Higelin, *Vi läser svenska tidningar*, was published gratis by Sveriges Radio in 1966; broadcasts begin in 1967.

DICTIONARIES

Standard orthography

SVENSKA AKADEMIEN. Ordlista över svenska språket. 9. uppl. Stockholm, Svenska Bokförlaget, Norstedts, 1951. xvi, 607 p. S.kr. 18.–

The standard dictionary giving spellings, parts of speech, genders, plurals, declensions, comparisons, etc. Very few definitions.

GUSTAFSSON, A. S.   Svensk ordlista; utgiven av Artur Almhult, Nils Ivan. 10. uppl.   Stockholm, A. V. Carlsons Bokförlag, [1965]. S.kr. 2.50.

A smaller dictionary of the same type, containing some 22,000 words. Gives inflexions, some simple definitions, and simple indication of stress. Agrees with the 9th ed. of *Svenska Akademiens ordlista*.

Also large-print ed. available (*Specialupplaga för synsvaga*) S.kr. 10.–

Translating dictionaries (in descending order of size)

HARLOCK, W. E., and others.   A Swedish-English dictionary, compiled by Walter E. Harlock with the collaboration of Arvid Gabrielson and others.   Stockholm, Svenska Bokförlaget, Norstedts, 1936–1951.   2 v.   [v. 1] A–K.   1936.   xv, 1,230 p.   S.kr. 49.–
[v. 2] L–R.   1951.   [4], 1,231–2,096, T16 p.   S.kr. 56.–

The publishers write (July 1966) that work on v. 3 has been abandoned, and it is unlikely that this dictionary will be completed.

As far as it goes, by far the fullest Swedish-English dictionary, giving a wealth of information about genders, plurals, parts of verbs, compounds, phrases and usage, etc. To compress this material into pages only 8 inches high a range of very small type faces has been used; this is far from easy on the eye. Under words with many meanings or compounds, etc., the articles are subdivided systematically, but they need close concentration if the user is not to lose track of the divisions.

T16 pages at the end of v. 2 consist of corrections and additions (*Rättelser och Tillägg*) to v. 1.

There is no other Swedish-English dictionary on the same scale, and no corresponding English-Swedish work. The fullest complete Swedish-English dictionary is:

HARLOCK, W. E. Svensk-engelsk ordbok. Skolupplaga, under medverkan av Arvid Gabrielson, John Holmberg, Margareta Ångström m.fl. 2. översedda upplagan. Stockholm, Svenska Bokförlaget, Norstedts, [1947]. viii, 1,048 p. S.kr. 27.–

1st ed. 1944. 2nd ed. is a reprint with minor corrections; several reprints since. Based on V. 1 of the big *Swedish-English dictionary* and such parts of the remainder as were available in proof or manuscript form. Although called a "school edition" it is very much more detailed than this would imply. As in the parent work, plurals and genders of nouns are given, and parts of verbs, and references from irregularly inflected forms are made to the main entry (e.g. from *böcker* (books) to *bok*). Many examples of phrases, compounds and usage are given. However, the reservations concerning the typography apply equally to this volume. No Swedish pronunciations.

The publishers state that it is to be superseded in 1967 by a completely revised edition being prepared under the editorship of Vincent Petti.

The corresponding English-Swedish volume is:

KÄRRE, K., and others. Engelsk-svensk ordbok. Skolupplaga. 3. omarbetade upplagan. Stockholm, Svenska Bokförlaget, Norstedts, [1960]. xvi, 973 p. S.kr. 27.–

ERNOLV, C., and others. Svensk-engelsk ordbok. 2. upplagan. Stockholm, Svenska Bokförlaget, Norstedts, [1942]. vi, 570 p. (Fickordböcker). S.kr. 11.–

Gives various translations for each word, but no examples of usage. No indication of genders, plurals, etc. Reliable; handy for the beginner, but Swedish usership is assumed.

The corresponding English-Swedish dictionary is:

WENSTRÖM E. Engelsk-svensk ordbok, fullständigt omarbetad av Ruben Nöjd och Anna C. Petterson. Stockholm, Svenska Bokförlaget, Norstedts, [1941]. viii, 648 p. (Fickordböcker). S.kr. 11.–

This, on the other hand, gives Swedish users information about irregular English plurals, etc. The first edition dates from 1894.

This pair of dictionaries is in the 50,000 word range; they are rather large for 'pocket' dictionaries.

FREUDENTHAL, F., and others. English-Swedish dictionary. 2nd rev. ed. London, Allen & Unwin, 1956. [viii], 348 p. 25s.

Based on *Engelsk-dansk ordbog*, by Haislund and Salling (1937). Printing could be better. Gives English pronunciations. Appendix I: English proper names, with pronunciations. Appendix II: English abbreviations.

The companion volume is:

REUTER, O. R., and others. Swedish-English dictionary. 2nd rev. ed. London, Allen & Unwin, 1966. [viii], 405 p. 35s. (B66–10378).

Intended for Swedes (Allen & Unwin imprint is merely for the British market). Gives no plurals or genders of nouns. The previous edition (1956; B56–7425) was also published as 2nd revised ed., being the *Swedish* 2nd ed. New ed. has some 1,700 additional entry words, mainly for modern technology, e.g. rockets, space, radio, TV, etc.

These volumes are published in Stockholm by Natur och Kultur.

NÖJD, R. Engelsk-svensk ordbok. Stockholm, Svenska Bokförlaget, Norstedts, [1939]. viii, 248 p. (Serielexikon). S.kr. 8.50.

First published by Åhlen & Åkerlund; many Svenska Bokförlaget printings. Only dates given are those of printing, e.g. 13th, 1965.

The corresponding Swedish-English dictionary is:

TORNBERG, A., and ÅNGSTRÖM, M. Svensk-engelsk ordbok. Stockholm, Svenska Bokförlaget, Norstedts, [1940]. iv, 220 p. (Serielexikon). S.kr. 8.50.

The two volumes are also available bound together, S.kr. 16.–

Vocabularies restricted. Very few compounds given, unless the translation is different from the translation of the constituent parts. Some English pronunciation given; no Swedish. No genders, plurals, etc., of Swedish words. These dictionaries are in the 25,000 word range.

CASSERBERG, T. Första engelsk-svenska ordboken. Stockholm, Svenska Bokförlaget, Norstedts, 1955. 174 p. S.kr. 4.80.

For Swedes beginning English. About 6,000 English words and expressions.

No corresponding Swedish-English volume. Svenska Bokförlaget also publish a *Miniatyrlexikon* series of very small dictionaries; both the English-Swedish and the Swedish-English volumes are by A. Klint. (S.kr. 4.50 and 3.75 respectively).

HILL, L. Hill's Swedish-English, English-Swedish pocket dictionary. [New enlarged ed.]. Stockholm, Jan-förlaget, 1965. 244 p. S.kr. 7.–

May be useful for the traveller at a loss for odd words; not recommended for the student. Very brief; no genders or plurals of Swedish words; one or two translations for each term; no phrases or usage.

Niloés engelsk-svenska och svensk-engelska lexikon; utgivet under medverkan av Orvar Lindén, Vincent Petti m.fl. Stockholm, Niloé, [1963]. 190; 192 p. S.kr. 9.50.

First published 1960. 2nd rev. ed. of Swedish-English section, 1962–63.

A tiny dictionary, far too expensive, but unusual in that it gives the International Phonetic Alphabet pronunciation of all entry words. Includes the 7,000 most-used English and Swedish words, and many important modern terms and words needed by tourists. Very brief definitions; no plurals or genders given for Swedish nouns. Swedish-English and English pronunciation by Petti; English-Swedish by Lindén; Swedish pronunciation by Hans-Olof Hagren and Erik Lindström.

There are several other pocket size dictionaries available, including Langenscheidt's Lilliput series, and innumerable phrase books. One further dictionary should not be overlooked:

ALLWOOD, M. S., and WILHELMSEN, I. Basic Swedish word list, with English equivalents, frequency grading and a statistical analysis. Rock Island, Ill., Augustana Book Concern, 1947. 48 p. [Fortress Press, 75c.].

This lists some 3,000 of the most-used Swedish words. (Not seen.)

Technical dictionaries

GULLBERG, I. E. A Swedish-English dictionary of technical terms used in business, industry, administration, education and research. Stockholm, Norstedts, 1964. xv, 1,246 p. S.kr. 145.–

Also Swedish title: Svensk-engelsk fackordbok för näringsliv, förvaltning, undervisning och forskning.

A large dictionary of the highest quality, covering a very wide field. 130,000 entries; excludes the general common non-technical vocabulary. Specifies subject fields. Distinguishes between British and American usage. Gives translations of the names of many organisations (including Danish, Finnish and Norwegian ones). The sole defect – especially regrettable in view of the thoroughness and attention to detail which otherwise characterise the dictionary – is the omission once again of any information about noun genders and plurals, and parts of verbs.

Enthusiastic review in *Babel* v. 11 (1965) no. 2, p. 91–2. An interesting article by Gullberg entitled *Some notes on dictionaries and dictionary-making, with particular reference to conditions in Scandinavia* also appeared in *Babel* (v. 11 no. 4, p. 168–74) and was reprinted in *Stechert-Hafner book news* (v. 21, no. 3 (November 1966) p. 33–5). This includes notes on the author's method of compiling his dictionary during the course of his work as official translator to the Swedish Foreign Ministry. Gullberg's next projects are a first supplement to his dictionary, with a bibliography of current dictionaries in more than 100 languages, a chronological bibliography of dictionaries, etc., 1440–1965, and a counterpart English-Swedish dictionary. Until this last makes its appearance, the standard technical dictionary will remain:

ENGSTRÖM, E. Engelsk-svensk teknisk ordbok. 10. uppl. Stockholm, Svensk Trävaru-Tidning, 1965. 851 p. S.kr. 65.–

The companion work is:

— Svensk-engelsk teknisk ordbok. 7. uppl. Stockholm, Svensk Trävaru-Tidning, 1964. 544 p. S.kr. 50.–

These are more conventional technical dictionaries, 'technical' being interpreted more narrowly than in Gullberg's work. They are frequently revised and enlarged (both volumes are more than twice the size of their first editions). The English-Swedish volume has some 100,000 words and expressions; the Swedish-English has *c.* 75,000, but the publishers state that an 8th edition the same size as the English-Swedish is to be published in Spring 1967. Well established, well regarded. Lacks grammatical information about Swedish words.

9

RUSSIAN

by A. J. WALFORD, M.A., PH.D., F.L.A., in consultation with
Mrs. O. L. GREEN

"Although French will remain the first business language for learning in the English-speaking community for the next ten or fifteen years, it will have lost some of its importance and Russian will have overtaken German and Spanish." So writes Max K. Adler, in discussing the problem facing language-teaching establishments[1].

English-speaking scientists have a major difficulty in dealing with Russian literature. "Although the situation is improving rapidly, the number of British scientists who have any knowledge of Russian at all is still less than 10 per cent, and in consequence most of the activity in the translation field has been directed at making scientists aware of what is being published in the Soviet Union, and at providing translations and information about translations of this material."[2]

Only in very recent years has prominence been given to the teaching of Russian. The 1955–56 annual report of the Advisory Council on Scientific Policy[3] urged the provision of more Russian language courses as well as improved facilities for making Russian scientific literature accessible to scientists in this country. The Hayter Committee report (1961)[4] worked on the assumption that by 1966 or 1971 enough pupils would be learning Russian at school for all universities to insist on an 'A' level qualification at entry for those wishing to take a Russian course. The report of the Annan Committee on the teaching of Russian, published in June 1962[5], recommended that an adequate force of Russian teachers should rapidly be built up. In the previous

[1] *Business language of the world* (London, The Institute of Marketing, 1966), p. 9.
[2] D. N. Wood, in *Chemistry in Britain*, v. 2, no. 8, August 1966, p. 346.
[3] *Ninth annual report* . . . (Cmnd. 11) (H.M.S.O., 1956), p. 2–3.
[4] University Grants Committee. *Report of the Sub-Committee on Oriental, Slavonic, East European and African Studies* (H.M.S.O., 1961), p. 95.
[5] *Teaching of Russian.* Report of the Committee appointed by the Minister of Education and the Secretary of State for Scotland in September 1960 (H.M.S.O., 1962).

year the first Russian 'language laboratory' was set up at Ealing
Technical College, with its teacher at the console and students in
soundproof cubicles with tape records.

The impetus is strikingly reflected in the number of Russian grammars, readers, dictionaries and similar books that have been published
since 1950. Here are the figures, based on entries in the *British national
bibliography*:

1950:	3	1959:	9
1951:	2	1960:	23
1952:	5	1961:	26
1953:	6	1962:	20
1954:	2	1963:	17
1956:	0	1964:	14
1957:	5	1965:	19
1958:	3	1966:	11

A number of these publications have U.S. imprints and are distributed in Britain; a few have Moscow imprints and are distributed by
Collet's. Even so, those with British imprints have shown a marked
increase.

In the lists that follow the great bulk of the items are in print and
have been examined at first-hand. Russian readers are normally excluded
unless they include a substantial amount of grammar.

For general background on the U.S.S.R., v. 50 of the *Bol'shaya
sovetskaya entsiklopediya* (1957. 647 p. 40s.) is an excellent source.
Information U.S.S.R., edited and compiled by Robert Maxwell
(Oxford, Pergamon Press, 1962. xii, 982 p. £10) is a translation.

Russian and the Slavonic languages, by W. J. Entwistle and W. A.
Morison (2nd ed. Faber & Faber, 1965. 407 p. 63s.), first published in
1949, is the first full account of the Slavonic languages group along
lines mainly historical and cultural rather than analytical.

GRAMMARS

The difficulties of learning Russian should not be minimised. As one
teacher[1] has put it: "Russian is a strongly inflected and, consequently,
difficult language. And, in addition, the teaching of Russian in this

---

[1] E. Koutaissoff, "Russian textbooks", in *Modern languages*, v. 38, no. 4, December 1957,
p. 143–4.

country is still a fairly new venture, with the result that authors of Russian courses have lacked that long experience which alone, after long years of trial and error, produces the ability of presenting linguistic material in a digestible form. Furthermore, these Russian courses were first written during or immediately after the last war, i.e. before Professor H. H. Josselson and his team at Wayne University, U.S.A., had completed the great task of compiling a word frequency list [*The Russian Word Count and Frequency Analysis of Grammatical Categories of Standard Literary Russian*, Wayne University Press, 1953]; so, inevitably, the initial vocabulary of these courses was selected at random."

Some of the main difficulties of Russian for English-speaking learners concern pronunciation and the verb. N. Lunan[1] has specified these difficulties thus:

"(a) A correct understanding of palatization

"(b) The mastery of inflexion patterns

"(c) The choice of verbal aspects in general

"(d) The choice of aspects in the basic verbs of motion."

Grammars for class use and self-tutors have been kept in one sequence below, since some grammars – usually the best of them – can be used for both purposes. A self-tutor is assumed to provide a key to the exercises set; it should be supplemented by either gramophone records, tape recordings or a broadcast series of lessons. The most widely used grammars are probably those by Semeonoff and Potapova. Grammars for scientists are appended.

Unless otherwise stated, stress is marked in these grammars.

BIRKETT, G. A.   A modern Russian course.   3rd ed., rev.   London, Methuen, 1946 (and reprints).   ix, 330 p.   13s. 6d.   Key to the exercises.   1957.   8s. 6d.

First published 1937. The author was at the time Lecturer in Russian at the University of Glasgow.

65 lessons, going as far as passive participles. Exercises consist of sentences into and from Russian. Vocabulary, each way, p. 284–327; index to grammar. Clear cyrillic type, without use of bold. On the lines of Semeonoff's grammar (q.v.). Presents serious difficulties to beginners, since irregular verbs are introduced in lesson 2. No guide to pronunciation; stories used as reading texts are uninspiring; sentences in exercises are laboured and old-fashioned.

[1] *A symposium on teaching Russian* (Oxford, etc., Pergamon Press, 1963), p. 121.

Bogatova, G., and others. Practical Russian. 2nd ed. Moscow, Progress Publishers, [1965]. 174 p. 5s.

18 sections, each with a descriptive passage and/or dialogue, vocabulary (particularly expressions) and exercises (mostly based on the Russian). Key to English-Russian exercises; Russian-English vocabulary. p. 130–74. No formal grammar is included; designed for English-speaking students who already have an elementary knowledge of Russian.

Bondar, D. Bondar's Simplified Russian method, conversational and commercial. 6th ed., revised by Louis Segal. London, Pitman, 1942 (and reprints). xxvi, 325 p. 15s.

First published 1932. A revised U.S. edition, by Mischa Fayer and others, has the title *Simplified Russian grammar* (New York, Pitman, 1957).

30 lessons; for class use, with graded passages for translation, questions, grammar drill and sentences, each way. Text matter and presentation decidedly old-fashioned. Commercial section, p. 221–97; vocabulary, each way; index to grammar. Good use of bold cyrillic type.

Boyanus, S. C., and Jopson, N. B. Spoken Russian: a practical course. Written and spoken colloquial Russian, with pronunciation, intonation, grammar, English translation and vocabulary. 3rd ed. London, Sidgwick & Jackson, 1952. xl, 366 p. 45s.

First published 1939. The author was formerly Professor of English Philology in Leningrad Institute of Philology and latterly Lecturer in Russian and Phonetics in the University of London. He died in 1952.

42 lessons. Designed as a 2-year course, with two 80-minute lessons per week. Special attention is paid to pronunciation (by use of phonetics) and intonation (by diagrams) throughout. Lessons consist of grammar, phrases and texts, with exercises. A short key to earlier exercises is appended. Also included are specimens of Russian handwriting. The vocabulary (p. 331–63) is Russian-English only; phonetic forms are given. Supplemented by a set of H.M.V. records made by Professor Boyanus, brilliantly done. But the grammar is hardly a self-tutor.

Brooke, K., and Forsyth, J. Russian through reading. London, Hutchinson, 1962. 344 p. illus. 30s.

66 reading passages with translation, grammar, vocabulary and notes. The authors are Head of the Department of Modern Languages, and Lecturer in Russian, respectively, at the University of North Staffordshire.

Designed as a self-tutor for the adult or teen-age beginner, and also for learners who have never studied a foreign language. Russian-English vocabulary (p. 285–340); index to grammar.

Callender, D. N. Learn Russian quickly. London, MacGibbon & Kee, 1962. 230 p. 21s.

28 lessons. A very simple presentation of the grammar on oblong pages. Vocabulary, each way; key to Russian-English exercises, which include drill and exercise in Russian handwriting. A stress-marking system is provided.

CHÉREL, A. Russian without toil. Godalming, Surrey, Assimil, [1957?]. xvi, 419 p. illus. 18s.

100 lessons. A lively presentation, with gay and amusing stories, and cartoons and extracts from current Russian material. Numerous short exercises, chiefly sentences, each way.

For self-study; can be used in conjunction with the Assimil gramophone records (see p. 199).

CORNYN, W. S. Beginning Russian. Rev. ed. New Haven, Conn. & London, Yale University Press, 1961. [xi], 312 p. $5. (Linguistic series).

First published 1960. Author is Professor of Slavic and Burmese Languages at Yale. 35 lessons. Designed to be used in the first-year Russian course at Yale University. Lessons comprise Russian sentences, pronunciation, grammar, drill on grammar, conversation and vocabulary (with imitated pronunciation). Russian-English vocabulary, p. 291–312. Large format; clear but unrelieved print.

DOHERTY, J. C., and MARKUS, R. L. First course in Russian. Boston, Heath, 1960–62; London, Harrap, 1961–62. 3 v. 25s.; 25s.; 37s. 6d.

V. 1 consists of 16 lessons, "geared to the needs of the high school student who may be studying a foreign language for the first time" (*Foreword*). Each lesson consists of reading, new vocabulary, grammar and a dozen exercises, including drill. Good illustrations; vocabulary, each way, p. 197–222; index to grammar; effective use of bold cyrillic.

DOMAR, R. A. Basic Russian: a textbook for beginners. New York, London, McGraw-Hill, 1961. xvi, 1], 516 p. illus. 56s. Workbook, 32s.; Teacher's book, 16s.

25 lessons. The author was at one time Professor of Russian at Columbia University.

Considered by the *Anglo-Soviet journal* (Spring 1962, p. 38–40) as excellent for a 2-year full-time course, i.e. for schools and colleges. Lessons consist of Russian text, vocabulary, grammar, exercises and questions. Particular attention is paid to verbs and prepositions; good illustrations. Vocabulary, each way; index to grammar. Has some highly questionable remarks on pronunciation, e.g. "There is one important general rule about Russian vowels: they are short." ... "The vowel ы is always pronounced like i in machine."

Exercises, on 7 tapes, £14; records, £6.

DUFF, C., and MAKAROFF, D. All purposes Russian for adults. . . .
London, English Universities Press, 1962. xx, 433 p. illus., diagrs.
25s.

> 46 lessons. Planned to meet the needs of the absolute beginner. Numerous
> passages for translation from Russian. No index to grammar, although there
> is a detailed contents-list. Vocabulary, each way, p. 375–433. Six word-lists
> are appended. Contains many misprints and incorrect Russian expressions.

DUFF, C., and MAKAROFF, D. First year Russian: a course for beginners. London, Cassell, 1960. xii, 121 p. 7s. 6d.

> 47 lessons. Intended for class use, with practice in conversation and dicta-
> tion. No key to exercises.

DUFF, C., and MAKAROFF, D. Second year Russian, with annotated
readings from Russian authors. London, Cassell, 1961. ix, 157 p.
12s. 6d.

> 35 lessons, taking the student to a little beyond G.C.E. 'O' level. Russian-
> English vocabulary only, p. 125–57; no index to grammar.
> Neither book can be recommended.

FAYER, M. H. Basic Russian. New York & London, Pitman, 1959–
61. 2 v., 18s.; 30s. Manual. 1959. 48 p. 7s. 6d.

> Book 1 has 28 lessons or 'units' in five major groups, – a 1-year course on
> traditional lines for secondary schools. Aims to "reduce all difficulties to the
> barest minimum" (*Introduction*). Vocabulary, each way, p. 253–90; no index
> to grammar. Book 2 includes more interesting reading matter.
> *Simplified Russian grammar*, by M. H. Fayer and A. Pressman (2nd ed.
> New York, Pitman, 1962, 425 p. $5. *Workbook*, $2.60) emphasises reading
> ability. Gramophone records available.

FENNELL, J. L. I. The Penguin Russian course: a complete course for
beginners. Harmondsworth, Penguin Books, 1961. xxiii, 343 p.
5s.

> An abridgement and adaptation of Potapova's *Russian: an elementary course*
> (q.v.); claims to be more adapted to the needs of English-speaking students
> than the original. 30 lessons; adequate grammar, examples and exercises,
> with key. Good use of bold cyrillic; rather brief on pronunciation; no
> detailed contents or index to grammar. Recommended for self-study for
> those with adequate linguistic background; a bargain at the price. In classes
> is best used for teaching graduates.

FORBES, N. Elementary Russian grammar. 2nd ed., by Elizabeth
Hill. Oxford, Clarendon Press, 1943. 174 p. o.p.

First published 1919. 30 lessons, with exercises in sentences, each way. Paradigms of nouns, pronouns and adjectives; hints on stress. Russian word, English word and grammar indexes.

For fuller treatment of declensions and verbs, and fuller vocabularies and exercises, students are referred in the Preface to Forbes's First, Second and Fourth Russian books and *Russian grammar*.

FORBES, N. Russian grammar. 3rd ed., rev. and enl. by J. M. Dumbreck. Oxford, Clarendon Press, 1964. xi, 438 p. 25s.

2nd ed. 1916 (iv, 275 p.). Dr. Forbes (d. 1929) was one of the pioneers of Russian studies in Britain. This enlarged edition bears the same paragraph numbers as the 2nd ed. but many have been substantially revised and extended. The new orthography is used. Essentially a practical reference grammar, with no vocabularies or exercises. Detailed study of the verbs (p. 218–352) and prefixes (p. 352–91). "The list of regular verbs, irregular comparatives, prepositions and prefixes are now, for practical purposes, complete", stated the reviser. Claimed to be "particularly useful to those who have completed an elementary course of Russian and are continuing their studies either in classes leading to a G.C.E. or university examination, or on their own with the aid of a Russian novel or a special reader". Bibliography; subject index of words and phrases (p. 408–35). Excellent typography.

FOURMAN, M. Teach yourself Russian. London, English Universities Press, 1943 (and reprints). xii, 276 p. 7s. 6d.

38 lessons. Intended for adults who wish to write rather than speak Russian. Exercises in English and Russian sentences, with key; prose and verse extracts appended. Vocabulary, each way, p. 165–211. Clear type, though sometimes small. Very old-fashioned.

HARLEY, N. Start Russian by talking. London, Bradda Books, 1963. 80 p. o.p.

40 reading passages; two sets of drill on these; vocabulary. Tables of personal and possessive pronouns; interrogative words; prepositions; the verbs *byt'* and *delat'*.

HARDING, J. C. Russian one: a first course for junior beginners. London, Harrap, 1965. x, 116 p. illus. 10s. 6d.

Stresses oral approach, with very limited grammar and only about 300 words of vocabulary. Treats the nominative, accusative, genitive and locative (or prepositional) cases, but not the dative or instrumental; simpler declensions and only the present tense of verbs. "Hardly suitable for more mature beginners" (*Modern languages*, v. 47, no. 2, June 1966, p. 88).

HAYWOOD, A. A. A first Russian book. New ed. London, Harrap, 1959. 194 p. illus. 10s. 6d.

26 lessons. The author was at the time Modern Language Master of Firth Park Grammar School, Sheffield. Designed for secondary school beginners.

HAYWOOD, A. A. A second Russian book. London, Harrap, 1960. 271 p. illus. 12s.

23 chapters, going up to G.C.E. 'O' level. Sentences, English into Russian, and Russian into English; drill in grammar. Clear print; good half-tone illustrations.

HAYWOOD, A. A. 'O' level Russian. London, Harrap, 1965. 207 p. 12s. 6d.

Intended for use in the final year of 'O' level Russian. Book I consists of (a) 35 passages for translation from Russian, plus passages for translation from English, using similar but not identical vocabulary, and a related subject for free composition; (b) 35 passages for use as comprehension tests; (c) questions concerned mainly with the family, home and school. Book II is a reference grammar, with exercises, vocabulary and indexes. The reviewer in *Modern languages* (v. 47, no. 1, March 1966, p. 41) suggests using Book I for 'O' level and Book II for 'A' level; this book may, as a result, well prove to be "a very valuable contribution to Russian studies in our schools".

HINGLEY, R. Russian for beginners. Rev. ed. London, B.B.C., 1960. 73 p. 5s.

First published 1959. A quarto pamphlet used in conjunction with a 40-lesson course broadcast in 1959 and 1960. Vocabulary is adult and idiomatic, and conversation is stressed. Lacks index and overall vocabulary.

HINGLEY, R., and BINYON, T. J. Russian: a beginner's course. London, Allen & Unwin, 1962. 330 p. 25s.

40 lessons. After reaching lesson 17, students should begin to read elementary Russian texts. Many examples of usage; up-to-date material. Sentences, each way. Clear lay-out and good use of bold type. Vocabulary, each way, p. 287–327. Index to grammar. Good examples of 'copperplate' Russian handwriting. Particularly good on pronunciation. Presumes some linguistic background on the part of the beginner. According to the review of *Anglo-Soviet journal* (v. 24, no. 2, Summer 1963, p. 45), is likely to be very useful for revision and gives practical hints on difficulties apt to be met by English students.

HUGO'S LANGUAGE INSTITUTE. Russian grammar simplified: an easy & rapid self-instructor. Standard ed., rev. and re-written. London, the Institute, [1957?]. [ii], 238 p. 6s.

26 graded lessons, with a pair of exercises (sentences, each way) after each part of a lesson. No connected passages for translation. Key to exercises; index to grammar; brief vocabulary, the lessons having 734 words of vocabulary in all; imitated pronunciation. Clear cyrillic type. Conceivably of use to the tourist but inferior and old-fashioned as a self-tutor. Hugophone gramophone records are available for use with this course (see p. 120).

KHAVRONINA, S. A.   Russian as we speak it.   Moscow, Progress Publishers, 1966.   268 p.   (Collet's 8s. 6d.).

Chapters consist of reading passage, idiomatic dialogue, abundant exercises and a conversational passage for translation, plus notes on points of idiom rather than grammar. A storehouse of Russian idiom for the English-speaking learner who has grasped the fundamentals.

The Russian material is available on tapes for £8 8s.

KOLNI-BALOZKY, J.   A progressive Russian grammar.   London, Pitman, 1938 (and reprints).   xii, 477 p.   18s.   Key. 1947.   86 p.   8s. 6d.

The author was at one time Senior Lecturer and Head of the Russian Department at the University of Leeds.

38 chapters, with appendices. Pt. 1, 26 lessons, claims to provide sufficient grammar and exercises to enable the student to acquire a practical knowledge of Russian in one academic year. A formidable, boring and somewhat confusing volume: vocabularies are scattered and there is no general index to grammar. Old-fashioned vocabulary. Probably more useful to the teacher than to the student, in that it is valuable for reference on minute points of grammar.

LUNT, H. G.   Fundamentals of Russian (first Russian course).   The Hague, Mouton, 1958.   x, [1], 320 p.   48s.

22 lessons, plus 9 short supplementary lessons; appendix (declensions, diminutives, etc.). Vocabulary, each way, p. 285-320. Lessons consist of conversation (English given), grammar and drill. Lengthy exercises in sentences, each way. Some connected Russian passages in supplementary lessons. Lessons 1-4 stress pronunciation (using phonetic forms), handwriting and stress, and include use of italics cyrillics. Essentially for class use. No index to grammar, but full contents. Good use of bold cyrillic.

MALTZOFF, N.   Russian reference grammar.   New York, London, Pitman Publishing Corpn., 1965.   xix, 332 p. $7.50.

Author is Adviser on Russian courses, United States Military Academy. 12 chapters (chapter 7, Verbs, p. 142-248). Plenty of examples. A reference grammar is not expected to have exercises or vocabularies, but the absence of an index to the grammar is a grave drawback. The detailed contents list (p. ix-xix) is no real substitute. Bibliography, p. vii-viii.

MILLER, L. S. Russian by yourself: a quick course in reading, for adult beginners and others. London, Bell, 1947. xii, 180 p. o.p.

Pt. 1: Grammar, p. 1–48; pt. 2: Russian extracts, prose and verse; pt. 3:

Chronology (in Russian); conversations; vocabulary (Russian-English only, p. 142–80). No exercises, either way. Claims, quite unjustifiably, to be a self-tutor.

MOORE, E. A., and STRUVE, G. Practical Russian. London, E. Arnold, 1946–57. illus. 2 v. ea. 8s.

The two volumes (Books 1–2) aim to provide a full course up to Matriculation standard. Book 2 can be used on its own by any student with a fair knowledge of Russian case-endings, and of the most common forms and tences of verbs. Each book has 12 chapters: Russian text; questions; grammar; exercises, each way. After lessons 4, 8 and 12 there are revisions of vocabulary. Russian-English general vocabulary; index to grammar. Very good as readers but inadequate as grammars. Use in conjunction with Potapova or Hingley or Ward.

NORMAN, P. Russian for today. London, University of London Press, 1965. 351 p. 25s.

Author is lecturer at the School of Slavonic and East European Studies, University of London.

A detailed grammar (50 lessons), with adequate treatment of verbal aspects. Emphasis on points where Russian usage differs from English. Russian-English vocabulary; key to exercises; index to grammar. Short lively dialogues between two characters using up-to-date idioms are a feature. Recommended for adult learners anxious to speak the language.

A set of four 10″ 33⅓ r.p.m. records is available.

POTAPOVA, N. Learning Russian. Moscow, Progress Publishers, [1964]. 4 v. illus. 18s. 6d.

An excellent, cheap course for beginners. Book 1 (50 lessons) concentrates on pronunciation and elementary grammar; book 2 (50 lessons), on grammar, with vocabularies and exercises, introducing commonly used Russian sentences; book 3 (35 lessons) introduces the student to Russian literature, with passages by contemporary authors; book 4 is a reference grammar, with tables, key to exercises, vocabulary each way, and index to grammar in all 4 volumes. Each volume has a detailed list of contents. Plenty of drill; good line-drawings.

A set of records to accompany this course has been announced.

POTAPOVA, N. Russian: an elementary course. 2nd ed., rev. Moscow, Foreign Languages Publishing House, 1959. illus. 2 v. 7s. 6d.; 9s. 6d.

72 lessons in all. An excellent, very thorough and well-balanced grammar.

Up-to-date texts and vocabulary; very full drill; most of the exercises have a key. This course will enable the student to read and understand Russian newspapers as well as easy fiction. Valuable as a self-tutor as well as for classes, especially if used with the Potapova gramophone record course (see p. 199).

Book 2 begins with Perfective verbs, presenting the more advanced beginner with formidable difficulties. Before starting book 2, the beginner could profitably consolidate his working knowledge of Russian by plenty of conversation and story-reading (e.g., N. Harley's *Easy Russian stories.* Nelson, 1961. viii, 71 p. 3s. 6d.). 48 graded stories, with vocabulary; those from 31 onwards are suitable for a normal second year's study. For adults as well as grammar- and secondary-school courses.).

PUL'KINA, I. M. A short Russian reference grammar, with a chapter on pronunciation. Edited by P. S. Kuznetsov. Moscow, Foreign Languages Publishing House, 1960. 267 p. 12s. 6d.

A revised and adapted translation of the author's *Kratkiĭ spravochnik po russkoĭ grammatike* (5th ed. 1959). 10 chapters; intended for self-instruction as well as for teachers of Russian. Comprehensive and cheap, in these qualities resembling Potapova's *Russian: an elementary course.* Typography is largely unrelieved. No index, but full contents list. Few cross-references. According to Neiswender (q.v.), "unrivalled as a systematic, non-theoretical exposition of grammar for the student and teacher". Largely supersedes F. J. Whitfield's *A Russian reference grammar* (Cambridge, Mass., Harvard University Press, 1944. ix, 222 p.).

PUL'KINA, I. M., and ZAKHAZA-NEKRASOVA, E. B. Russian for English-speaking students: a teaching grammar for students in the second and subsequent years of Russian course. V. 1, translated by D. G. Fay. New York, Pergamon Press, 1961. 308 p. $9.50; 63s.

A translation of Pt. 1 (Morphology) of the 1938 edition of the authors' textbook of the Russian language for foreign students (*Uchebnik russkogo yazyka dlya studentov-inostrantsev*). Recommended for the more advanced student; well translated; near-print type. Costly, like several other publications by Pergamon.

ROZENTAL, D. E. Modern Russian usage. Translated by M. A. Green. Edited by C. V. James. Oxford, Pergamon Press, 1963. x, 131 p. (Russian teaching aids, 3). 12s. 6d.

An English version of the Russian textbook *Kultura rechi* (Moscow, 1959). A practical reference guide to correct everyday modern Russian rather than a philological study. Four chapters: 1. The choice of words (with references to some of the major Russian dictionaries). – 2. The choice of grammatical forms and constructions. – 3. Pronunciation (especially for loan words). – 4. Stress (with a valuable list of short adjectives and verbs in the past tense stressed on last syllable in feminine singular). Misprints are fairly common, states the reviewer in *Modern languages* (v. 44, no. 3, September 1963. p. 127).

SEELEY, F. F., and RAPP, H.   The gateway Russian course.   London, Methuen, 1963–64.   2 v.   (283 p.; 397 p.).   12s. 6d.; 32s. 6d.

A clearly printed and attractively illustrated new course. Book 1 (a two-year course for beginners) has 42 lessons (Russian passage; grammar; exercises, English into Russian; vocabulary), including 6 recapitulatory; vocabulary, each way. Book 2 (presumably up to 'O' level), lessons 43–70 (summary of grammar; Russian grammatical terms (p. 315–7), to encourage a few to turn sooner to some of the larger Russian dictionaries); vocabulary, each way (Russian genders not shown; helpful notes on cases following prepositions); no index to grammar.

SEGAL, L., and WHIBLEY, K. H.   Elementary Russian grammar. London, Lund Humphries, 1961.   xii, 340 p.   25s.

A revision of the 9th ed. of *Russian grammar and self-educator*, by L. Segal (1944). 28 lessons, and appendices. Exercises consist of sentences, each way, and some passages for translation. Vocabulary, each way, p. 267–336; index to grammar. Phonetic pronunciation; vocabulary decidedly old-fashioned. The *Anglo-Soviet journal*, Spring 1962 (p. 38, 40) complains of the complicated arrangement of lessons: the student is plunged straight away into the intricacies of grammatical rules.

SEMEONOFF, A. H.   A new Russian grammar.   13th revised ed. London, Dent, 1960.   xxvii, 323 p.   13s. 6d.   Key.   1938 (and reprints).   vii, 63 p.   9s. 6d.

First published in 1934. The author was teacher of Russian in the George Watson's Boys' College, Edinburgh.

Pt. 1 consists of 25 lessons, with adequate grammar, numerous examples and exercises in translating sentences, each way. Only Lesson 25 has connected Russian prose. Vocabulary is rather old-fashioned and phraseology rather laboured; confusing treatment of verbs. To be used by a very experienced teacher with a perfect knowledge of English. Bold cyrillic type is not particularly legible. Pt. 2 provides a valuable reference grammar. Vocabulary each way; index to grammar. The *Key* includes a 'Table of endings'. A widely used grammar that lacks the thorough treatment and variety provided by Potapova.

SEMEONOFF, A. H.   Russian syntax, being part 3 of "A new Russian grammar".   London, Dent, 1962.   xv, [1], 245 p.   18s.

A comprehensive exposition, with numerous examples drawn from classical and contemporary Russian literature. It is a pity that these are not translated. No index to the subject matter, only to the authors cited; full contents list. "Unfortunately ... not entirely satisfactory, either as a practical manual for the student or as an academic exposition" (*The incorporated linguist*,

v. 4, no. 1, January 1965, p. 26). This review quotes examples of misstatement and lack of cross-references, adding that, while the book contains much useful information, it is too badly organised to be recommended.

Russian syntax: aspects of modern Russian syntax and vocabulary, by F. M. Borras and R. F. Christian (London, Oxford University Press, 1959. xi, 404 p. 35*s*.), the standard work, provides both vocabulary and subject indexes.

Exercises in Russian syntax, with explanatory notes, by V. S. Belevitskaya-Khalizeva and others, provides exercises as well as source material for the advanced student.

SENN, A., and ROZHDESTVENSKY, A. A. Cortina's Russian in 20 lessons: intended for self-study and for use in schools. 4th ed., rev. New York, Cortina; London, Collins, 1964. v, 444 p. illus. $2.95; 21*s*.

Each lesson consists of vocabulary and conversational exercises; simulated pronunciation. 3,700-word Russian-English vocabulary appended, with a reference grammar and an index to the grammar. Makes a bulky volume.

SERGIEVSKY, N., and BULAZEL, I. Modern Russian: how to read, write and speak it. 3rd rev. ed. New York, Ungar; London, Constable, 1960. xi, 272 p. illus. 16*s*.

First published 1945. 47 lessons. Lessons comprise Russian text, with translation; grammar drill; sentences, each way; grammar. Pt. 3 is a prose and verse reader. Vocabulary, each way, p. 212–56.

SHEVALDISHEV, A. N., and SUVOROV, S. P. Elementary Russian in patterns. London, Collet's, 1965. 665 p. 7*s*. 6*d*.

Intended for beginners, particularly those who wish to visit Russia and to get along without an interpreter. Two main parts: (1) "Elementary course" (outline of grammar, pronunciation guide to each word, and a few exercises, but no index); (2) Sentence patterns. The reviewer in *Modern languages* (v. 46, no. 2, June 1965, p. 86) finds the first part baffling and frustrating but praises the second part (v. 441–665), which is a detailed phrase book on hotels, motoring and getting about. Certainly cheap enough, and it gives teachers of Russian up-to-date examples of useful grammatical expressions. An accompanying tape would have helped.

STILMAN, G., and HARKINS, W. E. Introducing Russian grammar. New York, London, Blaisdell: Ginn, 1964. xi, 559 p. 84*s*.

Both authors are of Columbia University. A solid book in 27 units (grammar; pattern sentences; drill; translation each way; readings; vocabulary; conversation). Plenty of exercises; stress on pronunciation and grammar (e.g., verbal aspects, p. 206–55 (units 14–17)). Four appendices: declensions; diminutives; index of prepositions; suffixes. Large white page; clear typography, with good use of bold; expensive.

UNBEGAUN, B. O. Russian grammar. Oxford, Clarendon Press, 1957. 345 p. 30s.

The author was Professor of Comparative Slavonic Philology in the University of Oxford. Concentrates on the interdependence of inflection and word-formation. A scholarly reference grammar rather than a working tool. No syntax or exercises.

VON GRONICKA, A., and BATES-YAKOBSON, H. Essentials of Russian. 4th ed. Englewood Cliffs, N.J., Prentice-Hall, 1964. xii, [1], 399 p. illus. 48s.

First published 1948. The 30 lessons, each in 7 parts, include questions, grammar, exercises and passages for reading and translation. Lesson 30 covers passive participles and the passive voice. This edition gives fuller treatment to verbal aspects (lesson 16 onwards), has a new section on verbs of motion and adds examples of Russian script. Emphasis is on reading ability. Vocabulary, each way; index to grammar. Not well printed; only two illustrations, apart from end-paper map.

WARD, D. The Russian language today: system and anomaly. London, Hutchinson University Library, 1965. 297 p. diagrs. 25s.

Not a formal grammar but an engrossing study of modern usage and trends. Pt. 1, Sound and symbol (phonetics; stress; orthography); pt. 2, Forms and usage (syntax; parts of speech; sources of words; substantives; adjectives; genitive-accusative and negative genitive; verbs (p. 221–66)); the Russian language today; bibliography. No exercises or vocabulary, but index of Russian words discussed and an index to grammar. Most examples are drawn from writings of Russian authors and in periodicals of the past 30 or 40 years. Well produced.

WARD, D. Starting Russian. London, B.B.C., 1962. viii, 456 p. o.p.

Essentially an accompaniment to the B.B.C. broadcast course, 1962–63, and also a basis for self-study. 41 lessons, comprising grammar, phrases, reading exercises, and passages for translation, each way. Key to exercises, vocabulary, each way, p. 417–52, and index to grammar follow. Well produced.

The same author's *Keep up your Russian: an anthology*, with grammar commentary by Dennis Ward and translations into English by Ariadne Nicolaeff (2nd rev. ed. London, Harrap, 1963. 176 p. illus. 15s.) was originally published by the B.B.C. in 1960.

ZAWACKI, Z., and ZBIGNIEW, F. Intermediate Russian: readings, exercises and grammar review. London, Prentice-Hall International, 1962. x, 179 p. 30s.

The authors are both of the University of Wisconsin. 25 lessons. Primarily a reader; the lengthy reading passages have vocabulary and exercises appended. Russian-English vocabulary, p. 141-79.

Russian grammars in Russian

Apart from the standard three-volume Russian reference grammar, *Grammatika russkogo yazyka*, published by the Academy of Sciences (1960), there is the two-volume work with the same title by V. Shcherba (Moscow, Uchpedgiz), which is used in Russian schools. Like Pul'kina's grammar, which has been translated into English (q.v.), the textbook by N. G. Khromets and A. P. Kelsmar, *Spravochnik po russkoĭ* (1960, Collet's, 5s.) is specially designed for foreign students. It concentrates on verbs, as does also M. Ya. Federov and I. P. Kriukova's *Spravochnik po glagol'nomu upravleniyu v russkom yazyke* (3rd ed. Moscow, Uchpedgiz, 1961. 254 p. 5s. 6d.).

Special aspects of grammar

Pronunciation. Orthography. Handwriting. The authoritative work on pronunciation and stress is *Russkoe literaturnoe proiznoshenie i udarenie. Slovar' spravochnik*, edited by R. I. Avanesov and S. I. Ozhegov (1960. 708 p. 10s. 6d.), a dictionary guide to the pronunciation of *c.* 58,000 words, including noun cases, conjugated parts of verbs and short forms of adjectives. D. Ward's *Russian pronunciation illustrated* (Cambridge, University Press, 1966. 101 p. 8s. 6d.) contains 4-12 illustrations per page, plus Russian caption and phonetic transcription and is intended to provide material for practice, particularly in language laboratory work. J. Forsyth's *A practical guide to Russian stress* (Edinburgh, Oliver & Boyd, 1963. x, 150 p. 25s.) is scholarly and includes a select bibliography and an excellent 28-page reference index.

The fullest dictionary of Russian stress and orthography is *Orfograficheskiĭ slovar' russkogo yazyka* (1965. 1,040 p. 12s. 6d.), listing *c.* 104,000 words. Irving J. Saltzman's *Writing Russian script: a self-instructional program* (New York, McGraw-Hill, 1964. iv, 258 p. 23s.; 46s.) is timed to take about 10 hours for completion.

Phrases. A. V. Kunin's *Anglo-russkiĭ fraseologicheskiĭ slovar'* (2nd ed., 1965. 1,455 p. 200s.) gives Russian equivalents for *c.* 25,000 English phrases. For the tourist, there is the portable oblong *English-Russian phrase-book*, by S. V. Neverov (2nd ed., 1956. 181 p. 2s. 6d.) and the small paperback *Traveller's Russian: the phrase book + dictionary in one* (London, Cape, 1965. 141 p. 6*s*.), in which the phrases occupy p. 15–61. J. Burnip's *The teach-yourself Russian phrase book* (English Universities Press, [1957]. xiii, 3–180 p. 2*s*. 6*d*.) and I. B. Faden's *A book of Russian idioms* (Methuen, 1960. 64 p. 6*s*. 6*d*.) are other lists.

The verb. A. Vigelminina's *The Russian verb* (Collet's, 1963. 80 p. 4*s*. 6*d*.) tabulates verb tenses, moods and aspects, and adds exercises and a key. A. B. Murphy's *Aspectival usage in Russian* (Oxford, Pergamon Press, 1965. xiii, 158 p. 21*s*.) deals with a point of major difficulty for the student. The text is enriched with quotations from more than thirty contemporary Soviet writers.

Grammars for Scientists

A recent review of a Russian grammar for scientists in *Nature*[1] contained a statement that an elementary knowledge of the Russian language, plus a good dictionary, should suffice for reading Russian scientific texts. This view calls for considerable qualification: it is not as simple as that. J. W. Perry's *Scientific Russian*, for example, provides a valuable bridge between the elementary grammar and the translating of a scientific text.

BERESFORD, M. Complete Russian course for scientists. Oxford, Clarendon Press, 1965. xvii, [1], 227 p. 25*s*.

The author, lecturer in Russian, University of Manchester, maintains that Russian, though highly inflected, "is not much more difficult to learn for reading purposes than either French or German". 20 lessons, with grammar, exercises and reading passages. Lesson 20 deals with suffixes and roots. Guidance in looking up difficult forms in a dictionary. Supplements on Russian roots, last letters of words (table) and verbs (table). End vocabulary of *c*. 2,500 words; index to grammar. Intended primarily for sixth-form and university use, but can be used as a self-tutor by those who wish to read Russian, either technical or non-technical, or as a work of reference. Valuable and reasonably priced.

BUXTON, C. R., and JACKSON, H. S. Translation from Russian for scientists. London, Blackie, 1960. xix, 299 p. 30*s*.

The authors are on the Department of Modern Languages, Manchester College of Science and Technology, and the Faculty of Technology, University of Manchester, respectively.

Sections: A. Grammar (p. 1–89). B. Sentences for translation (both ways).

[1] V. 196, no. 4857, dated 1st December 1962, p. 872.

C. Annotated texts. D. Physics and electrical engineering. E. Chemistry and chemical technology. Vocabularies, Russian-English only, p. 252–96; index to grammar. Stresses are not marked; cyrillic type is small, but clear. 185 texts in all. The summary of grammar could be used by students requiring Russian for purposes other than reading scientific Russian.

CONDOYANNIS, G. E.   Scientific Russian: a concise description of the structural elements of scientific and technical Russian.   New York, Wiley; London, Chapman & Hall, 1959.   xii, 225 p.   diagrs. Ring binding.   30s.

12 lessons, giving a summary of the grammar and Russian passages for translation, plus notes on these and some drill in Russian words. No vocabulary, although there is a high-frequency word-list of some 200 words; also master verb-tables and a 'List of troublesome words'.

DRESSLER, A.   Introduction to Russian science reading.   London, English Universities Press, 1961.   x, 161 p.   20s.

Provides a short, systematic grammar, notes on how scientific terms are translated *into* Russian, 20 graded passages on general subjects, plus a basic vocabulary of 650 words, hints on dictionaries, and some more difficult scientific passages.

FOURMAN, M.   Science Russian course.   2nd ed.   London, University Tutorial Press, 1961.   viii, 285 p.   13s. 6d.

First published 1949. The author is University Lecturer in the Department of Slavonic Studies, University of Cambridge.

A science Russian reader rather than a course book. The basic grammar (p. 1–47) is followed by 84 extracts from Russian journals and textbooks in the fields of physics, chemistry, mathematics, botany, zoology, physiology and medicine. Many of the extracts are dated 1946 and earlier. The extensive Russian-English vocabulary (p. 233–85) has about 4,000 entries. Good, clear cyrillic type; stresses are marked.

HOLT, A.   Scientific Russian: grammar, reading and specially selected scientific translation exercises, and an extensive glossary.   London, Chapman & Hall, 1962.   xv, [1], 195 p.   36s.

Pt. 1 (p. 1–78) consists of 22 lessons, giving the main features of Russian grammar, plus passages from appropriate scientific texts. Pt. 2 consists mainly of 37 Russian passages for translation, in chemistry, physics and biology. Russian-English vocabulary; index to grammar. Good quality paper; clear cyrillic type.

MAGNER, T. F.   Manual of scientific Russian.   Minneapolis, Burgess Publishing Co.; Englewood Cliffs, N.J., Prentice-Hall, 1958.   iii,

101, [1], p., with 1 p. insert. Ring binding. $3.95. (London, Bailey Bros. & Swinfen. 36s.)

The author is Head of the Department of Slavonic and Oriental Languages, University of Minnesota.

Sections: 1. The structure of Russian (basic grammar). 2. Paradigms (declensions; conjugations). 3. Reference (easily identifiable grammatical data). 4. Vocabulary help (word derivations; prepositions, etc.). 5. Technique of translation. 6. Russian texts and glossary (10 selected passages). The glossary (p. 89–105) is followed by an index to grammar. Unusual treatment and format; good layout.

PERRY, J. W.   Chemical Russian self-taught.   Easton, Pa., Journal of Chemical Production, 1948.   vii, [1], 221 p.   (Contributions to chemical education, no. 4). $3.   (London, Bailey Bros. & Swinfen. 44s.).

The author is now at the College of Engineering, University of Arizona.

7 sections: 1. Aptitude for learning languages. 2. Suggestions for study methods. 3. The vocabulary problem. 4. Inorganic chemical nomenclature (p. 47–67). 5. Organic chemical nomenclature (p. 68–121). 6. Russian grammar (p. 122–66). 7. Glossary of Russian technical terms (about 1,800 terms, with helpful breakdown of compound nouns, verbs, etc.). No stress marks; no exercises or extended Russian passages; no index to grammar.

PERRY, J. W.   Scientific Russian: a textbook for classes and self study. 2nd ed.   New York, Interscience Publishers, 1960 (London, 1961). xxvi, 565 p. $9.50; 79s.

40 lessons, giving detailed grammar, numerous examples of phrases, reading exercises (with notes) and exercises for translation, English into Russian. Russian abbreviations; extensive vocabularies, each way (p. 486–555), and index to grammar. Useful 'Notes on study methods', p. 2–4. Stress is marked; cyrillic type is small but clear. A slight drawback is the profusion of footnotes and cross-references; the vocabularies are each preceded by prefatory notes. According to Neiswender (q.v.), "still the most comprehensive Russian grammar-reader available".

STARCHUK, O., and CHANAL, H.   Essentials of scientific Russian. Reading, Mass., London, etc., Addison-Wesley Publishing Co., Inc., 1963.   xv, 300 p. illus.   45s.

By Head of Slavonic Division, Department of Foreign Languages, University of Alberta, and Former Assistant Professor of Russian, University of Alberta. Claims to be a "textbook which develops the scientific style within the framework of the language as a whole" (*Preface*). Parts: 1. Introduction (with notes on pronunciation). 2. Grammar (15 lessons; p. 19–147). 3. Readings (16 branches of science and technology, p. 151–225, taken from Russian books and periodicals of the period 1955–61). 4. Appendix (conjugation; declension; etc.). 5. Glossary (Russian-English, about 2,500 words, p. 251–93). Russian index; English index. Attractively produced, with good use of bold type.

TURKEVICH, J., and TURKEVICH, L.   Russian for the scientist.   Princeton, N.J., Van Nostrand, 1959.   x, 255 p. $5.95; 30s.

The authors are respectively Professor of Chemistry, Princeton, and Lecturer in Russian at Princeton.

20 lessons, comprising grammar, passages for reading and exercises. Fields of aeronautical engineering, physics, chemistry and biology are covered. The Russian-English vocabulary is followed by a short English-Russian glossary. Appendices include a summary grammar; index to grammar. Well organised; clear lay-out.

WARD, D.   Russian for scientists.   London, University of London Press, 1960.   204 p.   15s.

19 lessons. The author is Head of the Russian Department and Senior Lecturer in Russian, University of Edinburgh.

The grammar covered provides a good general introduction, as in the case of the book by Buxton and Jackson. Each lesson consists of reading matter in science and technology, vocabulary and exercises, Russian into English (32 in all). Russian-English vocabulary, p. 175–200; index to grammar. Good use of bold cyrillic. Sound and comparatively cheap.

WYVILL, P. L.   Russian for chemists.   London, Royal Institute of chemistry, 1966.   vi, 347 p.   18s.

Author is lecturer in physical chemistry, Northern Polytechnic, London. 24 lessons, substantially those published in 24 monthly issues of the *Journal of the Royal Institute of Chemistry*. Each lesson consists of grammar, sentences and passage(s) for translation from Russian, sentences for translation into Russian, lengthy vocabulary and a key to the exercises. Lesson 24 deals with word order. Russian word index, p. 331–47; no index to grammar. Attractive layout and clear typography.

There are a number of scientific Russian readers which assume that the user has some knowledge of Russian grammar. *Scientific Russian reader*, compiled by M. A. Syniawska (New York, Columbia University Press; London, Oxford University Press, 1961. xiii, 177 p. 40s.) is of this type. Extracts are from current Soviet periodicals dated 1957–60; three model translations are included. Another is *Modern Russian reader for technical college students*, edited by N. S. Fidel (London, Pergamon Press, 1961. 134 p. o.p.). N. D. Gershevsky's *Scientific Russian reader* (2nd ed. New York, Pitman, 1960. 266 p. $4; 25s.) and M. and S. A. Emery's *Scientific Russian guide* (New York & London,

McGraw-Hill, 1961. vii, 191 p. $4.50; 44s.) consist largely of only slightly edited Russian texts, and they are expensive.

Wall Charts. *Elementary Russian grammar on one sheet* (19" × 26"), by I. Freiman (3s. 6d.) and *Russian phonetic tables*, by N. A. Lobanova and I. P. Slesareva (28 sheets, ea. 27" × 2", 20s.), are both available at Collet's. Neiswender mentions a *Russian declension chart*, compiled by L. E. Bratt (London, Pitman, [n.d.]. 5s.).

GENERAL DICTIONARIES

The best general English-and-Russian dictionaries are undoubtedly those published in the U.S.S.R. itself, usually with the imprint 'Moskva, Gosudarstvennoe Izdatel'stvo Inostrannykh i Natsional'nykh Slovareĭ' – State Publishing House of Foreign and National Dictionaries – and distributed by Collet's, London. They are cheap, at the expense of poor paper and binding. These dictionaries mark stress but do not give phonetic or other aids to pronunciation of Russian entry-words.

Two small (4⅞" × 3¾") dictionaries that are excellent value for the beginner are by O. S. Akhmanova, – *Russko-angliĭskiĭ slovar'* (7th ed., 1959. 492 p. 6s.) and *Anglo-russkiĭ slovar'* (11th ed., 1959. 590 p. 6s.). They have entries for about 25,000 and 20,000 words respectively, usually give single-word equivalents, but include idioms and have an appendix of geographical names. Specially designed for English-speaking students are: B. A. Lapidus and S. V. Shevtsova (*A Russian-English dictionary for the foreign student of Russian* (1962. 563 p. 7s. 6d.; c. 11,000 entry-words), and S. Folomkina and H. Weiser (*The learner's English-Russian dictionary for English-speaking students* (1962. 655 p. 7s. 6d.; c. 3,500 entry-words).

Medium-sized octavo dictionaries, published by Izdatel'stvo "Sovetskaya Entsiklopediya", Moscow, each with c. 34,000 entry-words, are: A. M. Taube's *Russko-angliĭskiĭ slovar'* (1965. 1,052 p. 17s. 6d.) and V. D. Arakin's *Anglo-russkiĭ slovar'* (7th ed. 1965. 988 p. 17s. 6d.).

For reference, the best one-volume current Russian dictionary is A. I. Smirnitskiĭ's *Russko-angliĭskiĭ slovar'* (1965 ed. 766 p. 35s.). This is a large volume (10½" × 8"), with about 50,000 entries. It gives genders of Russian nouns, refers from perfective forms of verbs, marks stress for both Russian and English words, numbers and categorises different applications of terms, and designates colloquial, idiomatic and technical expression. The appendixes cover geographical names, English grammar, 'The Russian sound-system and the Russian alphabet' and 'Notes on Russian grammar'. Every library should find a place for it. The companion English-Russian dictionary is by V. K. Myuller (1961 and reprints, 1,192 p. 35s.), with 70,000 entries.

Two older dictionaries which are still used were compiled by V. K. Myuller and S. Boyanus, – *Russko-angliĭskiĭ slovar'* (Moscow, Gosud. In-t. 'Sovetskaya entsiklopediya', 1935. 1,643 cols.) and *Anglo-russkiĭ slovar'* (1931. 1,390 cols.), with 60,000 and 40,000 entries (rather cramped) respectively. A war-time reprint of the first was published by Lawrence & Wishart in 1943 (822 p.); typography is rather muddy.

L. Segal's *English-Russian, Russian-English dictionary* (Lund Humphries, 1953. 2,160 p. 52s. 6d.) is fairly attractively produced and includes many technical terms, but it has also many omissions, and equivalents are often not well rendered. M. A. O'Brien's *New English-Russian & Russian-English dictionary* (Allen & Unwin, 1958. xii, 363, xx, 344 p. 25s. or 2 v., ea. 12s. 6d.) has very small type but it does contain handy grammatical information.

A well-recommended Russian-Russian dictionary in one volume is S. I. Ozhegov's *Slovar' russkogo yazyka* (4th ed., revised and enlarged. Moscow, 1960. 900 p. 30s.); it contains about 53,000 entries and gives principal parts and irregularities of verbs.

For the tourist and others who want a two-way dictionary in one volume there is the excellent Bantam Books paperback: *Akhmanova Russian dictionary* (1961. 820 p. $.95), with some 60,000 entries. Also pocket-sized is *Kratkiĭ russko-angliĭskiĭ i anglo-russkiĭ slovar'*, by S. G. Zaimovski (1957 ed. 431 p. 5s. 6d.), with about 18,000 entries in all. Almost as cheap is Collins' Russian gem dictionary, by W. Schapiro (Rev. ed. Collins, 1963. 768 p. 5s.). This gives phonetic pronunciation of Russian words. Langenscheidt's *Russian-English, English-Russian dictionary*, by E. Wedel and A. Romanov (London, Methuen, 1964. 480 p. 18s.), with a total of over 35,000 entry-words, has many virtues: phonetic transcription; graphic symbols and categories; stress marks; conjugation index number for Russian verbs (linked with appendix tables); and comparative cheapness. *The E.U.P. concise Russian and English dictionary*, by J. Grosberg (London, English Universities Press, 1957. xvii, [1], 271 p. 10s. 6d.), has some 18,000 brief entries in all, is well produced and has helpful introductory notes for the user. P. Waddington's *A basic Russian-English vocabulary* (London, Methuen, 1962. xvi, 355 p. 21*s.*; 30*s.*), compiled with the assistance of members of the Association of Teachers of Russian, is supported by an English-Russian index which makes the 3,300 word dictionary virtually two-way, and it includes a list of the 1,300 most essential words for 'O' level. The U.S. War Department *Dictionary of spoken Russian, Russian-English, English-Russian* (New York, Dover; London, Constable, 1958. vi, [1], 573 p. 22*s.*) is a reprint of the war-time *Dictionary of spoken Russian* (Technical manual TM 30–944). It includes many colloquialisms and has a United States and army slant. The Russian-English part has 7,700 word-entries and a grammatical introduction. Type is clear but minute.

Russian abbreviations: a selective list; compiled by Alexander Rosenberg (2nd revised and expanded edition, 1957. ix, 513 p. $2.75), published by the Library of Congress, Washington, D.C., is a valuable adjunct to the above dictionaries.

Pictorial Dictionaries

A good example of an illustrated vocabulary is the *Bildwörterbuch deutsch und russisch* (Leipzig, Verlag Enzyklopädie, 1959. 754 p. 15*s.* 6*d.*). The illustrations are detailed and well drawn and provide a visual aid to some 15,000 names of objects. It is fully indexed. *Russian through pictures*, by I. A. Richards and others (New York, Washington Square Press, 1961. 28, 189 p. 3*s.* 6*d.*) is a paper-back with several hundred single-object illustrations and a Russian-word index.

In Russian schools Z. V. Vlasova's *Anglo-russkiĭ slovar' s illyustratsiyami* (1962. 771 p. 15*s.*) is much used for Russian children learning English, but it could very well be used in reverse by English students of Russian, thanks to the Russian-English index. *Picture dictionary of the Russian language*, by Yu. V. Vannikov and A. N. Shchukin (Moscow, 1965. 441 p. 10*s.* 6*d.*) is for older school-children and adults, and can serve as a supplementary Russian course. For younger Russian children learning their own language a popular pictorial aid is the *Kartinnyi slovar' russkogo yazyka*, by N. V. Chekhov and others (Moscow, Uchpedgiz, 1959. Book 1, R.2.10; Book 2. R.1.60). Each has about 50 pages of illustrations, some in colour. They provide a useful elementary drill in the names of objects, cases governed by prepositions, numerals, etc., working up to short sentences in Book 2. Small children in

Russian schools use *Bukvar'* (11th ed., 1963. 3s. 6d.), an illustrated introduction to letters, sounds and word-building. V. M. Chistiakov's *Nagliadnoe posobie k izucheniyu sintaksisa russkogo yazyka* (3rd rev. ed. Moscow, Uchpedgiz, 1959. 118 p. 9s.) is a visual aid to the study of Russian syntax for upper forms in Russian schools.

Technical Dictionaries

The best and most up-to-date general Russian-English technical dictionary is Ludmilla Ignatiev Callaham's *Russian-English chemical and polytechnical dictionary* (2nd ed. New York & London, 1962. xxxii, 892 p. 147s.), first published in 1947. It has about 30,000 main entries, with many sub-entries, and covers most aspects of science and technology. Different applications of terms are categorised. The volume is particularly easy to use, thanks to good typography. The older and out-of-print *Russian-English scientific-technical dictionary*, by A. Bray (New York, International University Press, 1945. 551 p.) is less comprehensive (c. 22,000 entry-words), but it contains words not in the 1947 Callaham. L. N. Kondratov's *Russko-angliĭskiĭ politekhnicheskiĭ slovar'* (Moscow, Gostekhizdat, 1948, and reprints (e.g., 1963). 348 p. Flegon Press. 40s.) needs to be brought up to date. A basic vocabulary of 3,250 entry-words is found in *Concise Russian-English scientific dictionary*, by A. Blum, Senior Lecturer in Russian at Ealing Technical College, London (Oxford, Pergamon Press, 1965. 124 p. 12s. 6d.; 20s.). The up-to-date companion to (and in part reversal of) Kondratov is A. E. Chernukhin's *Anglo-russkiĭ tekhnicheskiĭ slovar'* (Collet's, 1962. 663 p. 30s.), with c. 75,000 entry-words. *Soviet Russian scientific and technical terms: a selective list* (Washington, Library of Congress, Reference Department, Aerospace Information Division, 1963. [v], 668 p. $3.50) has 26,000 entries, – generally "terms which cannot be found in standard dictionaries, or which have a special meaning when used in a particular field". Many names of Soviet organisations are included.

In specialised fields the following are notable Russian-English dictionaries:

CARPOVICH, E. A.   Russian-English biological and medical dictionary. New York, Technical Dictionaries, 1958.   398 p. $12.

32,650 entries, including words in common usage. Does not include abbreviations or state genders, plurals or indicate stress, but it gives direct adjective-noun entries. Particularly valuable for biological terms that frequently appear in the medical literature and are not found in any other work. Applications of terms are categorised.

EMIN, I.   Russian-English physics dictionary.   New York & London, Wiley, 1963.   xxx, 554 p.   105s.

25,000 entry-words, with English equivalents. Includes terms in allied fields, the dictionary having its origin in 4 preliminary glossaries (1957–58) covering acoustics and ultrasonics, electronics and physics, nuclear physics and engineering, and solid state physics. Reference section has notes on Russian technical word endings, verb formation and the like. Clear typography.

JABLONSKI, S.   Russian-English medical dictionary; edited by Ben S. Levine.   New York & London, Academic Press, 1958.   xi, 423 p. $11; 88s.

About 29,000 entries. More strictly medical-technical than Carpovich and lists frequently used Russian medical abbreviations (categorised). Particularly good for pharmaceutical terms. Carpovich and Jablonski are considered to supplement each other very well.

KONARSKI, M. M.   Russian-English dictionary of modern terms on aeronautics and rocketry.   Oxford, Pergamon Press, 1962.   ix, 515 p.   £10.

More than 14,500 numbered Russian terms currently used in Soviet aeronautics, radio, electronics, meteorology and air photography, with English equivalents and an index of English terms. Meticulously accurate but includes some padding (ordinary technical terms). Costly.

SMITH, R. E. F.   A Russian-English dictionary of social science terms. London, Butterworth, 1962.   xil, 495 p.   95s.

Compiler is Research Fellow, Department of Economics and Institutions of the U.S.S.R., University of Birmingham. About 10,000 entry-words, including entries for abbreviations; c. 35,000 definitions, some with explanations. Includes terms from sociology, politics, economics, accountancy, public administration, welfare and education. Considered by the reviewer in *Babel* (v. 9, no. 4, 1963, p. 197) to be an important contribution to an area in which terminology is often equivocal or difficult to render into English. Clear layout.

SOFIANO, T. A.   Russko-angliĭskiĭ geologicheskiĭ slovar'.   Moscow, Fizmatgiz, 1960; London, Collet's, 1961.   559 p.   30s.

About 30,000 entry-words, covering geology, geophysics, hydrogeology, mineralogy, stratigraphy, tectonics, palaeontology, geochemistry, etc. Short list of abbreviations.

A 2nd edition of Sofiano's *Anglo-russkiĭ geologicheskiĭ slovar'* appeared in 1960.

Usovskiĭ, B. N., and others.   Russko-angliĭskiĭ sel'skokhozyaistvennyi slovar'.   Moscow, Fizmatgiz, 1960.   504 p.   20s.

> More than 30,000 Russian entry-words, with English equivalents, in agriculture and related subjects. Botanical Latin names of plants are given. Appendix of abbreviations and symbols.
> The complementary *Anglo-russkiĭ sel'skokhozyaistvennyĭ slovar'* had its 3rd ed. in 1956.

Voskoboinik, D. I., and Tsimmerman, M. G.   Russko-angliĭskiĭ yadernyĭ slovar'.   Moscow, Fizmatgiz, 1960.   334 p.   20s.

> More than 20,000 Russian nuclear terms, with English equivalents, appendix list of abbreviations and table of elements and isotopes. Russian genders and stress are shown. Not so in the complementary volume, *Anglo-russkiĭ yadernyĭ slovar'* (1960. 400 p. 20s.).

An interesting study of the coverage of some eighty Russian-English technical dictionaries is Professor A. F. Hubell's *Russian-English scientific and technical dictionaries: a survey* (New York, National Science Foundation, 1960. 20 p. 40cs.). This helpfully notes, for example, the way in which the Carpovich and Jablonski dictionaries complement each other.

There has been a spate of English-Russian scientific and technical dictionaries published in the U.S.S.R. for Russian specialists. A few of them carry Russian indexes.

GRAMOPHONE RECORDS

Two of the best-known gramophone record courses are those that accompany grammars: Potapova's *Russian course on records* (four 10″ L.P. records, with 78-page booklet. Collet's 90s.), to accompany the two-volume *Russian: an elementary course;* and the Assimil 20-lesson preliminary and advanced course (twenty 10″ 78 r.p.m. or ten 7″ 45 r.p.m. records, £14), to accompany Chérel's *Russian without toil.* S. A. Khavronina's *Russian as we speak it* (new edition in preparation) is on tape, – three 5″ reels or two 5¾″, at 3¾ i.p.s. £8 8s.). The Linguaphone course consists of 16 L.P. 45 or 78 r.p.m. records, plus a course-book, at £17 4s. 1d.; it is also available on tape (two 5″ spools, at 3¾ i.p.s., 2-track recording). The Harrap-Didier Audio-visual language course, Méthode audio-visuelle de russe, is designed to teach by the

Direct Method, integrating a series of situations on film strips with dialogues on records and tapes, plus a student's handbook (price on application to Harrap Audio-Visual Aids). The "Daily Express" issues a 'Basic conversational Russian' course, consisting of two 12″ 33⅓ r.p.m. L.P. records, with an illustrated phrase book, at £6 5s.

There are various shorter courses. Dover have a 'Listen and learn Russian' course on two 12″ L.P. discs, at 58s. The 'Instant' Russian course is on two 12″ L.P. records, accompanied by two word-books and a 25,000-word dictionary (Rainbow Hi-fi Records, £3 10s.). The Hugophone record (12″ L.P. 33⅓ r.p.m. 33s. 6d.) – "not a language course, but an advanced help to pronunciation" – is accompanied by two dialogue cards. The Conversaphone 'C' language course in Russian also consists of one record (10″ L.P.), with instruction manual, at 30s. 6d. Intended for pronunciation practice, "Russian: 200 basic words" (Saga Records) consists of one 7″ 45 r.p.m. record at 7s. 6d.

Collet's Russian teaching aids catalogue, 1966, gives details of Russian-published audio-visual aids, tapes and film strips. It is supplemented by a quarterly list, 'Russian literary recordings & film strips'.

BIBLIOGRAPHY

The following bibliographical aids are recommended to those who require a fuller survey of Russian grammars, dictionaries and philology in general.

NEISWENDER, R. Guide to Russian reference and language aids. New York, Special Libraries Association, 1962. iv, 92 p. (Special Libraries Association bibliography, no. 4). $4.25.

   A comprehensive, up-to-date and well annotated guide to some 450 items, with an index to authors, subjects and titles. Sections: Textbooks and readers. – Language records. – Dictionaries and glossaries. – Encyclopedias and encyclopedic dictionaries. – Geographical reference works. – Bibliographies, indexes and other reference sources. U.S. imprints and prices are given.

UNBEGAUN, B. O., and SIMMONS, J. S. G. A bibliographical guide to the Russian language. Oxford, Clarendon Press, 1953. xi, [2], 174 p. 35s.

   Particularly valuable for historical works; academic approach. 1,043 numbered items, most of the entries being annotated. Chapters 7 and 8 deal respectively with modern literary Russian grammars (especially items 606–625) and modern literary Russian vocabulary.

HORECKY, P. L., ed.   Basic Russian publications: an annotated bibliography on Russia and the Soviet Union.   Chicago, University of Chicago Press, 1962.   xxvi, 313 p. $6.50; 48s.

> Five main sections: 1. Bibliography. – 2. Serials. – 3. Modern Russian language. – 4. History of the Russian language. – 5. Dialectology. Section 3, p. 175–86 (items 880–952), is by Professor B. O. Unbegaun. The detailed index covers authors, titles of publications and principal subject headings.

POCKNEY, B. P., and SOLLOHUB, N. S.   Bibliography of Russian teaching materials.   Prelim. ed.   London, Nuffield Foreign Language Teaching Materials Project; Association of Teachers of Russian, June 1966.   43 p.   Mimeographed.   Unpriced.

> Contains only items at present available in Britain, in 14 classes of books, records tapes, etc. Most of the titles have been published in the last six years and are a testimony to the increased interest in Russian. 48 publishers are listed; no author index.

Critical reviews of new Russian grammars, dictionaries, etc., appear in such periodicals as *Babel, The incorporated linguist, Soviet studies* and *The Anglo-Soviet journal.*

10

FINNISH

by J. E. O. Screen, M.A., A.L.A.

The Finnish language has a reputation for peculiarity and difficulty. Many people know that it is a Finno-Ugrian language and, as such, related to Hungarian. Less common is the realization that Finnish and Hungarian have been developing separately since perhaps about 2,500 B.C., and that the relationship between them is thus exceedingly distant. The introduction to a recently published Finnish grammar quoted a Finn who said, with forgivable exaggeration, "We have the world's most private language." This linguistic isolation increases the need for Finns to learn foreign languages and is reflected in the style of linguistic dictionaries published in Finland, in which features intended to assist the foreigner are relatively rare. The lack of up-to-date foreign language dictionaries has caused concern in Finland, and proposals for linguistic research during the period 1966–80 include the establishment of a research institute to co-ordinate the compilation of a new series of dictionaries.[1]

Although the 'private' nature of Finnish diminishes the incentive to foreigners to learn it, interest in the language is growing and some useful introductory works have appeared during the last few years, both in Finland and the United States. In spite of the sixteen cases governing nouns and adjectives, the absence of definite and indefinite articles and grammatical gender, the paucity of consonants and abundant use of vowels, an elementary knowledge of spoken Finnish is not difficult to acquire. Unfortunately, there are few opportunities to do so in this country, except by private tuition or working on one's own. There are, however, indications that classes in Finnish may be instituted regularly in London. In addition, some instruction in Finnish will be introduced as part of the Hungarian degree course at the School of Slavonic and East European Studies (University of London) from October 1967.

---

[1] Kansallisten tieteiden kehittämisohjelma, 1966–80. *Suomi*, 112i, 1965. p. 32–35. Economic difficulties have seriously retarded the implementation of this programme.

The student who has passed the elementary stage will find the following readers helpful and interesting: Austerlitz, R. *Finnish reader and glossary*. Reprint, corrected. (Bloomington, Indiana university, 1966. (Uralic and Altaic series, 15). $6); Heiskanen, T. J., and Magoun, F. P., ed. *Graded Finnish reader* (Helsinki, Suomalaisen kirjallisuuden seura, 1957. 3 v. ea. 4.45 Fmk.). More demanding linguistically, but valuable as a representative selection of Finnish prose and verse writing, is: Ravila, P., ed. *Finnish literary reader, with notes* (Bloomington, Indiana university, 1965. (Uralic and Altaic series, 44). $2.50). A standard work on the language itself is: Hakulinen, L. *The structure and development of the Finnish language;* translated by J. Atkinson (Bloomington, Indiana university, 1961. (Uralic and Altaic series, 3 . $7).

GRAMMARS

AALTIO, M. H.   Essential Finnish.   London, University of London Press, 1964.   315 p.   32s. 6d.   Published in Helsinki by Otava as *Finnish for foreigners*.

The primary aim is to teach the beginner spoken Finnish. Divided into an introduction on pronunciation, orthography and syllable division (p. 15–18), 40 lessons (p. 19–283), and appendices containing paradigms and a key to most of the exercises (p. 285–315). The lessons consist of a dialogue or narrative, structural notes, reader, exercises and vocabulary. Most of the dialogues deal with practical situations and have parallel translations (American English). The structural notes are not intended as a complete grammar but are sufficient to meet the book's secondary aim of providing an introduction to the written language with its different constructions. The length of exercises and vocabularies is well judged. Some illustrations. A fresh and imaginative work: highly recommended. The 2nd Finnish edition (1966), which contains minor revisions and corrections and adds an index, is unlikely to be issued in this country before 1968.

ATKINSON, J.   Finnish grammar.   2nd ed.   Helsinki, Finnish Literature Society, 1961.   131 p.   6.75 Fmk.

Aims "to provide, in as brief a compass as possible, a comprehensive description of Finnish together with rules for the formation of all parts of speech." A careful, traditional grammar, divided into 25 lessons. To keep the cost of production down, few readings have been included and there are no exercises. Excellent for reference and for acquiring quickly a basic knowledge of grammar for reading the language. Very useful guide for English teachers of Finnish.

HARMS, R. T.   Finnish structural sketch. Bloomington, Indiana university, 1964. vii, 105 p. (Uralic and Altaic series, 42). $3.

"The final or morphophonemic stage of a transformational grammar of spoken standard Finnish." A list of rules, with examples, for stem formation, suffix-allomorph selection, morphophoneme sequence and phonetics. There are indexes of symbols and suffixes, a glossary, and illustrative paradigms. For the student of linguistics only.

LEHTINEN, M.   Basic course in Finnish. (Supervised and edited by T. A. Sebeok.) Bloomington, Indiana University, 1963. xxxiii, 657 p. (Uralic and Altaic series, 27). $15.

A radical revision of Sebeok's *Spoken Finnish* (1947). Designed to be used in intensive first-year Finnish courses, involving at least 5 hours class-work a week plus additional work in a language laboratory. Five of the 33 chapters review topics like the formation of words and finite verb forms, the others follow a pattern: basic sentences, dialogues covering daily situations, grammar, and drills to test fluency. Helpful explanations of Finnish manners and customs. Appendix I summarises various grammatical points and gives declensions and conjugations. Appendix II consists of songs with translations. The glossary (p. 619–657) lists all the words used in this massive work. A good course for class instruction in spoken Finnish.

TUOMIKOSKI, A., and DEANS, H.   Elementary Finnish; translated and adapted from Eero K. Neuvonen's 'Éléments de finnois' (2nd ed.). Helsinki, Suomalaisen kirjallisuuden seura, 1952. 85, [2] p. 2.20 Fmk.

Pt. I: Easy texts (p. 5–25). Pt. II: Selected passages (p. 26–38). Pt. III: A short Finnish grammar (p. 39–70). Glossary (p. 71–85). The "easy texts", consisting of a few sentences, of practical as well as grammatical utility, are linked to the grammar by reference to the paragraph numbers of Part III. The grammar is concise but clear; the selected passages varied and entertaining.

WHITNEY, A. H.   Teach yourself Finnish. Reprint. London, English Universities Press, 1964. xii, 13–301 p. (Teach yourself books). 10s. 6d.

"Covers the whole of the grammar of the present-day standard language" (p. v). An introduction on pronunciation, consonant modification and vowel assonance precedes 20 lessons, each arranged in a set pattern: grammatical notes, vocabulary, exercise (Finnish into English, with key at end of book), and reading. The readings form a connected story. The amount of vocabulary for each lesson is intimidating – 150 words is typical and 250 occasional – and the grammatical notes, because of their comprehensiveness, are also long and hard-going for the beginner working on his own.

GENERAL DICTIONARIES

ALANNE, V. S. Suomalais-englantilainen sanakirja. [2nd ed.] Porvoo, Söderström, 1962. xxxiv, [i], 1,111 p. 31 Fmk.

An extensive revision, dating from 1956, of the author's Finnish-English dictionary published in 1919. Some more recent terms incorporated in the addenda in 1962 (p. 1,108–1,111). Many examples of usage. Some colloquialisms. Features especially valuable to the English user include the indication with an asterisk of words subject to consonant gradation, the citation alongside the infinitive of the present tense first person singular where this is irregular, and, in some cases, references to infinitives from other verb forms. For the Finnish user there is a detailed guide to English pronunciation and a list of differences between English and American usage. The best large Finnish-English dictionary.

HALME, P. E. Suomalais-englantilainen sanakirja. Helsinki, Suomalaisen kirjallisuuden seura, 1957. 632 p. (Suomalaisen kirjallisuuden seuran toimituksia, 255). 17.80 Fmk.

Finnish-English dictionary designed for Finns, giving the principal parts of English irregular verbs, and including appendices on British currency, temperature scales and weights and measures, but with no guidance on pronunciation. The number of examples of the usage of words like *saada* is relatively few. No indication of consonant modification. Effectively meets its aim to cover the practical linguistic needs of everyday life. Excellent typography.

HART, K. A., and LAHTINEN, A. T. K. Englantilais-suomalainen idiomisanakirja. I osa: verbit. English-Finnish dictionary of idioms. Part one: verbal idioms Helsinki, Otava, 1965. 340 p. 20 Fmk.

Contains the Finnish equivalents of a good variety of English verbal idioms both formal (e.g. "keep house") and informal (e.g. "blow one's top"). The index from Finnish to English (p. 333–340) makes it possible to find English equivalents of some Finnish verbal idioms. A companion volume on substantival, adjectival and adverbial idioms is to be published in late 1967 or early 1968.

RIIKONEN, E., and TUOMIKOSKI, A. Englantilais-suomalainen sanakirja. [3rd ed.] Helsinki, Otava, 1967. 832, [3] p. 32 Fmk.

Reprint of a medium-sized English-Finnish dictionary first published in 1964, and aiming to cover the development of the language in the last decades. Smaller in size and scope than Tuomikoski and Slöör, with correspondingly fewer examples of usage and idiomatic expressions; its advantage lies in the use of more modern sources and the inclusion of up-to-date vocabulary: in these respects it complements the larger work. Helps the

Finnish user by giving the pronunciation of English words and referring from irregular word forms.

TUOMIKOSKI, A., and SLÖÖR, A.   Englantilais-suomalainen sanakirja. [4th ed.]   Helsinki, Suomalaisen kirjallisuuden seura, 1964.   xiii, 1,100 p.   (Suomalaisen kirjallisuuden seuran toimituksia, 212). 20 Fmk.

This is a reprint of the 2nd revised edition (1948), which added some new material (p. 1,069–1,100) to an English-Finnish dictionary first published in 1939. Although its broad scope ensures its continued value, some words now in regular use are lacking (e.g. 'computer'). Numerous examples of usage and many idiomatic phrases. Some slang. Subject fields are distinguished by abbreviations and symbols. Useful features for the Finnish user include assistance with English pronunciation, references from irregular word forms, indication of etymology, and appendices of abbreviations, proper names, and tables of British and United States weights, measures and money.

VUOLLE, A.   Englantilais-suomalainen pienois-sanakirja.   [10th ed.] Porvoo, Söderström, 1961.   458 p.   2.40 Fmk.

VUOLLE, A.   Suomalais-englantilainen pienois-sanakirja.   [10th ed.] Porvoo, Söderström, 1959.   362 p.   2.40 Fmk.

Miniature dictionaries for use by Finns, but with conversations, numerals and a menu that might be helpful to English visitors to Finland. Less satisfactory in format and content than *Suomi-englanti-suomi*.
The author's name is also spelled Wuolle.

WUOLLE, A.   Englantilais-suomalainen sanakirja.   [10th ed.]   Porvoo, Söderström, 1964.   x, 535, [1] p.   6 Fmk.

WUOLLE, A.   Suomalais-englantilainen sanakirja.   [10th ed.]   Porvoo, Söderström, 1966.   [viii], 440 p.   6 Fmk.

These valuable medium-sized dictionaries, suitable for the needs of the small library and most students, are frequently reprinted – the reprints being called editions – and were both revised in 1964. The vocabulary is up-to-date (e.g. there is an entry for anti-missile missile), and there is a good range of examples of usage. The English-Finnish volume gives the pronunciation of English words.

WUOLLE, A.   Suomi-englanti-suomi.   [5th ed.]   Porvoo, Söderström, 1965.   [iv], 176, 180 p.   (Punaiset sanakirjat).   4.50 Fmk.

More modern than the miniature dictionaries. A Finnish-English and English-Finnish pocket dictionary convenient for the English traveller although it contains no features designed to assist him.

SPECIAL DICTIONARIES

AIRAS, V., and others, ed.   Tekniikan sanasto, saksa-englanti-suomi-ruotsi-venäjä. [2nd ed.] Helsinki, Otava, 1950–52. 2 v.   108s. the set.

V. 1 (xxiv p., 1,518 cols.) is a German-English-Finnish-Swedish-Russian technical dictionary; v. 2 provides English, French, Swedish and Russian indexes. About 35,000 entry-words. No genders given. About a hundred graphic symbols are used to categorise terms.

ARO, P., and others, ed.   Suomalais-ruotsalais-saksalais-englantilainen metsäsanakirja . . .   Finnish-Swedish-German-English forest dictionary. Helsinki, Otava, 1944. 37, [174], 51, 65, 76, 6 p. 20 Fmk.

Dictionary of terms used in forestry, comprising 9,440 Finnish entry words with Swedish, German and English equivalents. Separate Swedish, German and English indexes refer to the Finnish entry by column and line number. Also an index of Latin words. Forestry is interpreted widely. Symbols are used to denote technical and industrial terms.

JÄÄSKELÄINEN, M., comp.   Suomalais-ruotsalais-englantilais-saksalais-ranskalainen kauppasanakirja. 23476 suomalaista ja vieraskielistä hakusanaa sekä lyhennysten luettelo. Helsinki, Otava, 1957. 397 p.   19 Fmk.

A compact dictionary of commercial terms with 23,476 Finnish and foreign entry-words. Two parts: Finnish words with their Swedish, English, German and French equivalents (p. 11–176), and a single sequence of all non-Finnish words referring to the Finnish terms (p. 179–385). Appendix of abbreviations (p. 386–397).

MALI, L., comp.   Maatalouden sanakirja. Lantbrukets ordbok. Landwirtschaftliches Wörterbuch. Agricultural dictionary. Suomen maataloustieteellisen seuran toimeksiannosta laatinut; compiled under the auspices of the Scientific agricultural society of Finland. Helsinki, Otava, 1958. xxviii, [300], 177 p. 50 Fmk.

Covers a wide range of terms relating to agriculture, forestry and fishing. Main sequence of Finnish words with Swedish, German and English equivalents. Subject fields are denoted by symbols. Separate indexes for Swedish, German and English, referring to the column and line number of the equivalent Finnish term. Additional index of Latin scientific terms.

Miss Mali is on the point of completing a dictionary of terms used in domestic science.

SULONEN, K., and LEIKKOLA, U. Urheilusanakirja; englanti-saksa-ruotsi-suomi. Sportlexikon; engelska-tyska-svenska-finska. Dictionary of sports; English-German-Swedish-Finnish. Sportwörter-buch; englisch-deutsch-schwedisch-finnisch. Porvoo, Söderström, 1952. xxx, 1,003 p. (Valtion urheilulautakunnan julkaisuja).

Emphasises athletics, although a variety of sports mentioned. The main sequence is of English words, with German, Swedish and Finnish equivalents. and separate indexes.

TALVITIE, Y. Englantilais-suomalainen tekniikan ja kaupan sanakirja. [2nd ed.] Lahti, Tietoteos, 1960. xi, [748] p. £15.

Comprehensive English-Finnish scientific, technical and commercial dictionary, with over 100,000 entry words, printed in double columns (cols. 1–1,450). There is also an extensive list of abbreviations, with three columns per page (cols. 1,451–1,507).

GRAMOPHONE RECORDS

There are very few Finnish language courses on records. The extensive Linguaphone course comprises 16 L.P. 78 r.p.m. records, plus a course-book, at £17 4s. 1d. The short Conversa-phone 'C' course consists of one 10″ L.P. record and an instruction manual, at 30s. 6d.

II

CHINESE

by A. C. Barnes, b.a.

INTRODUCTION

Standard Chinese (i.e. the Mandarin dialects as a whole) is spoken by five hundred million people and is being taught as a matter of Government policy in the non-Mandarin speaking areas of China (roughly, the area south of the Yangtse and east of 110° E.).

Structurally, Chinese resembles English: the morphology has been streamlined to about the same extent, and word-order rather than morphology is used to express grammatical relationships. The lexis is almost entirely native and, unlike English, Chinese draws on its own lexical resources, ancient and modern, for the formation of new technical terms. Most words are of two or three syllables, though usually analysable into invariant monosyllabic morphemes (living or dead), hence the old misleading description of Chinese as a "monosyllabic language". Phonetically, it presents very few difficulties: the tonal element is far less important than the layman is given to understand and may be ignored with very little loss of intelligibility (it is ignored, for instance, in Chinese shorthand), and, as in English, there is a strong word-stress.

If the language itself (apart from the completely unfamiliar vocabulary) is relatively easy, the script is a nightmare of complexity and inefficiency and constitutes the principal deterrent to the study of Chinese. It is syllabic, with no word-division, and nowadays written from left to right except for special purposes such as spine-titling. Most syllabic signs (characters) consist of a phonetic element with or without the addition of a determinative element that often gives a clue to the meaning of the syllable represented; but the script reached its present form over two thousand years ago, since when Chinese phonology has changed drastically, words have undergone extensions of meaning, and characters have been re-used as phonetic loans, with the result that phonetic and determinative clues now offer little assistance to the student, who is confronted with the learning of several thousand apparently arbitrary syllabic signs (four thousand are adequate for most purposes). This represents a considerable investment of time and effort, and unless one is prepared to go all the way with the learning of the script, the return in terms of fluent reading ability will be small.

An added complication is that the script (like the Japanese script after the Second World War) is being simplified by government decree. The simplified forms have been decided upon but the rate at which the 'old' characters have been replaced by individual printers has been very uneven. This means that the student has to learn both the old and the 'new' forms (actually most of the 'new' printed forms are hand-written abbreviations of long standing). He will, for instance, be confronted with a word printed in simplified characters in a newspaper and be unable to find it except in a dictionary printed in traditional characters. The simplifications are of two kinds: (*a*) the abolition of 1,821 characters representing variant spellings of other characters, (*b*) the simplification of 506 individual characters (of which 132 occur as elements of more complex characters) and of 14 elements occurring only in combination. Since the latter 146 elements occur in thousands of characters and since no limit has been placed on the number of characters ancient and modern, common and rare, in which they may be replaced by the simplified forms, it is impossible to say how many characters will be affected altogether. On the average, every third character in a piece of running text will be partly or wholly simplified by the omission or replacement of constituent elements.

The principal systems of romanization in current use in textbooks and dictionaries are (1) Wade-Giles, the traditional English system, (2) the Yale University system, (3) Gwoyeu Romatzyh (G.R.), the old official Chinese system, which indicates tonal difference by differences in spelling, and (4) Pinyin Zimu, the new official Chinese system. Others encountered are the Cyrillic system in Russian-language publications, the French and German systems, and (still in use in China) the old Chuyin Tzumu alphabet based on elements from the Chinese script. A detailed description of transliteration systems is about to be published and will probably become the standard work of reference: *Guide to transliterated Chinese in the modern Peking dialect;* compiled and introduced by I. L. Legeza (Leiden, Brill, 1967).

V. 1: *Conversion tables of the currently used international and European systems. With comparative tables of initials and finals.*

The two main methods of arrangement of Chinese entries in dictionaries and indexes are (*a*) by the sound of the word, and (*b*) by the shape of the character. For the former purpose one of the above-mentioned romanisations is usually employed and presents no special problems. The latter may be subdivided into two types: (*a*) the traditional arrangement, and (*b*) various new systems. With the traditional arrangement, characters are classified primarily under 'radicals' and secondarily under the number of strokes in the character. The 'radicals' are 214 character-elements, largely coinciding with the determinative elements, though sometimes quite arbitrarily chosen. The new systems are based on the shapes of the strokes taken in the order in which they are written (the Russian system takes them in *reverse* order) and/or the number of strokes. Since the new simplified characters often have no traditionally recognised 'radical', Chinese lexicographers and indexers are having to abandon the traditional system in favour of one of the newer systems, though of course the traditional system must be known if one is to use any but the latest works of reference.

A knowledge of written Chinese provides a basis for the rapid acquirement of written (but not spoken) Japanese, since the bulk of the written vocabulary is common to both languages, though the grammar is very different.

Modern written Chinese, based largely on the spoken language, has come into general use since the First World War, almost entirely superseding the Classical Chinese that had until then been in use for all writing except some fiction. The term "Classical Chinese" is applied to the language of all Chinese writing of the past two and a half millennia up to the First World War, including the Confucian Classics. Though developing various widely divergent styles, this classical language remained remarkably consistent, especially over the last two millennia. It was abandoned on the pretext of being an inadequate vehicle for twentieth-century ideas, despite the fact that it had proved admirably adaptable to an immense variety of technical and artistic purposes. Though modern written Chinese is largely based on the colloquial so far as its grammar and basic vocabulary are concerned, the inevitable poverty of the exising colloquial dialects has forced modern Chinese writers to fall back on the abundant resources of the Classical language, and even to borrow from Japanese, for creating new terms and even for composing political slogans. And with the spread of literacy and education, this new written language is enriching the spoken language and providing a channel back to life for elements from the ancient written language. This means that one cannot study modern Chinese without paying some attention to the Classical language (richly rewarding in itself), though this may be deferred to a later stage of one's studies. Twentieth-century academic writing is particularly prone to mixed Classical-and-Modern styles, and it is no longer possible to draw a dividing line between the two languages.

Modern Chinese is moderately well documented, though not always in European languages. The best lexicography is in Japanese (e.g. Kuraishi, Takeshirō. *Chūgokugo Jiten*. Tokyo, Iwanami Shoten, 1963), and the fullest reference grammars are in Chinese (e.g. Li, Chin-hsi. *Hsinchu Kuoyü Wenfa*. Shanghai, Commercial Press, 1924; 19th edition 1954).

Classical Chinese, on the other hand, is still inadequately documented. The largest dictionary of Classical Chinese is in Japanese (Morohashi, Tetsuji. *Dai Kan-Wa Jiten*. 13 v. Tokyo, Taishūkan, 1955–1960), and the fullest reference grammar is in Chinese (Chou, Fa-kao. *Chungkuo Kutai Yüfa*. Taipei Institute of History and Philology of Academia Sinica. v. 1–3, 1959–62; v. 4 awaited).

Whereas for Modern Chinese we are now well provided with elementary courses of systematic grammatical and syntactic drill, thanks mainly to the stimulus of military and political requirements, no such course has yet been published for Classical Chinese.

Since 1949 the Chinese language has changed a great deal, particularly in its vocabulary. Unfortunately, these changes are not reflected in re-editions of textbooks published before 1949, nor in the majority of textbooks published since that date in the United States. The social situations and atmosphere portrayed in these books are similarly out of date and a Chinese under thirty would find the language and subject-matter quaint and old-fashioned. For instance, one could cause great offence by following de Francis's *Beginning Chinese* (1963) and *Intermediate Chinese* (1964) and addressing a waiter as 'huoji' instead of the normal 'tongzhi' ('comrade'). Worse than this, a student could spend several years working through current American textbooks without ever meeting this universal form of address for stangers, the current

Chinese counterpart of 'monsieur'. The most urgent need in the field of textbooks of current Chinese is something comparable to the Yale courses but presenting the language of today rather than of the last generation. It seems unlikely that such courses will be produced in the United States for some years to come, and Chinese departments in European universities lack the large staffs and funds necessary to produce such courses.

What, then, is the would-be student of modern Chinese to do? He should take full advantage of the available material for mastering the phonetics, grammar and syntax of the language, then, as soon as possible, turn to current Chinese publications (with the aid of translations where available) for the study of contemporary vocabulary and idiom. This is admittedly unsatisfactory, but it is the best that can be done for the time being.

TEXTBOOKS, GRAMMARS AND READERS OF THE MODERN LANGUAGE

The largest integrated series of textbooks is the Mirror Series published by the Institute of Far Eastern Languages of Yale University. These are so planned that the student can concentrate on a spoken or a written course or on both as he prefers. They also permit specialisation after the groundwork has been laid. They are pedagogically sound, though in some of them misprints are more frequent than they should be in books which may be used for self-tuition. For the most part they use pre-reform script. The romanisation is the Yale system throughout. One drawback is that the language and subject-matter of most of them are a little dated. The following titles do not represent all the material available. The serial number of each work in the Mirror Series is given after the title:

TEWKESBURY, M. G. Speak Chinese. (No. A/1). New Haven, Yale University Press, 1948. xvi, 189 p. 24s.

For beginners. The approach is from sentence-patterns, i.e. exercise material is limited to sentence structures already taught. Each of the 24 lessons introduces new vocabulary and sentence-patterns, which are exercised systematically. Romanisation only is used. One disadvantage is that almost all exercise material is accompanied by a translation printed beside it, which means that for class use additional materials need to be devised. There is a vocabulary with references to first occurrence and a useful index to the grammatical notes.

WANG, F. Y.   Chinese dialogues.   (No. A/5).   New Haven, Yale University Press, 1953.   vi, 385 p.   32s.

Intended as a continuation of the preceding work. Again, romanisation only is used throughout. Each of the 24 lessons consists of a Chinese dialogue without an English translation, new vocabulary with examples, sentence structures introduced, and exercises involving translation in both directions. An index to notes on sentence structure is appended, and also a vocabulary with references to first occurrence. The subject matter is social and domestic.

WANG, F. Y.   Read Chinese: a beginning text in the Chinese character. (No. A/4).   New Haven, Yale University Press, 1961. xxiii, 236 p.   25s.

Intended to be preceded by at least the first 12 lessons of Tewkesbury, M. G. *Speak Chinese*. The 20 lessons consist of new vocabulary in large brushed characters and text-matter (sentences and anecdotes) employing only the characters met so far; the parts of the text represented by characters not yet met are given in romanisation, resulting in a mixture of characters and romanisation in which the proportion of the former to the latter progressively increases. A stroke-order list and a vocabulary are appended.

WANG, F. Y.   The lady in the painting.   (No. A/23).   New Haven, Yale University Press, 1957.   vi, 87 p.   12s.

A Chinese folk-tale retold using a vocabulary of 300 characters, intended to follow the preceding work. The characters are legibly written with a pen. A list of vocabulary not occurring in *Read Chinese* is appended.

CHANG, R. I.   Read Chinese.   Book 2.   (No. A/24).   New Haven, Yale University Press, 1958.   x, 223 p.   25s.

To follow F. Y. Wang's *Read Chinese*. A second 300 characters are introduced, with occasional romanisation in the text in place of characters not yet introduced. Characters are pen-written, and the vocabularies are given in large brushed characters. The 15 lessons contain, apart from vocabulary, sentences and anecdotes as in *Read Chinese*. A vocabulary arranged by number of strokes is appended.

CHANG, R. I., and WANG, F. Y.   Read Chinese.   Book 3 (No. B/3). New Haven, Yale University Press, 1961.   xiv, 57, 84, 101 p. 25s.

Intended to follow the preceding work, introducing an additional 400 characters. The 20 lessons consist of passages in Chinese legibly pen-written and notes mainly on vocabulary. A vocabulary arranged by number of strokes is appended.

LEE, P. C.   Read about China.   (No. 16).   2nd ed.   New Haven, Yale University Press, 1958.   iv, 72, 92 p.   25s.

Intended to follow *Read Chinese*, introducing a second 300 characters. Characters not yet met replaced by romanisation, though the characters are given in the notes. The work consists of 20 connected passages each followed by sentences using the same material, the whole legibly pen-written. These are followed by vocabulary and notes comprising more than half of the book.

These introductory textbooks serve as a preparation for more specialised works, of which some are given below.

CHIH, Y. J. A primer of newspaper Chinese. (No. A/12). New Haven, Yale University Press, 1956. ix, 219 p. 24s.

A knowledge of about 800 characters is assumed. Legibly pen-written throughout. The 23 passages included are news-items from the Chinese press, each accompanied by a vocabulary, grammar notes and exercises in Chinese-to-English translation. Appendices include common surnames, the transliteration of foreign names, the organisation of the Governments of China and Taiwan, correspondences between literary and colloquial vocabulary, and a list of 800 basic characters arranged by radical.

CHIH, Y. J. Advanced Chinese newspaper readings. (No. B/32). New Haven, Yale University Press, 1960. iii, 161 p. 25s.

Intended to follow the preceding work. The 12 selections from the Chinese press consist of editorial matter reproduced photographically, each accompanied by notes, mainly on vocabulary, legibly pen-written. Since the texts are photographically reproduced, simplified characters occurring in them are inevitably kept, though their older counterparts are also given. A glossary arranged by stroke-order is appended.

LIU, W. C., and LI, T. Y. Readings in contemporary Chinese literature. V. 1: Plays and poems. (No. C/7). New Haven, Yale University Press, 1953. xxxv, 110 p. 25s.

The text of 5 short plays and 13 poems, photographically reproduced from printed editions, sometimes with loss of legibility that might cause the student difficulty.

LIU, W. C., LI, T. Y., and WAN, G. Notes to readings in contemporary Chinese literature. V. 1: Plays and poems. (No. C/10). New Haven, Yale University Press, 1957. xii, 109 p. 12s.

Notes to the preceding, mainly on vocabulary but including biographical notes on the authors of the works included.

LIU, W. C., and LI, T. Y. Readings in contemporary Chinese literature. V. 2: Stories. (No. C/8). New Haven, Yale University Press, 1953. xxvii, 234 p. 25s.

The text of 14 short stories, photographically reproduced, sometimes with slight loss of legibility.

LIU, W. C., LI, T. Y., and WAN, G.   Notes to readings in contemporary Chinese literature.   V. 2: Stories. (No. C/11).   New Haven, Yale University Press, 1958.   x, 141 p.   16s.

Vocabulary notes and biographical notes to the preceding work.

LIU, W. C., and LI, T. Y.   Readings in contemporary Chinese literature.   V. 3: Essays.   (No. C/9).   New Haven, Yale University Press, 1953.   xxi, 133 p.   25s.

The text of 20 essays, photographically reproduced with slight loss of legibility.

Apart from the Mirror Series, Yale University has begun the production of a new series of textbooks which are in many ways an improvement on the Mirror Series. There has been an attempt to make the subject-matter more lively and entertaining right from the start. Vocabulary is introduced over the series in order of frequency. The Mirror Series approach through sentence-patterns is maintained. Subject-matter is domestic and social, but as in the Mirror Series the language and social situations are on the whole those of a generation ago. Characters are pre-reform, but the new official Chinese transcription (Pinyin Zimu) is used instead of the Yale system of the Mirror Series. A series of three consecutive works is planned, each accompanied by a character text and a reader, making nine works in all. Of these the following have been available at the time of writing:

DE FRANCIS, J.   Beginning Chinese. Rev. ed.   New Haven, Yale University Press, 1963.   xxxi, 498 p.   18s. 6d.

Four units of six lessons each, every sixth lesson being a revision of the preceding five. 600 vocabulary items. Sentence-stress and breath-groups marked (an unusual feature in textbooks of Chinese). Excellent, very full exercises of all kinds. Romanisation only used in this volume. A vocabulary is appended, also an introduction to the Chinese script.

DE FRANCIS, J.   Character text for beginning Chinese.   New Haven, Yale University Press, 1964.   436 p.   18s. 6d.

References to pagination of preceding work enabling the student to use them in conjunction. Very clearly handwritten. 494 characters are introduced at this stage. A stroke-order chart is included, as well as four indexes arranged from lesson to radical number, from stroke number to lesson, from radical to lesson, and from pronunciation to lesson.

DE FRANCIS, J.   Beginning Chinese reader.   New Haven, Yale University Press, 1966.   2 v.   xxxii, 1,004 p.   37s.

48 lessons consisting of eight sets of five lessons each introducing ten

characters plus one revision lesson. Each lesson contains, apart from new vocabulary, illustrative sentences (Chinese text with English translation) and Chinese texts without an English translation (these constitute the bulk of the material). The characters are printed and are large and clear; characters in vocabularies are brushed and larger still. A supplementary lesson gives some practice in the simplified script in current use, though not without errors. Charts of stroke order are included, and also indexes of characters by lesson, number of strokes and radical, variant forms of characters, and finally an alphabetically arranged vocabulary with characters and references.

DE FRANCIS, J. Intermediate Chinese. New Haven, Yale University Press, 1964. xii, 542 p. 18s. 6d.

A continuation of *Beginning Chinese*, arranged on the same pattern. Very full exercises of all kinds. Appended is a glossary of new vocabulary only (*c.* 1,000 items), with references.

DE FRANCIS, J. Character text for intermediate Chinese. New Haven, Yale University Press, 1965. iv, 434 p. 18s. 6d.

Magnetic tapes are available for many of the works in the Mirror Series at 3 guineas per 7" reel (speed 3¾). Six 7" tapes to accompany *Beginning Chinese* are available at a price of 10 guineas for the set.

Apart from these two large series, the following are some of the other textbooks available for the modern language:

CHAN, S. W. Elementary Chinese. 2nd ed. Stanford, Stanford University Press, 1959. xxx, 508 p. 76s.

An excellent textbook. The Chinese characters are printed in clear type (they were hand-written in the first edition). Wade-Giles romanisation. Each of the 60 lessons consists of new vocabulary, with the stroke order of characters clearly marked, reading material in both characters and romanisation, clearly written grammar notes, and exercises involving translation in both directions in both characters and romanisation. Appended are an index of characters and compounds with references, arranged alphabetically, a list of radicals and hints on using radical dictionaries, and a list of simplified characters not used in the body of the work.

CHAO, Y. R. Mandarin primer: an intensive course in spoken Chinese. Cambridge, Mass., Harvard University Press, 1948 (reprinted 1957). vi, 336 p. 48s.

Uses romanisation (Gwoyeu Romatzyh) throughout, but a character text to accompany it is available (see next entry). The work consists of (1) an introduction covering the Chinese language in general, pronunciation and romanisation, an outline of grammar, character structure and recommended methods of study. This introduction constitutes an excellent outline of Chinese by an acknowledged authority on the subject. (It is of interest to note that a translation of the chapter on grammar has been published in China without acknowledgement of authorship or source and that this in turn has been quoted by a leading Russian sinologist.) (2) Foundation work, consisting of thorough drill in tones, difficult sounds, the system of sounds and tone sandhi. Nothing comparable to this is available elsewhere. (3) 24 lessons, each consisting of (*a*) romanised text with translation on facing page, consisting mainly of dialogue, (*b*) grammatical and etymological notes to the text, and (*c*) good exercises of all kinds. (4) Vocabulary and index (over 3,000 entries). The emphasis throughout is on the spoken language, with even grunts and 'ers' realistically reproduced. Though the material is excellent, the length of the lessons reduces its value for class use.

CHAO, Y. R.   Character text for Mandarin primer.   Cambridge, Mass., Harvard University Press, 1954 (reprinted 1963).   142 p. 38s.

"This character text is for the Chinese teacher, who usually reads much more easily in characters than in romanisation, and for the student, who, sooner or later, should learn to read in characters." Apart from a clearly hand-written character version of the text of the lesson, it contains a key (not complete) to the exercises, written in a very cursive script intended to be legible to the teacher only.

CHI, W. S.   Readings in Chinese Communist documents.   A manual for students of the Chinese language.   Berkeley and Los Angeles, California University Press, 1963.   xvi, 478 p.   76s.

Consists of 15 texts (policy documents, etc.) arranged in chronological order and covering the period 1949 to 1959. The texts are photographically reproduced from printed sources with some loss of legibility, and each text is provided with an introduction and with a vocabulary legibly brush-written. The romanisation used in the vocabularies is Wade-Giles and great care has clearly gone into the selection of English equivalents. Two glossaries are appended, one arranged by romanisation, with references to number of lesson and serial number within lesson-vocabulary, and the second by radicals. This work provides an excellent stepping-stone from the general run of textbooks to the reading of current newspapers and political writing in general and it can be unreservedly recommended for this purpose.

Modern Chinese reader.   Compiled by the Chinese Language Special Class for Foreign Students in Peking University.   2 v. Peking, Epoch, 1958.   786 p.   18s.

This work is unusual in that it is bilingual throughout, thus facilitating its use with a Chinese teacher. The characters are partly simplified. Romanisation (Pinyin Zimu) is used only in the vocabularies. Stress and tone are marked on the characters throughout. Each of the 72 lessons contains new vocabulary, grammar and exercises, and a stroke order chart. Appended are a general review of basic grammar, an alphabetically arranged vocabulary with references, a table of characters with the compounds in which they occur, a table of simplified characters, and rules for word-division. One feature of this work that recommends it is that the language is up to date, though the amount of exercise material is far from sufficient, particularly exercises involving translation into Chinese. For class use it is necessary for the teacher to provide additional exercises.

SIMON, W., and LU, C. H. Chinese sentence series. London, Probsthain, 1942–4 (reprinted 1956.) 3 v. 230, 166, 55 p. 24s. 6d.

V. 1 contains the text in romanisation (Gwoyeu Romatzyh) with a translation on the facing page. V. 2 contains the text in characters, legibly brush-written. V. 3 is a glossary in romanisation. The Gouin method is adopted, i.e. the text is mainly a present-tense commentary on the actions of the speaker, intended to be acted out by the student, accompanied by the utterance of the text, in conjunction with daily domestic routine.

SIMON, W., and LU, C. H. Chinese national language (Gwoyeu) reader and guide to conversation. London, Lund Humphries, 1943. (2nd rev. ed., 1954). viii, 195 p. 20s.

Intended as a continuation of the Chinese Sentence Series. The 50 lessons consist of a Chinese character text (pen-written) on the left-hand page, with a romanised version (Gwoyeu Romatzyh) facing it, and with an English translation below. Again the Gouin method is followed. The subject matter concerns travel to and in China and domestic routine.

TENG, S. Y. Conversational Chinese, with grammatical notes. Chicago, Chicago University Press, 1947 (6th impression 1962). ix, 441 p. 68s.

Pre-reform characters (printed and brushed), very legible, and Wade-Giles romanisation. The 47 lessons contain vocabulary, text in both characters and romanisation, notes on the text, exercises involving translation in both directions, and grammar notes with examples. A romanised character index and a general index are appended. This is a very solid textbook, but the romanisation in places leaves something to be desired and the language and contents are naturally somewhat dated.

TENG, S. Y. Advanced conversational Chinese. Chicago, Chicago University Press, 1965. xv, 293 p. 41s.

Follows the pattern of the preceding work. It consists of "Part I, five lessons dealing with political and geographical terms; Part II, five lessons on religious and historical terms; Part III, two short plays." Again a romanised character index is provided. Despite its more recent appearance this work is dated in its language and contents as its predecessor was (for instance, Lesson 1 contains the statement that "The Chinese central government includes a president and five presidents of yuan", which ceased to be true in 1949). Translation is very literal; while this is not out of place in an elementary work, a freer translation would seem more appropriate at this stage.

WILLIAMSON, H. R. Teach yourself Chinese. London, English Universities Press, 1947 (latest impression, 1966). viii, 530 p. 10s. 6d.

This work consists principally of 40 dialogues on social and domestic topics. The romanised (Wade-Giles) text is printed syllable by syllable, with no indication of tone, stress or word boundaries. It is faced by a translation and vocabulary. A character text is appended, together with grammar notes and indexes. The introduction on phonetics contains serious elementary errors and the vocabularies also contain errors. The grammar notes are disappointing in the extreme. It is not possible to recommend this work for beginners in view of the deficient and erroneous romanisation (for instance the vocabulary of dialogue 1 contains sixteen errors of pronunciation), the lack of adequate grammatical information and the lack of systematic exercises. The language and subject matter are dated.

TEXTBOOKS OF THE CLASSICAL LANGUAGE

GABELENTZ, G. von der. Chinesische Grammatik, mit Ausschluss des niederen Stiles und der heutigen Umgangssprache. 4th ed. Halle, Niemeyer, 1960. xxviii, 549 p. 60s.

First published 1881. All materials are given both in characters and in romanisation, which is the author's own system, basically Mandarin but including certain sound-distinctions obtaining in earlier stages of the language and in other dialects. This is a systematic treatment of the grammar of the Classical language, not a textbook with exercises. Parts of it have become outdated by subsequent research, though virtually all this research is available only in learned journals. Much subsequent research has been summarised in Chou Fa-kao's grammar (in Chinese) but not yet in any textbook in a European language. Until this is done, Gabelentz's work will remain a useful stand-by for the European reader.

HAENISCH, E. Lehrgang der klassischen chinesischen Schriftsprache. 4th ed. Leipzig, Harrassowitz, 1956–57 (4th edition). 4 v. 164; x, 242; 133; vi, 260 p. 85s.

A unique, graduated course based on texts selected from Chinese school readers in Classical Chinese in use at the beginning of this century, progressing from simple, specially-written texts in v. 1 to actual extracts from Chinese literature and historiography in v. 3. Although the choice of these texts has obliged the author to follow the traditional Chinese method of teaching the Classical language by explaining grammatical features haphazardly as they crop up, his course is extremely useful. It could best be preceded by a course of systematic exercises in Classical Chinese grammar, but unfortunately no such course is available. The texts (v. 1 and 3) are very legibly brushed; characters in the notes and vocabularies (v. 2 and 4) are in printed style, small and not always clearly legible to a beginner. German romanisation. Stroke order is shown clearly in the table in v. 2. Apart from vocabularies for individual texts, v. 2. and 4 contain vocabularies arranged by radicals, with romanisation, translation and references.

DICTIONARIES

ALDRICH, H. S. A topical Chinese dictionary. New Haven, Yale University Press, 1945. x, 182 p. 25s.

This is reprinted from v. 2 of *Practical Chinese* (first published 1942). It is a topical glossary containing 5,000 entries under 75 heads, mostly concrete nouns, with the emphasis on the domestic and professional needs of foreigners in pre-1949 China (e.g. 29 pages devoted to food). Alphabetical English-Chinese arrangement under each head. Equivalents given in romanisation (Wade-Giles) with stress marked and in printed characters, small but reasonably legible.

CHAN, S. W. A concise English-Chinese dictionary. Stanford, Stanford University Press, 1947. 2nd ed. 1955. xvii, 416 p. 52s.

Estimated 11,000 entries (English key words). Wade-Giles romanisation and pre-reform characters, legibly hand-written. A useful beginner's dictionary, particularly since romanisation is given as well as characters.

CHAN, W. H., and others. A daily use English-Chinese dictionary. Shanghai, World Book Co., 1936 (reprinted frequently). x, 1,950 p. 16s. 6d.

Estimated 33,000 main entries, 52,000 exemplary sentences and phrases. Pre-reform characters, no romanisation. Minute print, particularly difficult to read in the photographic reprints currently available. Intended for Chinese studying English. The Chinese versions of examples are often very literal and unidiomatic, and their style varies from the colloquial to the classical, usually a compromise with the colloquial predominating. The equivalents given in the main entries are often outdated or inaccurate.

CHAO, Y. R., and YANG, L. S. Concise dictionary of spoken Chinese. Cambridge Mass., Harvard University Press, 1947 (3rd impression 1957). xxxix, 292 p. 52s.

Chinese-English only. Arranged by radicals. Both Gwoyeu Romatzyh (with extra indication of ancient and dialect features) and Wade-Giles romanisations. This is a dictionary of morphemes (estimated 5,000 character-entries) with some polysyllabic words exemplifying them. It further indicates which morphemes are bound and which are free; in this respect this work is unique and marks a great advance on the traditional morpheme-dictionaries. This indication of bound or free refers only to the modern language. By its very nature this work will not be particularly useful for determining the meaning of polysyllabic words. A Gwoyeu Romatzyh index and a list of classifiers and units of measurement are appended.

CHEN', Ch. Kh., and others.   Russko-kitaĭskiĭ slovar'.   3rd rev. ed. Moscow, Gos. Izd. Inostrannykh i Natsional'nykh Slovareĭ, 1953. xvi, 975 p.   12s. 6d.

26,000 entries. Pre-reform characters and Cyrillic romanisation throughout. A list of geographical names and Russian grammatical tables for the use of Chinese readers are appended. The language is up to date.

CHENG, Y. L., and TSAO, C. S.   A new English-Chinese dictionary. Shanghai, Shenghuo-Tushu-Hsinchih Sanlien Shutien, 1950 (Peking reprint 1963).   15, 36, 2,144 p.   25s.

Estimated 50,000 main entries. Pre-reform characters, no romanisation. Pages 1,523 to the end contain a Chinese index giving page and part-of-page references, which can be used (though very laboriously) as a Chinese-English dictionary. The characters in the currently available reduced photographic reprints are very small but fairly clear. This work is intended for Chinese users. The language is more modern than that of the Daily Use Dictionary mentioned above, but it contains far fewer examples. An attempt has been made to match the style of the Chinese equivalent to that of the English entry, especially in the case of colloquialisms. The entries contain much ephemeral slang, especially American, e.g. s.v. 'chin' are given 'chin-armor, chin-buster, chin-mauler (industry), chin-music', etc.

Dictionary of spoken Chinese.   (Compiled by the staff of the Institute of Far Eastern Languages, Yale University).   New Haven, Yale University Press, 1966.   xxxix, 1,071 p.   105s.

This is a revised version of the War Dept. Technical Manual of the same title published in Washington, D.C. in 1945. It consists of two main parts: (1) Chinese-English (295 p.) estimated 2,300 characters. Arranged by first syllable of entry, Yale romanisation with cross-references from Pinyin Zimu. Simplified characters are given in brackets and also in the index. Full pronunciation included, with stress indicated. Many examples (characters only). Indication of bound and free morphemes, parts of speech and appropriate classifiers. (2) English-Chinese (737 p.) estimated 2,300 entry-words (five pages for 'get', six for 'come', two for 'by'). Romanisation only. Copious examples. Appendices include weights and measures, radical index, conversion tables from Wade-Giles to Pinyin and Yale romanisations. Legibility excellent. This is a unique reference work for the colloquial language, though it does not reflect the changes that have taken place in Chinese since 1949.

HUANG, P. F., ed.   IFEL vocabulary of spoken Chinese.   New Haven, Yale University Press, 1954.   xvi, 347 p.   40s.

A revised edition of *Vocabulary for airmen* (Yale, 1952), representing vocabulary met in a one-year intensive course at the Institute of Far Eastern Languages and contained in *Speak Chinese, Chinese dialogues, Read about China*, and two texts for airmen. Despite its sources it is not a specialist vocabulary, but of general usefulness. The English-Chinese part contains an estimated 5,000 items, Yale romanisation only, no characters. The Chinese-English part is arranged by Yale romanisation, with hand-written characters (some loss of legibility in reproduction) for main entries only. Parts of speech indicated, also source of item. Estimated 3,800 entries.

MATHEWS, R. H.   A Chinese-English dictionary.   Rev. American ed. Cambridge, Mass., Harvard University Press, 1947 (9th impression 1963).   xxiv, 1,226 p.   80s.

The largest Chinese-English general dictionary currently available, with over 100,000 entries under 7,773 characters. The entries have been taken indiscriminately from all periods and styles of spoken and written Chinese without indication. No indication of whether a given syllable is a free or bound morpheme. Much current vocabulary is not included. All entries are serially numbered. The radical index refers to these, as does the separately published English-Chinese index (see below). A number of useful tables (e.g. chronological, cyclical) are appended, and a full radical index. Legibility is good despite the small type.

MATHEWS, R. H.   A Chinese-English dictionary: revised English index.   Cambridge Mass., Harvard University Press, 1947 (3rd impression 1954).   186 p.   27s.

Index to the preceding work. Reference is to the serial number of the entry. Estimated 34,000 entries.

OSHANIN, I. M., ed.   Kitaĭsko-russkiĭ slovar'.   Moscow, Gos. Izd. Inostr. i Nats. Slovareĭ, 1952 (2nd rev. ed. 1955).   900 p.   45s.

Estimated 67,000 entries under 9,075 characters (serially numbered). Entries arranged by the shape of the characters, working backwards from the last stroke (the system is set out in the end-papers). Cyrillic romanisation with all entries. Pre-reform characters, legibly printed. The 2nd edition seriously attempts to bring the vocabulary up to date, for example by including the vocabulary in v. 3 of Mao Tse-tung's Selected Works. A list of simplified characters and a list of MS abbreviations of character-elements are appended.

SIMON, W.   A beginners' Chinese-English dictionary of the national language (Gwoyeu).   London, Lund Humphries, 1947 (3rd rev. ed. 1964).   cxl, 880, 194 p.   50s.

14–15,000 polysyllabic entries (consisting of romanised form and radical-numbers of characters) arranged alphabetically in conjunction with 4,741 character entries. For each character the following information is given: frequency (one of four degrees), radical and stroke numbers, four-corner number, cross reference to other readings. No indication of whether bound or free, or of part of speech (except as implied in translation). Characters are brushed, whereas beginners will have greater need for printed style or pen-written style in which the structure is better seen. There is a radical index. The many useful appendices include mnemonics for radical-numbers, classifiers, weights and measures, cyclical terms and chronological tables, G.R. – Wade-Giles – Chuyin Tzumu transcription tables, the four-corner system of arranging characters, geographical names and simplified characters.

ZHANG, Q. C., and CAI, W. Y.   A concise English-Chinese dictionary. Peking, Commercial Press, 1965.   xxii, 1,252 p.   21s.

Intended for use by Chinese. 26,150 entries. Characters are small, sometimes not very legible. The characters represent the first stage of simplification. Pronunciation of the English words is indicated, but not that of the Chinese, of course. The compilers have aimed at conciseness and practicality, so there is not much "dead wood". The English is old-fashioned in spite of the attempt to be up to date, but the Chinese equivalents are an improvement on early dictionaries of this kind. Appendices include proper names, English phonetics with technical terms, ranks in the armed forces, weights and measures, twenty Duden-style vocabularies in conjunction with pictures, and other items.

Technical Dictionaries

Modern Chinese-English technical and general dictionary. New York, McGraw-Hill, 1963.   3 v.   (vii, 152; vii, 1,900; vii, 1,788 p.) £18.

212,000 entries, of which "more than 80% . . . are common scientific and technical terms". V. 1 consists of tables: conversion from Wade-Giles to Pinyin Zimu, from abbreviated to full characters, radical index (telegraphic code) to Pinyin and Wade-Giles, Pinyin to characters and telegraphic code.

V. 2 and 3 comprise the main body of the dictionary, each containing the same material differently arranged. V. 2 is arranged by the Standard Telegraphic Code in numerical sequence, and v. 3 by Pinyin Zimu romanisation in alphabetical sequence, so that an entry may be found either from the character or from the pronunciation. No characters are included in v. 2 and 3. This very large work contains a wealth of useful data, but it is marred by frequent errors of transcription (resulting in entries becoming 'lost' when processed by the computer used to arrange the material) and also by the poor quality of many of the translations, which may very possibly have existed in the glossary materials from which the work was compiled.

KOLOKOLOV, V. S., ed.   Kitaĭsko-russkiĭ slovar' nauchnykh i tekhni-
cheskikh terminov.   Moscow, Institut Nauchnoĭ Informatsii Aka-
demii Nauk SSSR, 1959.   iii, 568 p.   42s.

32,000 terms arranged by the same system as that used by Oshanin (*see
above*) and here also set out in the end-papers. No romanisation. Pre-reform
characters, brushed and not very legible for a beginner. A list of simplified
characters is appended. Though it contains much useful data, this work is on
the whole disappointing. There are serious gaps (for example the Chinese
term for 'servo-' is not included). Many out-of-date terms are included, on
the other hand. There are many quite unnecessary entries, for example
nineteen examples of "sulphide of X" on p. 473-4, all deducible from the
constituent parts, but no separate entry for "sulphide of . . .". This inclusion
of unnecessary compound entries at the expense of important elements used
in compound-building is a striking feature of this dictionary.

GRAMOPHONE RECORDS

The Linguaphone Chinese course comprises 16 78 r.p.m. records, plus
a course book, at £17 4s. 1d. It was recorded before 1931 and is somewhat dated in content. Artificial diction; some very common words
mispronounced. Not recommended for students of current Standard
Chinese. The brief Conversa-phone CX Mandarin Chinese course
(not heard) consists of one 12″ L.P. record and an instructional manual
at 37s. 6d.

INDEX